P W Preston
Birmingham 2015

LOST IN CHINA?

Rule of law is a core Hong Kong value, providing a defensive wall around the territory and protecting its way of life against 'mainlandisation'. Before the 1997 retrocession to China, fears were widespread that the rights and freedoms enjoyed under colonial rule would be eroded, that the rule of law would be weakened and that corruption would increase. Soon, the first blows were struck against the rule of law via a NPCSC ruling that overturned the judgement of the Court of Final Appeal. Successive interventions by Beijing in Hong Kong's legal and political affairs have given rise to fears about the loss of the rule of law and loss of identity. These fears have subsequently provoked mass street demonstrations, including the 'Umbrella Revolution' of 2014. But, as this book shows, Hongkongers also use less explicit arts of resistance to maintain their identity.

CAROL A. G. JONES taught at universities in Hong Kong from 1990 to 2002 and remains involved academically there. She has written extensively about the role of law in Hong Kong's history and society, and she has a particular interest in how ideas about the law have shaped and been shaped by Hong Kong's colonial and postcolonial development.

CAMBRIDGE STUDIES IN LAW AND SOCIETY

Cambridge studies in law and society aims to publish the best scholarly work on legal discourse and practice in its social and institutional contexts, combining theoretical insights and empirical research.

The fields that it covers are: studies of law in action; the sociology of law; the anthropology of law; cultural studies of law, including the role of legal discourses in social formations; law and economics; law and politics; and studies of governance. The books consider all forms of legal discourse across societies, rather than being limited to lawyers' discourses alone.

The series editors come from a range of disciplines: academic law; socio-legal studies; sociology; and anthropology. All have been actively involved in teaching and writing about law in context.

Series editors

Chris Arup *Monash University, Victoria*
Sally Engle Merry *New York University*
Susan Silbey *Massachusetts Institute of Technology*

A list of books in the series can be found at the back of this book.

LOST IN CHINA?

Law, Culture and Identity in Post-1997 Hong Kong

CAROL A. G. JONES

CAMBRIDGE
UNIVERSITY PRESS

CAMBRIDGE
UNIVERSITY PRESS

University Printing House, Cambridge CB2 8BS, United Kingdom

Cambridge University Press is part of the University of Cambridge.

It furthers the University's mission by disseminating knowledge in the pursuit of education, learning and research at the highest international levels of excellence.

www.cambridge.org
Information on this title: www.cambridge.org/9781107093379

First published 2015

A catalogue record for this publication is available from the British Library

Library of Congress Cataloguing in Publication data
Jones, Carol A. G., author.
Lost in China? : law, culture and society in post-1997 Hong Kong / Carol Jones.
pages cm. – (Cambridge studies in law and society)
ISBN 978-1-107-09337-9 (Hardback)
1. Law–Social aspects–China–Hong Kong. 2. Law–China–Hong Kong–Chinese influences.
3. Hong Kong (China)–Politics and government–1997-
4. Hong Kong (China)–Civilization. I. Title.
KNQ9306.J66 2015
951.2506–dc 3 2014042961

ISBN 978–1–107-09337-9 Hardback

In memory of
Robert Staunton
(1936–2009)

CONTENTS

ACKNOWLEDGEMENTS

Thanks are due to Professor Jerome Cohen, who first suggested that I write this book. I am also grateful to friends, family and colleagues in Hong Kong, the United Kingdom, and at Eura Conservation for their assistance and support. The Taiwan Research Centre at the London School of Economics and the Department of Sociology at the University of Hong Kong both provided stimulating intellectual environments in which to test and develop ideas. The comments of anonymous readers at Cambridge University Press undoubtedly improved the text. Finally, I owe a lasting debt to the remarkable staff at the Abraham Darby Comprehensive School (1965–1973) who gave a working-class schoolgirl the opportunity and confidence to ask big questions.

ABBREVIATIONS

BOR	Bill of Rights
CE	Chief Executive of the Hong Kong Special Administrative Region
EXCO	Hong Kong Executive Council
HKSAR	Hong Kong Special Administrative Region
ICCPR	International Covenant on Civil and Political Rights
LEGCO	Hong Kong Legislative Council
NPCSC	National People's Congress Standing Committee
PRC	People's Republic of China
RTHK	Radio Television Hong Kong
SCMP	South China Morning Post

1

Introduction: the lie of the land

At his inauguration on 1 July 1997, the first Chief Executive of the Hong Kong Special Administrative Region (HKSAR), Tung Chee-hwa, declared that 'for the first time in history, we, the people of Hong Kong, will be master of our own destiny'.[1] On 1 July 2014, the anniversary of Hong Kong's retrocession to China, almost 500,000 people took to the streets protesting against Beijing's governance of Hong Kong. A week earlier, 800,000 voted in an informal referendum for the right to freely choose their government. Clearly, they did not feel that they were masters of their own destiny.

The protest on 1 July 2014 was the latest in what has become a tradition of anti-mainland and anti-government marches. Each year since 1997, the anniversary of the handover has been a day of mass demonstration, accompanied by banners, chants slogans, a variety of art works, videos and performances – even a mock tomb symbolising the death of democracy and a mock wedding signifying a forced union. Lawyers dressed in black mark the death of the rule of law. Hong Kong, city of law, has become a theatre of protest.

Lawyers and the rule of law play a central part in these protests. In recent years, the role of lawyers as fighters for political freedom has become of interest to law and society scholars. It is not a new role; as Halliday, Karpik and Feeley demonstrate, when the foundations of

[1] J. M. Carroll, *A Concise History of Hong Kong* (Plymouth: Rowman & Littlefield, 2007), p. 206.

liberal politics were laid down in eighteenth- and nineteenth-century Europe, lawyers were in the vanguard.[2] In a variety of ways, they argue, the legal profession has 'sought the moderation of state power via judicial independence, the creation and mobilisation of a politically engaged civil society, and the vesting of rights in subjects as citizens who would be protected by judiciaries'.[3] This is exactly the part currently played by lawyers in the fight against the demise of liberalism and the rise of authoritarianism in post-1997 Hong Kong.

As a British colony, Hong Kong inherited the English system of common law. Before 1997, its legal system was characterised by a separation of powers, an independent judiciary, due process, habeas corpus and the right to own property, as well as freedom from arbitrary arrest, freedom of speech, freedom of association and of assembly, freedom of religion and freedom of travel – what Halliday and others call basic legal freedoms and protections. Much like nineteenth-century England, however, these did not include the right to vote. For a variety of reasons – including opposition from China – Britain never introduced democracy into Hong Kong. Historically, in England itself political rights did not automatically accompany the rule of law. Universal suffrage was only won after long political struggle, though its eventual adoption owed much to the state's need to incorporate a discontented population whose marginalisation threatened its 'right to rule'.

As I have argued elsewhere, in Hong Kong a regime of legal liberalism developed in the 1970s, and when it did, it played a similar role to the ideology of rule of law in eighteenth- and nineteenth-century England, absorbing demands for political change by offering, instead, justice, rights and equality before the law.[4] Limited democratic rights were later developed in Hong Kong by the Patten administration but these, along with administrative channels of consultation developed in the 1970s, were systematically dismantled by China after 1997. Only the rule of law remained intact. However, this too has suffered attack, and it is now unlikely that legal liberalism alone can repeat

law, not democ

[2] T. Halliday, L. Karpik and M. Feeley (eds.), *Fighting for Political Freedom: Comparative Studies in the Legal Complex and Political Liberalism* (Oxford: Hart, 2007), pp. 1–2.

[3] Halliday, Karpik and Feely, *Fighting for Political Freedom*, pp. 1–2.

[4] C. A. G. Jones, 'Politics postponed: law as a substitute for politics in Hong Kong and China', in K. Jayasuriya (ed.), *Law, Capitalism and Power in Asia: The Rule of Law and Legal Institutions* (London: Routledge, 1990), pp. 45–68.

its 1970s performance as a safety valve for sociopolitical grievances. It is nevertheless the case, as I argue here, that rule of law has become deeply embedded in Hong Kong's culture. Indeed, partly because of China's attacks upon it, rule of law has become the ruling idea of the time.

THE POLITICAL CONTEXT

In 1997, when Hong Kong was handed back to China, its inhabitants were promised a 'high degree of autonomy' and the introduction of universal suffrage for the elections of their Chief Executive (CE) and their political representatives in the Legislative Council (LEGCO). By 2014, they were still waiting for the right to vote, and a White Paper issued by Beijing placed their 'high degree of autonomy' on notice. Unanticipated by China, Hong Kong had become a highly politicised city. For Beijing, however, Hong Kong's value lies partly in its status as a marker on the road to the (re)creation of 'One China', a forerunner to reunification with Taiwan. Nonetheless, events in Hong Kong since 1997 have made it unviable as a blueprint for Taiwanese reunification, and Hong Kong's usefulness now lies primarily in its role as an international financial centre and conduit to global commerce. Hong Kong enjoys world standing as an international financial centre, and Beijing supposes this to depend upon stability, 'Stability and Prosperity' having become the mantra of the Communist Party since the repression of the pro-democracy movement of June 1989. 'Stability' in this sense means the maintenance of one-party rule; 'instability' means anything that challenges it. From this view, democracy is politically dangerous. It cannot be allowed in Hong Kong lest it subvert Communist Party rule on the mainland.

However, even amongst those with the greatest investment in Hong Kong's prosperity – the business elite – there is no longer a consensus that democracy is harmful to economic success. In 2014, for example, at the height of a row over Hong Kong's constitutional reforms, the Chinese Manufacturers' Association argued that universal suffrage would mean that Hong Kong's leaders would enjoy a stronger mandate to rule and that this would in fact be good for stability. Dozens of other financial and banking executives issued an open letter to President Xi Jinping demanding universal suffrage and the protection of Hong Kong's core values. Some – including hedge fund managers – even pledged to join the civil disobedience movement Occupy Central, which called for universal suffrage.[5] In an advertisement placed in several leading newspapers, the group stated that Hong Kong's political system 'has become the stumbling block to the city's long-term social, political and economic growth, and is the root cause of social division and disharmony'.[6] Other international corporations also declared their support for democracy on the basis that it offered greater stability in the long term. Pro-Beijing opponents responded with their own advertisement in three Chinese-language newspapers, arguing that Occupy Central would disrupt business and deter foreign investors. The 'Big Four' accountancy firms declared their opposition to Occupy Central, a position for which they were called to account by the British Parliament. In an unprecedented move, however, dozens of their employees publicly distanced themselves from these remarks, despite a warning that they might lose their jobs if Beijing retaliated by preventing accountants from doing business in the mainland. The proposed Occupy Central sit-in (of 10,000 people in the Central business district) was, they argued, likely to cause no more disruption to business than one of the strong typhoons that hit Hong Kong each summer. Pro-Beijing figures, however, warned of 'blood on the streets' and the deployment of the People's Liberation Army (PLA).

The lack of elite consensus left the government without its traditional centre of support and raised questions about whether, in the event of a Tiananmen-style crackdown on Occupy Central, it would be able to effectively validate its actions. Since its inauguration in 1997, the government of the Hong Kong Special Administrative Region (HKSAR) has adopted a restricted and statist interpretation of the rule of law. It has proved insistent, for example, that 'the law is the law' and that 'rule of law' means 'law and order'. Participants in protests – such as civil disobedience – are seen as law breakers and troublemakers. Mostly, what they have been protesting about since 1997 is the government's failure to guarantee the rights and freedoms associated with the liberal view of the rule of law. Since 1997, this tension has recurred, played out on the streets and in the courts of law. In court, lawyers have repeatedly challenged the government's somewhat statist interpretation of the law and called it to account for infringing the rights of citizens. Out of court, the Bar Association has been in the vanguard of civil

[5] T. Chong, 'Hong Kong business elite demand 2017 universal suffrage in open letter', *SCMP*, 23 April 2014.

[6] Chong, 'Hong Kong business elite'.

society's defence of the rule of law. In 2014, at the peak of the government's strong law and order rhetoric condemning the Occupy Central movement, the Bar Association's chairman reminded the government that the rule of law required: (i) checks on the legality of governmental discretion; (ii) guarantees as to protection of rights in the laws passed by the legislature; and (iii) an independent judiciary and an equally independent legal profession, free from control or influence of the government or business interests. In a reference to the 'law is the law' approach, he added:

> If all we have are laws and the machinery to enforce those laws against ordinary mortals, then 'law' will be nothing more than a mere tool to govern people, and the Government would be able to justify everything on the basis that it was only 'doing things according to law'. It would not be 'Rule of Law' but 'Rule by Law' ... [A]t the end of the day, the flourishing of the Rule of Law depends on the moral fabric of society and the civic qualities of its citizens. Some may call it the 'collective conscience' ... The moral fabric of a society is really what ancient wisdom called a sense of 'justice, righteousness and honour'. If it crumbles, it may take years to rebuild.[7]

Society, the chairman cautioned, needed to remain vigilant in defending the rule of law and the independence of judiciary; judges needed the support of citizens in the exercise of their constitutional function, even when their decisions were unpopular. Citing an English judge, he added, 'there are countries in this world where every judicial decision finds favour with the government, but they are not places where one would want to live.' He ended this speech with a rallying cry to lawyers to 'keep the faith'. On the face of it, this looks very much like Hong Kong lawyers in the vanguard of liberalism. However, Hong Kong has a split legal profession, and the leader of the Law Society – the solicitors' branch – publicly criticised the Bar's stance, opposing the Occupy Central campaign on the basis that it would be bad for business.

This conflict with the Bar is not new – on previous occasions when the Bar has led the charge against human rights infringements, the Law Society has preferred the status quo. As I argue here, this divergence of views very much reflects the different structural position of these two

[7] Paul Shieh, Speech of the Chairman of the Hong Kong Bar Association at the opening of the legal year 2014, 13 January 2014.

branches of the profession, solicitors having more to lose if they offend Hong Kong's new sovereign. One question for Hong Kong is whether (and how) this fragmentation of the legal profession limits lawyers' role in fighting the rise of authoritarianism after 1997.

AUTHORITARIANISM

On 10 June 2014, China's State Council issued a White Paper on the 'one country, two systems' policy in Hong Kong. This stated in no uncertain terms that China controlled Hong Kong.[8] It claimed, somewhat disingenuously, that the 'one country, two systems' policy under which China governed the HKSAR had the 'wholehearted support' of Hong Kong compatriots, was internationally recognised as successful and had secured Hong Kong's continuing stability and prosperity. Hong Kong had, it stated, benefitted from reunion with the Motherland – China had assisted in the fight against the 2003 SARS epidemic, in the Asian financial crisis and in the 2008 global recession.[9] The White Paper listed a swathe of statistics testifying to the health of the territory's fiscal and foreign exchange reserves; its international rating as a leading international banking centre, securities market, international port and financial development centre; and the level of its external merchandise trade and foreign direct investment. The list itself is a telling indication of how Beijing views Hong Kong and its inhabitants. Essentially, it regards the Hong Kong citizen as *homo economicus*, a self-seeker after wealth who will always trade political freedom for the freedom to make money.

Given this litany of successes, the question is why did Beijing feel the need, in the same document, to 'read the riot act' to Hong Kong in 2014?[10] The White Paper claimed that it was because 'some people' had a 'confused or lopsided' understanding of the 'one country, two systems' policy that needed to be corrected. Many 'wrong views' were rife in Hong Kong. The authors of the White Page reiterated that the central government held comprehensive jurisdiction over HKSAR,

8 For the full text, see www.scmp.com/news/hong-kong/article/1529167/full-text-practice-one-country-two-systems-policy-hong-kong-special.

9 Hongkongers remember, rather, that China sought to conceal the outbreak of SARS on the mainland. The epidemic reached Hong Kong via the border.

10 M. DeGolyer, quoted in A. Wong, 'Beijing's White Paper sets off a fire storm in Hong Kong', *SCMP* 11 June 2014.

that Hong Kong was just another administrative region in the People's Republic of China, and that 'one country, two systems' referred only to Hong Kong's retention of a capitalist economic system; it did not mean that the two systems were 'on a par'. Indeed, the 'two systems' was subordinate to 'one country'. Moreover, Hong Kong's 'high degree of autonomy' was neither inherent, nor full autonomy nor decentralised power. There was no such thing as 'residual power'. Any autonomy enjoyed by Hong Kong was held at the grace of Beijing. The clear implication was that what Beijing gave, it could also take away.

The tone of this warning was new, but its substance was not. In 2007, Wu Bagguo had already declared that the 'high degree of autonomy' was something bestowed by the central government; it was not a right.[11] Cheng Jie, another mainland scholar, also argued that the high degree of autonomy of the HKSAR was not inherent, there was no locus to counteract the Central Authorities and the HKSAR must accept their supervision.[12] The 2014 White Paper ratcheted up this rhetoric, reminding recalcitrant Hongkongers that all the executive, legislative and judicial practices in the HKSAR 'must conform to the Basic Law' and that all individuals, groups and organisations must obey it. It thus signalled an escalation in Beijing's determination to rein in Hong Kong, and it categorically contradicted Tung's promise that, after 1997, Hongkongers would be masters of their own destiny.

BATTLE LINES

The guarded optimism with which Hongkongers had greeted the 1997 handover had dissipated by 1999 and turned to anger by 2003. This culminated in a mass march on 1 July 2003, when 500,000 people demonstrated against a proposal to introduce mainland-type anti-subversion laws into the HKSAR. The size of the protest shocked the Central Government, which reacted with a mix of 'iron fist' and 'velvet' glove tactics, ranging from intensified efforts to inculcate patriotism at one

[11] The comments were made by Wu Bangguo, then head of the NPC. See J. M. Carroll, 'Ten years later: 1997–2007 as history', in Kam Louie (ed.), *Hong Kong Culture: Word and Image* (Hong Kong: Hong Kong University Press, 2011), p. 11.

[12] Cheng Jie, 'The Central Authorities' governing power and special administrative region's high degree of autonomy – using the delegation relationship under the basic law as the framework', *Legal Science* 8 (2007), 61–8, cited in Lo, *Judicial Construction of Hong Kong's Basic Law*, pp. 31–2.

extreme, to veiled threats to deploy the PLA against protestors at the other. The battleground in between was the courts.

What I have here termed 'the law wars' began soon after the handover. The 2014 White Paper was simply the latest in a series of skirmishes centring on interpretation of the Basic Law. The White Paper reminded Hongkongers that the power to interpret and amend the Basic Law was vested in the National People's Congress Standing Committee (NPCSC) and that although courts of the HKSAR had the power of final adjudication and could provide their own interpretation of matters that lay within the autonomy of the HKSAR, the NPCSC had the final power to interpret the law. The Basic Law might permit Hong Kong to be governed by 'Hong Kong people' but:

> There are lines and criteria to be observed in implementing 'Hong Kong people governing Hong Kong', that is what Deng Xiaoping stressed, Hong Kong must be governed by the Hong Kong people with patriots as the mainstay, as loyalty to one's country is the minimum political ethic for political figures. Under the policy of 'one country, two systems', all those who administrate Hong Kong, including the chief executive, principal officials, members of the Executive Council and Legislative Council, judges of the courts at different levels and other judicial personnel, have on their shoulders the responsibility of correctly understanding and implementing the Basic Law, of safeguarding the country's sovereignty, security and development interests, and of ensuring the long-term prosperity and stability of Hong Kong. In a word, loving the country is the basic political requirement for Hong Kong's administrators.[13]

This was the first time Beijing had explicitly stated that it considered judges to be 'administrators' who need to be 'patriots'. This was a step too far for Hongkongers, for whom judicial independence has become, as I seek to show, a core value. The immediate response was a silent protest by a legal profession dressed in mourning black. Civil society activists burned copies of the White Paper, and a firestorm of reaction followed. An estimated 500,000 attended the annual 1 July anti-government demonstration, the largest turnout since 2003, and almost 800,000 defied Beijing by voting in an unofficial Occupy Central referendum calling for constitutional reform. Hong Kong's *homo economicus* was, it seemed, no longer simply interested in money.

[13] State Council White Paper, *The Practice of 'One Country, Two Systems' in the Hong Kong Special Administrative Region* (Beijing: Xinhua), 10 June 2014.

By 2014, the legitimacy of the CE, C. Y. Leung, had hit a low point. A few months earlier, in December 2013, a toy wolf called 'Lufsig' flew off the shelves of Hong Kong stores, having become a symbol of protest. Leung is known as a 'wolf' in popular culture, and protestors threw the toy at the CE during demonstrations. The 2014 annual 4 June vigil to commemorate Tiananmen Square witnessed one of the biggest turnouts since 1997, with 180,000 people defying the government's exhortation to be patriots and 'put away the baggage of history'.[14] So low had Beijing's standing fallen that a poll conducted in March 2013 showed that, given the option, 91 per cent of respondents would opt to become a British overseas territory like the Falkland Islands.[15] In March 2014, a visit to Hong Kong by the former colonial governor, Chris Patten, attracted a crowd of 'Hong Kong People First' supporters carrying the colonial flag, singing the British national anthem, and calling for a complete break from Chinese rule. A similar display in March 2013 prompted Beijing officials to denounce the flag-wavers and warn that 'centrifugal forces' would not be allowed in the HKSAR.

The White Paper's release was sabre rattling in the face of this mounting discontent with Beijing's governance. Its publication was seen as an attempt to rewrite the Joint Sino-British Declaration and the Basic Law. The Joint Declaration 3(3) and Article 2 of the Basic Law promise that the HKSAR will enjoy executive, legislative, and independent judicial power. Beijing, however, declared that it alone held ultimate authority, that the NPCSC was free to interpret and amend the Basic Law as it wished and that, in the event of disturbances, it had the power to declare a state of emergency in Hong Kong.[16] International commentators warned that, should the Hong Kong unrest end as another Tiananmen Square episode this would:

> alarm Taiwan, disrupt Hong Kong's thriving and vibrant economy [and] destroy China's credibility as a partner that respects legally binding agreements. A violent crackdown would also alarm Japan, Vietnam, the Philippines, Malaysia and Brunei, which worry about China's

[14] Hong Kong is the only Chinese city where the law permits such a gathering.

[15] E. Tran, 'SCMP's Falkland's-inspired poll sparks Hong Kong colonial debate', *SCMP*, 15 March 2013.

[16] See M. C. Davis, 'With White Paper, Beijing may have achieved the opposite of what it wants', *SCMP*, 16 June 2014. That the White Paper breached the terms of the 1984 Joint Declaration was reiterated by Bao Tong, a former aide to Zhao Ziyang, who signed the treaty in 1984.

> belligerent posturing in the East and South China seas. Beijing must carefully weigh its Hong Kong options; ordering a violent crackdown is certainly not the best one.[17]

Though locally seen as an attempt to scare Hongkongers into silence, the White Paper's belligerence actually swelled support for the Occupy Central movement.[18] But there was also pessimism. Polls in June 2014 showed that fewer than half of the Hong Kong population thought that the 'one country, two systems' arrangement would last.[19] Politics had become more polarised. Pro-Beijing radical groups (such as Justice Alliance, Caring Hong Kong Power, and Defend Hong Kong) had emerged and were strident in their opposition to the democracy campaign. Violence broke out at political rallies. As one political commentator argued, 'the clashes we see on the streets now are a natural extension of [the] two line struggle approach, first advanced by the Red Army in the 1930s. In a nutshell, one is either a friend or an enemy'.[20]

MAINLANDISATION

What this and previous episodes of unrest illustrate is that, apart from a few short years after 1997, Beijing's resumption of sovereignty over Hong Kong has been beset by resistance to the mainland's attempts at legal, social, cultural and economic re-colonisation and subject (re)formation.[21] A number of writers have likened the processes of Hong Kong's reintegration to mainland China to re-colonisation, and certainly there are similarities to the strategies of colonisation.[22] Here,

[17] M. Mehta, 'Beijing's treatment of Hong Kong protests watched by a wary region', *SCMP*, 9 July 2014.

[18] Occupy Central is a campaign for universal suffrage. It promised a sit-in of 1,000 people in the Central business district if the government failed to produce proposals which accord with international standards.

[19] A. Wong, 'Beijing's White Paper sets off a firestorm in Hong Kong', *New York Times*, 11 June 2014.

[20] A. Cheng, 'Rise of the radical anti-democracy groups in Hong Kong', *SCMP*, 5 June 2014.

[21] See H. van Houtem, O. Kramsch and W. Zierhofer (eds.), *B/Ordering Space* (Aldershot: Ashgate, 2005).

[22] See, S. Lo, 'The mainlandization and recolonization of Hong Kong: A triumph of convergence over divergence with mainland China' in J. Y. S. Cheng (ed.), *The Hong Kong Special Administrative Region in its First Decade* (Hong Kong: City

I try to document some of the ways in which Hongkongers have responded to this and to what C. Wright Mills calls the 'remote transformations' and John Comaroff terms the 'force fields' within which human beings live out their lives'.[23] Globalisation, on the one hand, and mainlandisation on the other, combine in Hong Kong to make retention of local identity problematic. Global capital and its allies within both Hong Kong and mainland China seek to rearrange the economy, law, geography and society to suit their own imperatives.

In addition, Beijing wishes its successful reintegration of Hong Kong to be seen as one step in its 'Greater China' policy, an integration which demands that Hong Kong ceases to be different and becomes part of a homogenous nation. As with its aggressively expansionist policies in the South China Sea against Japan, Indonesia, the Philippines and Vietnam, the reunification of Hong Kong and Taiwan is partly related to the need to satisfy domestic critics and consolidate Communist Party rule. In essence, it would mean strengthening the nation in its rise to global power whilst trying to stave off domestic instability. China may be increasingly capitalist, but it is also resolutely authoritarian, under the control of a Communist Party, which sees rule by law as a core element of China's state-centred developmental strategy. The rule of law, certain freedoms and a liberal society are permitted in Hong Kong insofar as these are necessary for the continuance of capitalism. Beyond that, they have no intrinsic value and, to the degree that they impede economic success or threaten the stability of the nation, they are expendable.

Despite the promise that Hong Kong would remain unchanged for fifty years after 1997, both of these economic and political projects have driven changes in the HKSAR. A number of Hong Kong's institutions have been damaged by mainland interference and the mainlandisation

University Press, 2007); W. P. McNeill, 'Enjoy your rights! Three cases from the postcolonial commonwealth', *Public Culture* 23 (1997), pp. 377–93; S. Vines, *Hong Kong: China's New Colony* (London: Orion, 1999); G. C. H. Luk (ed.), *From a British to a Chinese Colony: Hong Kong in the Past and Today* (Berkeley: University of California Press, forthcoming); W. W. Law, 'The accommodation and resistance to the decolonisation, neocolonisation and recolonisation of higher education in Hong Kong', *Comparative Education* 33, no. 2, Special Number 19, *Education and Political Transition: The Implications of Hong Kong's Change of Sovereignty* (June 1997) pp. 187–209.

[23] J. Comaroff, 'Foreword' to M. Lazarus-Black and S. F. Hirsch, *Contested States: Law, Hegemony and Resistance* (New York: Routledge, 1994), pp. ix–xiii.

of everyday life. The result has been an outpouring of defiance and a flourishing of local culture. When, in March 2014, the Oxford English Dictionary included the term 'Hongkongers' for the first time to refer to a native or inhabitant of Hong Kong, it was seen locally as a victory for those opposed to the 'mainlandisation' of the HKSAR and a confirmation that the Hong Kong Chinese were internationally recognised as distinct from their mainland compatriots 'in cultural spirit and political identity'.[24] I try to document here some of the 'noise' heard on the cultural, legal and political wavebands since 1997, the sound of Hongkongers resisting 'mainlandisation'. Mainlandisation (a term seldom heard outside Hong Kong) in essence denotes: (i) the HKSAR's increased economic dependence upon the PRC; (ii) the undermining of its core freedoms, rights and values and the PRC's interference with the rule of law; (iii) the subordination of its culture; (iv) the weakening of its political institutions; and (v) the deterioration of everyday life. Lo defines mainlandisation as the process of making the HKSAR politically more dependent on Beijing, economically more reliant on the mainland's support, socially more patriotic towards the motherland and legally more reliant on the interpretation of the Basic Law by the PRC National People's Congress.[25] Kwong and Yu summarise mainlandisation as Hong Kong's 'ideological assimilation to mainland China at the expense of its core values, such as the rule of law and professionalism'.[26]

Economic integration – billed as Hong Kong's saviour in 2003 – is now seen as a Trojan horse. Though resented, it is the policy of the Central Authorities and, as such, must be supported by the HKSAR government however much it provokes public anger. In 2007, for example, the CE, Donald Tsang, exhorted Hongkongers to embrace the opportunities offered by greater economic integration with China.[27] In 2009, his successor, Leung Chun-ying, faced with rising

[24] C. Mo Man-ching, cited in J. Lam, '"Hongkonger" makes it to world stage with place in Oxford English Dictionary', *SCMP*, 19 March 2014.

[25] S. H. Lo, 'The mainlandization and recolonization of Hong Kong: a triumph of convergence over divergence with mainland China', in Cheng, *The Hong Kong Administrative Region*, pp. 179–231.

[26] K. M. Kwong and H. Yu, 'Identity politics', in Y. Zheng and C. P. Yew (eds.), *Hong Kong under Chinese Rule: Economic Integration and Political Gridlock* (Singapore: World Scientific Publishing, 2013), 135n27.

[27] Y. W. Chu, *Lost in Transition: Hong Kong Culture in the Age of China* (Albany, New York: State University of New York Press, 2013), p. 156.

opposition to the influx of mainlanders into Hong Kong (especially the high number of mainland mothers giving birth in local hospitals) sought to assuage public opinion by promising protective measures to reserve Hong Kong land for Hongkongers.[28] However, on being elected, he reneged on this undertaking, which led some activists to fashion a Pinocchio puppet of him. He announced that there would be no quota for mainland births at local hospitals and backed plans to build three new towns along the border, in the New Territories. This development was to prove very controversial, earning the ire not only of those immediately affected by village clearances but also of civil society activists concerned with mainlandisation. Whilst 6 per cent of the development was destined to provide much-needed public housing for Hongkongers, the remaining retail and accommodation units were all intended for the mainland market. One in a line of integration policies, this generated heated discussion, protests and continuing concerns about the effects of mainlandisation on Hongkongers' way of life.

As Vickers points out, Hongkongers' 'residual attachment to the Chinese race' has since 1997 come to sit alongside a strong antipathy to, and suspicion of, the mainland and its people.[29] Increasingly, Hongkongers resent the impact that 'mainlandisation' is having on their territory. Greenhouse, Yngvesson and Engel, writing of another place, describe how in the eyes of the inhabitants:

> the landscape bears the marks of this altered stream: housing developments or industrial areas where farms once were, old landmarks disappearing. On the street, they meet unfamiliar faces ... the distinction between people who are where they belong and people who are out of place is highly charged [and] evokes the image of rival moral orders sharing the same space, as if the local landscape were contested ground.[30]

This captured exactly the situation in Hong Kong in 2012. The policy of relaxing border controls, facilitating 'soft integration' and encouraging mainlandisation has produced a backlash against the degradation

[28] Kwong and Yu, 'Identity politics' in Zheng and Yew, *Hong Kong under Chinese Rule*, p. 138.

[29] E. Vickers, *In Search of an Identity: The Politics of History as a School Subject in Hong Kong, 1960s–2005*. (London: Routledge 2003), p. 244.

[30] C. J. Greenhouse, B. Yngvesson and D. M. Engel, *Law and Community in Three American Towns* (New York: Cornell University Press, 1994), p. 1.

of Hongkongers' everyday lives by millions of mainlander visitors. These visitors vastly outnumber the 7 million people who reside in Hong Kong.

Hongkongers have not taken to being treated as second-class citizens in their own city. Demonstrations have broken out concerning even minor perceived infractions of the rule that everyone should be treated equally. Shops and businesses thought to be showing favouritism to mainlanders or discriminating against Hongkongers find themselves at the centre of a storm.[31] More than a thousand people demonstrated outside the Dolce and Gabbana store, for example, which allegedly allowed mainlanders to take photographs outside but not Hongkongers; a 2012 article written by a school student arguing that the influx of mainlanders was harming Hong Kong 'went viral on Facebook and online forums'.[32] In April 2012, netizens expressed anger that menus in a local café (agnes b.) had adopted simplified mainland characters rather than the traditional Chinese used in Hong Kong: 'They dubbed this "invasion" by simplified Chinese'.[33] In certain areas of Hong Kong, residents felt that their neighbourhoods were being transformed by mainlanders. In To Kwa Wan, for example, shops and residential blocks had been turned into guest houses for visiting mainlanders, a trend set to continue as mainland tourism is projected to increase to between 70 and 100 million by 2023, especially after the opening of the Hong Kong-Macau-Zhuhai Bridge. Mainlanders – said to be attracted to Hong Kong because of its orderliness and cleanliness – were seen as ruining these very characteristics by their disorderly behaviour.[34]

These social infractions – though often minor – were interpreted as breaking the rules and frequently subsumed under the catch-all phrase as the 'breakdown of the rule of law'. As one social activist remarked in 2012, 'Hong Kong culture is basically a respect for the rule of law . . . in the end it's the rule of law. And we feel mainland people are abusing our tolerance.'[35] 'Integration Anxiety' was said to make Hongkongers worried about losing their cultural distinctiveness and their home becoming 'just another Chinese city'. There is 'a fear that Hong Kong

[31] Kwong and Yu, 'Identity politics', pp. 141–2.
[32] Kwong and Yu, 'Identity politics'. [33] Kwong and Yu, 'Identity politics'.
[34] Kwong and Yu, 'Identity politics'.
[35] M. Mo, quoted in V. England, 'Hong Kong suffers identity crisis as China's influence grows', *The Guardian*, 23 March 2012.

will no longer belong to Hongkongers ... the fear of colonisation by the mainland'.[36] The government was accused of remaining heedless to the complaints of local people badly affected by the 'locust invasion' of mainlanders and called upon to defuse the tensions caused by mainlandisation.[37] Given its obligations to uphold 'one country', however, it was never going to put Hongkongers' concerns first.

The over-arching image which came to symbolise how Hongkongers felt about mainlandisation first emerged in 2012, when a picture appeared on posters and across social media of a giant locust towering over the Lion Rock, symbolising mainland 'invaders' devouring Hong Kong. This followed a full-page advertisement in the *Apple Daily*[38] that summed up the feeling amongst many Hongkongers that their home was being destroyed and reshaped by mainlanders.[39] The general public has become hyper-vigilant for signs of the mainlandisation of everyday life. In 2012, public anger focussed on a number of targets. Mainland mothers were blamed for taking up beds in local hospitals. Mainland children were said to be 'swamping' local schools and nurseries, edging out local children. Overcrowding on the trains to Lo Wu was blamed on mainlanders carrying outsize baggage and boxes of goods bought for parallel trading over the border. Locals also complained of being unable to buy baby milk powder because mainlanders were buying all the stock to resell on the mainland, where baby milk has been contaminated by unscrupulous manufacturers. Hong Kong's 'home' bank, HSBC, was criticised for replacing the complex local script on its ATMs with the simplified characters of mainland China. Local newspapers blame mainlanders for everything from crime and disease to rising property prices and undercutting the job market.[40] A Tsim Sha Tsui East news stand owner complained of being abused by mainlanders for failing to speak Putonghua.[41]

36 England, 'Hong Kong suffers identity crisis'.

37 'Immediate government action needed', *Ming Pao*, 7 February 2012; 'Cross border conflicts calling for resolution', *Ming Pao*, 19 February 2012.

38 Kwong and Yu, 'Identity politics', p. 134.

39 J. H. C. Lau, 'Hong Kong is reshaped by mainlanders', *New York Times*, 24 June 2007.

40 C. Gao, 'HK gold retailers overwhelmed by mainland shoppers', *China Daily*, 2 May 2013.

41 'A Hong Kong newspaper vendor beaten for failing to speak Mandarin', *Dictionary of Politically Incorrect Hong Kong Cantonese*, www.badcanto.wordpress.com, 4 April 2012.

Mainlanders' distinctive dialects, habits and dress provide ammunition for an explosion of xenophobic sentiments. Photographs appear across social media of mainland children urinating on the Mass Transit Railway (MTR) and in the streets. A 'May Day Stink' protest in April 2014 parodied such incidents, with protestors pretending to defecate in the streets. Exhorted since the 1970s to 'Keep Hong Kong Clean', such uncivil behaviour was seen by Hongkongers as proof that mainlandisation was debasing their way of life. A 'Reclaim Sheung Shui' group protested against the mainlandisation of their area, and the police were again forced to intervene when scuffles broke out in Tsim Sha Tsui during another demonstration against mainland shoppers.

Kwong and Yu remind us that this rise in distrust of the Central People's Government in 2012 was not simply related to perceived degradations of life in Hong Kong. It was, they argue, partly related to events on the mainland – the trials of Bo Xilai, the harsh treatment of human rights activist Chen Guangcheng and the suspicious death in mainland custody of Tiananmen dissident Li Wangyang.[42] This reminds us that the mood in Hong Kong cannot be divorced from events in China and anxieties that similar things might happen in Hong Kong. Tellingly, a 2012 survey revealed that public confidence in the 'one country, two systems' formula had dropped back to 1993 levels. The collapse of the formula would mean Hong Kong was becoming more like mainland China, where bad things happened to dissidents and ordinary people. Rumours persistently circulate in Hong Kong of mainlanders trying to kidnap young children at MTR stations, fast food restaurants, playgrounds and schools. As Kwong and Yu say, though the reports could not be verified, 'child-grab' rumours still swept Hong Kong in 2012, signalling a 'deep sense of insecurity generated by the increasing numbers of mainland visitors . . . given that child-grab is perceived as common in mainland China'.[43]

Mainland visitors in Hong Kong have become surrogates for these 'Integration Anxiety' fears. Petersson warns that the existence of scapegoating phenomena like this can produce a 'highly explosive mix'.[44]

[42] Kwong and Yu, 'Identity politics', p. 136.

[43] Kwong and Yu, 'Identity politics', p. 147.

[44] B. Petersson, 'Combating uncertainty, combating the global: scapegoating, xenophobia and the national-local nexus' in B. Petersson and E. Clark (eds.), *Identity Dynamics and the Construction of Boundaries* (Lund, Sweden: Nordic Academic Press, 2003), pp. 103–4.

The stranger is taken to 'epitomise all that is bad, inferior, or deteriorating in society',[45] encapsulating an argument made by anthropologist Mary Douglas about the power of what is seen as 'pollution' to clarify and strengthen a symbolic order.[46] Dirt, Douglas argues, is simply 'matter out of place', and by placing the blame for it on some outside challenger, it clarifies the ambiguity that new elements create for the social order, 'an ambiguity that could throw doubt on reigning classifications'.[47]

A society's reaction to such infractions 'condemns any object or idea likely to confuse or contradict cherished classifications'.[48] The social consequences of some 'offences', Douglas argues, can 'ripple out in all directions and can never be reversed'.[49] In Hong Kong, instances of mainlanders spitting or urinating in the street produce outrage because such behaviour violates the accepted rules and norms of that society, reinforcing the felt need to reinstate the order of things. Hong Kong is, after all, a society where the rule of law has also come to embrace the following of rules and procedures deemed to operate for the common good. Any violation by 'outsiders' provokes a reaction, be that ridicule or moral condemnation. However, in 2012, the more extreme forms of anti-mainland xenophobia also produced condemnation, re-establishing the HKSAR as a place both orderly and liberal – and thus quite different from mainland China.

CROSS-BORDER CONTACT

If mainland tourists are intrigued by Hong Kong precisely because it is different, many Hongkongers visit the mainland for the same reason. In 1999, around 75,000 Hongkongers regularly travelled to the mainland to visit a spouse and/or children. In 2003, they made 52.6 million trips to the mainland, up by 34 per cent compared with 1998.[50] Children

[45] Petersson, 'Combating uncertainty'.

[46] J. C. Alexander and S. Seidman (eds.), *Culture and Society: Contemporary Debates* (Cambridge: Cambridge University Press, 1990), p. 19.

[47] Alexander and Seidman, *Culture and Society*, p. 19.

[48] M. Douglas, *Purity and Danger: An Analysis of Concepts of Pollution and Taboo* (Harmondsworth: Pelican, 1996), p. 35.

[49] Douglas, *Purity and Danger*, pp. 158–9.

[50] Department of Census & Statistics, Hong Kong Government, Transport, Communications & Tourism, 2003.

of Hong Kong families living in Shenzhen crossed the border daily for schooling or university; elderly people retired to Guangzhou, where the cost of living was cheaper, travelling back and forth to visit their relatives in Hong Kong; workers travelled across the border in both directions every day by fast bus, train or boat. Figures for 2006 showed that roughly 8,000 people took the Kowloon Canton Railway (KCRC) through-train from Hunghom to Guanzhou every day, whilst another 6,000 caught the ferry to Shenzhen and other coastal cities.[51]

Kwong and Yu note that mainland tourism to Hong Kong has also risen ten times between 1998 and 2011 and that, whereas in 1998 only 2.6 per cent of visitors were from the mainland, by 2011 this figure has risen to 67 per cent, twice the number of tourists from elsewhere.[52] In 2013, Hong Kong received 54.3 million visitors of whom 40.5 million came from the mainland; over 277 million passed through the territory's border control points. By 2014, an estimated 70 million mainlanders were visiting Hong Kong each year. This rise is due to a change of policy introduced by China in 2003. The Individual Visitor Scheme relaxed an existing rule that mainlanders might only visit Hong Kong as part of a tour group and allowed individuals to enter as single tourists. The policy was introduced to help boost Hong Kong's economy in the wake of the Asian Financial Crisis and the SARS outbreak, both of which had had a devastating effect on the tourist market. As a result, the land and sea borders with mainland China have become intensely busy places, seething with strangers. In an average month, more than 8 million passed through the border controls at Lo Wu and Lok Ma Chau, making these crossings by far the busiest on the mainland, if not the world. By 2012, it was clear that the number of mainlander visitors was giving rise to resentment. Whilst good for the economy in the retail and commercial sectors, ordinary Hongkongers felt they were being 'swamped' by mainlanders.

This resentment partly stems from a reversal of fortunes. Hongkongers have long seen themselves as more modern, sophisticated and superior to their mainland compatriots. Surveys in the 1990s found that Hongkongers saw mainlanders as 'poor, lazy, unfriendly, superstitious, coarse, uncultured, and unintelligent'.[53] However, the Asian Financial Crisis

[51] *SCMP*, 7 February 2006.

[52] Kwong and Hu, 'Identity politics' in Zheng and Yew, *Hong Kong under Chinese Rule*, p. 141.

[53] Carroll, *Concise History of Hong Kong*, p. 235.

and the SARS outbreak impacted negatively on Hong Kong's economy just as China's grew. Where once mainlanders were poor, 'country cousins', they are now often wealthy visitors indulging in conspicuous consumption of luxury goods. Their spending now symbolises the HKSAR's dependency upon mainland economic largesse, the 'golden handcuffs' that chain the HKSAR to the mainland.

This fear of life becoming different and more ambivalent is described by Bauman and May as heterophobia.[54] Normally, they observe, people believe that the state protects peace and order, and in doing so enables people to pursue their lives and plans. In Hong Kong, however, it is the state itself – local and national – which is seen as the cause of disorder, allowing millions of mainlanders to enter the territory, adversely affecting locals' life chances, and reducing the territory's status from a global city to a tourist destination. Mainlandisation was a ticking time bomb, the city 'being changed too fast' into something the population feared.[55] For most Hongkongers, the mainland system was 'totally at odds with their own core values'.[56] But integration is the state's hegemonic project, and so in a speech on 1 October 2012, the CE again exhorted the population to 'embrace every opportunity that the development of our country brings to Hong Kong',[57] arguing that greater integration with the Pearl River Delta region was in the city's 'best interests'. Not everyone agreed. One critic warned Hongkongers:

> When the [m]ainland sneezes, we don't just catch cold we develop pneumonia. Integration is a fact, and our future depends on it. But whilst we can't reject it wholesale, we can deal with problems such as reducing the numbers of pregnant mainland visitors and tourists . . . To our national leaders, I say many Hong Kong people love China. But they express it not through waving the flag or singing the national anthem, but by protesting for dissidents and against national education. Their sentiment is unlikely to change and will only harden. We must deal with it wisely so the gulf between protesters and governors does not become unbridgeable.[58]

[54] Z. Bauman and T. May, *Thinking Sociologically* (Oxford: Blackwell, 2001), p. 133.
[55] M. Chugani, 'Public eye', *SCMP*, 11 April 2012.
[56] M. Chugani, 'Hong Kong's fear of "mainlandisation" stems from everyday frustration', *SCMP*, 8 October 2012.
[57] C. Lee, 'Closer ties between HK, Mainland China "essential", says Leung', *SCMP*, 1 October 2012.
[58] A. Lo, 'Be a statesman CY, not a chameleon', *SCMP*, 3 October 2012.

A 2011 book, *Hong Kong as a City State*, caught the public mood. It asked, 'What is Hong Kong?' and 'Hong Kong belongs to who?'[59] It became one of the year's best-sellers and its text the programme of the Hong Kong City-State Autonomy Movement,[60] which sees its mission as the safeguarding of Hong Kong's autonomy by pushing for greater separation from the mainland.[61] Its supporters have garnered attention by waving the old colonial British flag during street demonstrations. On one occasion, a demonstrator carried a placard reading 'Chinese scram back to China'.[62] In the run-up to the 2012 LEGCO elections, a few candidates were even heard to chant 'down with the Communist Party'. In 2013, the group sent a letter to British Prime Minister David Cameron asking Britain to return to Hong Kong as its sovereign power. Chinese leaders were outraged. One told the protestors to 'love China or leave'; another suggested that the mainland should not wait until 2047 to effect Hong Kong's full reintegration but should fully impose its will on the territory with immediate effect.[63]

These anti-mainland feelings were mirrored in polls measuring how Hongkongers identified themselves. The percentage identifying primarily as 'Chinese' had peaked in 2008, the year of the Beijing Olympics,[64] but by 2012, a survey indicated that the number of respondents identifying as 'Hong Kongers' had reached its highest level since 1997, double the number identifying as 'Chinese citizens'.

THE RULE OF LAW

When Hongkongers talk of their way of life, one of the first things they mention is the rule of law. Its inhabitants are so attached to it that they risk incurring the wrath of Beijing to defend it. When, why and how did the rule of law become a central feature of Hong Kong's culture and identity? The answer lies in Hong Kong's 'peculiar socio-political

[59] Kwong and Yu, 'Identity Politics', p. 137.
[60] S. Lau, 'Crusade for Hong Kong to keep its distance from Beijing picks up', *SCMP*, 11 October 2012.
[61] Lau, 'Crusade for Hong Kong'. [62] Lau, 'Crusade for Hong Kong'.
[63] S. Lau, 'De-Sinification debate re-emerges in Hong Kong', *SCMP*, 26 September 2012.
[64] Kwong and Yu, 'Identity Politics', p. 126.

experience'[65] as a British colony, as a sanctuary from trouble in China and/or as a safe place from which to influence political events in China (such as the Republican Revolution of 1911). As a British colony, it inherited a concept of legitimacy whose etymology, as Mohr reminds us, suggests that it rests on the rule of law. Equally, however, Hong Kong has been subject to the countervailing influence of Communism, which regards the rule of law as part of the West's 'soft power' tool-kit for subverting one-party rule in China.

The aetiology of 'British' rule of law has its roots in early colonial attempts to establish Hong Kong as an attractive place of trade for Chinese as well as European merchants. As Munn has argued, to 'attach' the Hong Kong Chinese to colonial rule the first governor, Davis, promised them the 'protection of equal laws, and ... the best fruits of science and civilisation, transplanted direct from the European headquarters'.[66] At the Supreme Court opening in 1844, the attorney general told those assembled that 'English laws were not the laws of vengeance but were intended to protect the innocent by the punishment of guilt, not to punish guilty by mere vindictive feelings'.[67] The chief justice added that, as inhabitants of a British colony, 'one of the great privileges you enjoy is the right to a due and even-handed administration of the English laws, and I am satisfied that the more you become acquainted with these laws, the more you will learn to love and respect them'.[68]

As I have argued elsewhere, this exhortation of the merits of English rule of law was in part a reflection of the colonisers' sense of themselves as bringers of civilisation to the East, and part conscious strategy designed to establish a red line between life under British rule and life in what was then seen as a barbarous China.[69] The comparison would be redrawn repeatedly during British rule, most notably during the 1950s and 1960s, when the Hong Kong government sought to prevent the Cold War 'going hot' in the colony by extolling an even-handed

[65] J. F. Tsai, *Hong Kong in Chinese History: Community and Social Unrest in the British Colony, 1842–1913* (New York: Columbia University Press 1993).
[66] C. Munn, 'Scratching with a rattan: William Caine and the Hong Kong magistracy 1841–44', *Hong Kong Law Journal* 25, no. 2 (1995), p. 234.
[67] J. W. Norton Kyshe, *The History of the Laws and Courts of Hong Kong* (1898; Hong Kong: Vetch & Lee, 1971), p. 65.
[68] Munn, 'Scratching with a rattan', p. 233.
[69] C. A. G. Jones and J. Vagg, *Criminal Justice in Hong Kong* (London: Routledge, 2007).

application of law to rival political factions. In the 1970s, the administration would again turn to rule of law rhetoric to help solve its legitimacy crisis following the 1967 riots, whilst in the run-up to 1997, rule of law became a leading trope of the outgoing Patten administration.

These latter two periods are important for understanding the place of law in contemporary Hong Kong culture. The 1966 and 1967 riots reminded the Hong Kong government of the need to reattach the Chinese to colonial rule by revealing the lack of legitimacy of an unrepresentative colonial power. Repairing this deficit with democracy was not an option – China herself stringently opposed such a move. Nevertheless, there was an urgent requirement to restructure the way in which Hong Kong was governed. The answer was a wholesale, top-down, re-engineering of civil society, which Turner (citing Brecht) captures in the phrase, 'The government, having lost the confidence of the people, has decided to dissolve the people and form a new one.'[70] Without directly decrying life in Communist China (something the diplomats opposed) the colonial government set about making life in Hong Kong vastly more attractive than that in the People's Republic. As a result, the 1970s have gone down in folk memory as 'The Golden Years' of colonial rule. An extensive new consultative machinery provided grassroots people with readier channels of access to government; a large-scale programme of welfare colonialism provided free education, health care, mass public housing and an improved environment. Free festivals lifted morale and helped to establish a sense of 'belonging', whilst regular mass mobilisation in government campaigns to 'Keep Hong Kong Clean' and 'Fight Crime' established a view of Hong Kong as a clean, safe and civilised city. As Ng points out, for years this is the way in which the Hong Kong government has:

> organised the lives of the population to inculcate a set of values such as the work ethic, hygiene, civility and consumer etiquette, prescribing appropriate behaviour and comportment of Hong Kong's citizenry ... parks, waterfront promenades, even streets, are all structured to systematize or modify the people's behaviour and ... nurture civic virtue. These efforts produce and support a particular international image of Hong Kong people as polite, disciplined, and professional.[71]

[70] M. Turner, 'Sixties/Nineties', Art Installation, Hong Kong Arts Centre, 1996.

[71] J. Ng, *Paradigm City: Space, Culture, and Capitalism in Hong Kong* (Albany, New York: State University of New York Press, 2009), p. 11.

Much of the civic virtue now seen as undone by mainlandisation stems from this period of 1970s hegemonic restructuring. The government pursued what was known as a 'Rose Garden' strategy to enhance the city's environment and cultivate new kinds of citizens (Ng calls them 'bourgeois') for whom 'Red China' presented a far less appealing 'homeland'. The ideology of the rule of law was absolutely critical to this message. The 1970s witnessed a frenzy of legislation ushering in substantive legal and social change, particularly in the field of labour relations and employment law. Procedural fairness was crucial to the message that law was applied in an even-handed, transparent fashion. Hongkongers were not given political rights, but they were given legal rights. In place of political accountability, they were promised legal accountability, with government and its officials becoming more accountable than ever before to the law. In place of political transparency, they were to have legal transparency. Instead of political redress, they would have legal redress.

These universalising norms of law promised to cut through corruption, cronyism and patronage, creating a level socio-economic playing field upon which everyone (not just an elite few) could compete equally on merit to achieve prosperity and success. Rational legal administration meant that people would be treated impartially, on their merits rather than according to their status, whilst vast increases in legal aid also ensured that those with limited means would be able to claim their new legal rights. This dovetailed with the promise of rule of law ideology that everyone was equal before the law, that no one was above the law and that everyone would be treated openly and equally on the fair field of law. From this point onwards, Hong Kong developed a strong sense of itself as a 'city of law', a place in which the subjects of British colonial rule – though denied political rights – nevertheless enjoyed a wide range of liberal rights and freedoms. It was a self-image confirmed by the contrast in 1989 between Hong Kong, city of law and peaceful demonstrations in support of the democracy movement in China, and Beijing, city of tanks.

By such means, the colonial government created a Hong Kong identity centred on fairness, justice and rule of law. Procedural justice – the *way* things were done and goods distributed – became as (if not more) important than the substantive outcomes of the legal process. Nor was the rhetoric of rule of law an empty rhetoric: corruption, cronyism and patronage – once deemed an ineradicable aspect of Chinese society – *were* dramatically reduced by the Independent

1967 + rule of Law

Commission Against Corruption (ICAC); the courts *did* bring government to account, sometimes in spectacular fashion; citizens *did* enjoy a means of redress for their grievances; government *was* moderated by a liberal legal system.[72]

Lawyers were, however, generally conspicuous by their absence from this shift to liberalism, and effective restraints on state power and the kinds of the rights and freedoms associated with this kind of liberal society were all established without the kind of political struggles with which they are associated elsewhere. In addition, when in 1991 Hongkongers were granted a Bill of Rights, they became beneficiaries of a raft of wide-ranging internationally recognised freedoms and rights. Between its enactment in 1991 and 1997, the Bill of Rights enabled constitutional, civil rights and public interest lawyers to deliver some body blows to power. In a series of landmark cases, government officials were publicly called to account by the courts in unprecedented fashion. In the same decade, just as Britain was departing, Hongkongers were allowed the first opportunity to vote for number of LEGCO members on the basis of geographical (as opposed to functional) constituencies. By the end of colonial rule, moreover, the franchise had been further extended, as 2.7 million people were given the right to vote.

Unfortunately, since 1997, many of these gains have been lost, curtailed or squandered. Hong Kong's powerful elites have repeatedly flouted the law, and the public, noting this, has become increasingly vocal in its critique of their fitness to rule. The struggle of the Hong Kong courts to restrain the rulers has also generated doubts about whether law offers sufficient protection against Beijing's assaults. As I hope to demonstrate, these assaults on law have backfired, turning it into a 'core value' of Hongkongers' identity and a cherished marker of distinctiveness from mainland China. By looking at the years in the run-up to the handover, I try to show how, when and why Hongkongers became so hyper-vigilant about mainland incursions, a vigilance that has intensified in recent years. There is a growing sense that, as 'mainland ways' creep in, standards in Hong Kong public life have worsened – even the highest of Hong Kong officials have violated such cherished norms as 'everyone must be treated equally' and 'no-one is above the law'.

[72] See Halliday, Karpik and Feeley, *Fighting for Political Freedom*.

These norms were fully established between 1992 and 1997, partly by the Bill of Rights and partly by the discourse of rights of the then-Governor, Chris Patten. In the last years of British rule, he sought to construct a narrative of colonialism that would compensate for its many past deficiencies. He did this by impressing upon Hongkongers the importance of the rule of law. In his speeches, he repeatedly stressed the importance of the rule of law, the freedom of the press, freedom of expression, religious liberty, judicial independence and the right to call the government and its officials to account. The rule of law was, he insisted, 'the foundation of Hong Kong's way of life', as well as its economic success.[73] This ideology of the rule of law gave Hongkongers a sense of entitlement to equal, fair and just treatment that does not sit easily with their post-1997 status as subjects without power. Upon its resumption of sovereignty, China reduced the franchise by 90 per cent, introduced corporate voting, dismantled old channels of consultation and replaced them with united front organisations, and restored the Hong Kong polity to a 1960s-style centralised, executive-led, plutocracy. It was a system highly suited to the CCP's doctrine of democratic centralism but which, ironically, made the post-1997 government even less representative than its colonial predecessor. Within two years, international observers began to talk of the 'death of the rule of law' in Hong Kong.

CULTURE AND RESISTANCE

The exclusion of critics, limitations on the power of LEGCO, dismantling of previous channels of communication and attacks on law have left the public with nowhere to go but the streets. Mass marches now punctuate what have become routine demonstration days, such as the 1 July anniversary of the handover and the 4 June commemoration of Tiananmen Square. This, a new tradition of dissent, has provided new experiences of popular political participation. Spontaneous demonstrations occur at a moment's notice, organised via social media. The rules about public protests require prior notice to, and permission from, the police but, Cartier observes, these 'flash protests' frequently fail to abide

[73] L. S. Ngan, 'More than a war of words: identity, politics and the struggle for dominance in the recent "Political Reform" period in Hong Kong', *Economy & Society*, 24 (1 February 1995), pp. 67–100.

by the legal requirements.[74] They range from protests by small groups of artists and cultural workers to 'hundreds of thousands of people' expressing local, regional and national concerns. Some focus on the government's 'raze and develop' policy, which has seen local landmarks such as the Queen's Pier and Star Ferry Clock Tower demolished, eviscerating 'places of people's experience and local memory'.[75]

Hong Kong's political landscape has become more complicated, divided, rowdy and unpredictable. Where once there were few political parties, there is now a proliferation but, due to the built-in majority of the government, none are capable of mounting a 'loyal opposition'. Without an effective voice in the formal machinery of government, the public has deployed a variety of other means to express its grievances and protect its culture. In addition to street demonstrations, a host of alternative forms of expression have flourished. They include politically-informed art, performance works, disrespectful cartoons and graffiti, short dramas, humorous skits, dance, song, satire, films, language, rumours, gestures, jokes, satirical parodies, irony, graffiti and insulting slang, all of which 'challeng[e] perceptions and lead . . . to the possibility of new perspectives . . . [conveying] meaning about ideas and social issues through creative composition in actions, words and images'.[76] Many are concerned with the theme of identity and the threat to the rule of law. Scott calls these the 'fugitive political conduct' of subordinate groups, often adopted out of prudence when speaking truth to power carries real risks for the transgressor.[77]

By such means, Scott argues, the subordinate manage to artfully imply that they are grudging conscripts to the performance of the official script of the powerful, constructing a shared critique of the 'self-portrait of the elites as they would have themselves seen'.[78] For Ng, the 'tactile guile' or stratagem appeals because it is also able to 'elude ideological control . . . The inventiveness of the culture of the quotidian opens up social spaces, no matter how fragile or fleeting'.[79] Thus, she notes, the 'hard sell' of nationalism in Hong Kong has often been countered by irony, sarcasm

[74] C. Cartier, 'Power plays: alternative performance art and urban space in the political life of the city', in Louie, *Hong Kong Culture*, pp. 25–40.

[75] Cartier, 'Power plays', p. 27. [76] Cartier, 'Power plays', p. 29.

[77] J. C. Scott, *Domination and the Arts of Resistance: Hidden Transcripts* (New Haven: Yale University Press, 1992).

[78] Scott, *Domination and the Arts of Resistance*, pp. 15–18.

[79] Ng, *Paradigm City*, pp. 17–18.

and derision in newspaper essays and comic strips'.[80] These are all what I refer to here as 'boundary-making practices'.

PATRIOTISM

This theatre of politics is part of an increasingly sophisticated repertoire of resistance to what Ku and Pun call the central government's hegemonic project to remake the 'citizen-subject' of Hong Kong.[81] Where under colonial rule Hong Kong people had some – albeit limited – ability to influence state activity through law and partial democracy, since 1997, they have become less able to participate in what Bauman and May call 'the definition and management of "law and order"'.[82] Citizen's rights cannot be exercised fully if the activities of the state are surrounded by secrecy and if the 'ordinary people' have no insight into the intentions and the doings of their rulers. Relations between the state and its subject will become strained, they argue, if the state tends to treat its subjects 'as if they were unable to determine what is good for them and act in a manner that serves their best interests'.[83] Since 1997, however, Beijing has insisted that only 'patriots' know what is good for Hong Kong.

The word 'patriot' has appeared more frequently in official discourse since 1997. Patriotism is defined as 'loving the country', and according to Deng Xiaoping, only 'patriots' should be permitted to govern Hong Kong. This begs the question, who or what is a patriot? Deng's answer to this was that a patriot:

> respects the Chinese nation, sincerely supports the motherland's resumption of sovereignty over Hong Kong and wishes not to impair Hong Kong's prosperity and stability ... Those who meet these requirements are patriots, whether they believe in capitalism or feudalism or even slavery. We don't demand that they be in favour of China's socialist system; we only ask them to love the motherland and Hong Kong.[84]

[80] Ng, *Paradigm City*, pp. 145–6.

[81] A. S. Ku and N. Pun, 'Remaking citizenship in Hong Kong', in A. S. Ku and N. Pun (eds.), *Remaking Citizenship in Hong Kong: Community, Nation and the Global City* (Abingdon: Routledge, 2006), pp. 1–16.

[82] Bauman and May, *Thinking Sociologically*, pp. 137–8.

[83] Bauman and May, *Thinking Sociologically*.

[84] Deng Xiaoping, 'Remarks on "one Country, two Systems"', 23–24 June 1984, in *Important Documents concerning the Hong Kong SAR Basic Law of the People's Republic of China* (Beijing: The People's Press 1990), p. 6.

However, it has become clear that Beijing's definition of patriotism also requires a 'love of the Communist Party', which most Hongkongers do not share; after all, many of them fled Communism in the 1950s and 1960s. They are now expected to demonstrate patriotism overtly – those who do so are friends of China and enjoy the benefits of this connection to the state; those who fail to do so (or fail to do so with sufficient enthusiasm) are 'enemies within', 'criminals' or subversives, deemed 'unpatriotic' by the party faithful keen to demonstrate their own credentials. This assimilation crusade tends to breed resentment in the very people it aims to convert.[85] Their resistance is something I try to capture here by delineating some of the skirmishes being fought in what I have termed 'the culture wars'.

Hong Kong culture is multi-faceted. There is, however, a recognised core and rule of law is at the heart of this. Amongst sociologists and anthropologists, the term 'culture' is the subject of some debate. Traditionally, 'culture' connoted the reproduction, transmission and reception of symbolic and/or cultural forms, including norms, beliefs, practices and values.[86] This, however, suggests the transmission to passive receptors of a conservative form of culture. But culture is not simply a set of received norms and beliefs. It is a process through which a world view is constructed and modified, a set of expressive symbols that can be organized to fit new needs. In their classic text, *The Social Construction of Reality*,[87] Berger and Luckman argue that people are not merely powerless recipients of culture – they actively create, shape and use it. Increasingly, the sociology of culture seeks to examine the conditions surrounding the production of cultural symbols (such as law) and the characteristics of the cultural symbols themselves.[88]

The social constructionist approach to law and culture adopted here seeks to understand how particular legal and cultural configurations have arisen in Hong Kong. As Thomson points out, grasping the 'hidden history' of present appearances gives people a powerful tool 'to reveal how things could be otherwise and thus to overcome

[85] Bauman and May, *Thinking Sociologically*, p. 144.
[86] *The Polity Reader in Cultural Theory* (Cambridge: Polity Press, 1994), pp. 1–2.
[87] P. L. Berger and T. Luckman, *The Social Construction of Reality: A Treatise in the Sociology of Knowledge* (New York: Doubleday, 1966).
[88] D. Crane, 'Introduction', in D. Crane (ed.), *The Sociology of Culture* (Oxford: Basil Blackwell, 1994), p. 13.

powerlessness'.[89] Here, I explore how political, social and legal factors shape – and are shaped by – Hong Kong's 'culture creators'. What need does the rule of law as a cultural symbol express? Have the law's inadequacies encouraged people to construct other forms which better answer their needs?

As Fletcher argues, 'of all the dreams that drive men and women into the streets, from Buenos Aires to Budapest, it is this popular defence of "the rule of law" which is the most puzzling'.[90] The role of lawyers as carriers of this culture is an important part of the explanation, but the belief in the rule of law has escaped the confines of the legal system and, like some genetically modified crop, has permeated Hong Kong society, where it now carries a host of meanings, from 'justice' and 'fairness' to simply demanding that people – and governments – do things 'by the rules'.

In the courtroom, political freedoms and rights have been extended since 1997 and made part of a broader social environment and political community.[91] In the streets and in multiple cultural formats, the public has mobilised around law, freedom and rights. There has emerged a broad alliance across political and class lines rallying around the defence of the rule of law. This includes social groups, the Catholic Church, pro-democracy lawyers and politicians, trade unionists, welfare and environmental campaigners, social activist groups and school children, as well as myriad grassroots community organisations and individuals. Whilst there have been arguments and fissures within these groups as to tactics, they have unified around the rule of law (and, recently, universal suffrage) their commitment only enhanced by Beijing's attempts at repression. At the same time, however, channels for airing grievances have narrowed. Ma Ngok points, for example, to the degree to which China has co-opted the owners of the mass media in Hong Kong, lowering the possibility that grievances will receive fair coverage in the press.[92] With LEGCO unable to leverage public

[89] A. Thomson, 'Critical legal studies in Britain', in P. Fitzpatrick and A. Hunt (eds.), *Critical Legal Studies* (Oxford: Blackwell, 1987), p. 192.

[90] G. P. Fletcher, *Basic Concepts in Legal Thought* (New York: Oxford University Press, 1996), p. 4.

[91] J. Priban, 'Sharing the paradigms? Critical legal studies and the sociology of law', in R. Banakar and M. Travers (eds.), *An Introduction to Law and Social Theory* (Oxford: Hart, 2002), p. 126.

[92] Ma Ngok, 'Press relationship in post-1997 Hong Kong: constant negotiation amidst self-restraint', *The China Quarterly*, 192 (December 2007), pp. 949–70.

grievances effectively, and the government listening principally to Beijing, the 'boundary making practices' of courts and culture provide spaces for the public voice.

B/ORDERING

What I have outlined above, and what this book attempts to explore, is the means by which Hongkongers have been constructing and defending their social world since 1997, their 'bordering practices'. For those 'inside' a border, van Houtem suggests, '(b)ordering practices' reflect a desire 'to distance oneself from the Other in order to uphold the (fantasy of the) self during feelings of fear or anxiety'.[93] What I call Hong Kong's 'walls of law' have their part to play in this, but the social world is defined by more than law, and in particular, it is defined by borders and those whom borders exclude. Maps, borders and nations are human-made products.[94] Beijing's way of talking about Hong Kong's retrocession has, however, the suggestion of immutability and inevitability about it, as if the order of the universe has been restored to its normal, 'natural' self. But this discourse masks the play of history and human intervention in China's territorial compass, glossing over the many disputes that remain within its borders as to what is and is not 'Chinese' territory.

In 1841, Britain secured a border with China when it took Hong Kong by force. That border stopped at Hong Kong Island, ceded in perpetuity to the British. In 1860, at the end of the second Opium War, a new border was created in Kowloon, at Boundary Street. In 1898, China granted the British a 99-year lease on land further north of Boundary Street, as well as outlying islands.[95] The border now shifted to the edge of the New Territories along the Shum Chun River. This border still separates the HKSAR from mainland China with a high wire fence, guards and sensors to detect intruders. It was the expiry of this lease that necessitated the retrocession of the whole of Hong Kong to China in 1997.

Until 2047, under the 'one country, two systems' formula, Hong Kong is both part and not part of mainland China. This temporal fix

[93] van Houtum et al., *B/Ordering Space*, pp. 675–7.
[94] van Houtum et al., *B/Ordering Space*, pp. 675–7.
[95] See P. Wesley-Smith, *Unequal Treaty: 1989–1997* (Hong Kong: Oxford University Press, 1998).

makes Hong Kong's existence all the more tenuous. Spatially and temporally, it is a land 'in between'. Both Communists and Nationalists have used it as a base from which to organise subversive activities inside China. Nineteenth- and twentieth-century cross-border mobilisations of labour and political activists also alarmed those in power (and still do). It was only in the 1950s, following Mao's victory, that the PRC became isolated. During the Cold War, the border became a fortified line through which very distinct geopolitical, socio-spatial and ideological differences were communicated.[96]

Hong Kong in the Cold War became the land between the 'open' world of the West and 'closed' world of Communist China. Crossing the border was a political act, fraught with danger. Some, attempting to swim across, were eaten by sharks, and at the height of the Cultural Revolution, bodies floated down the Shum Chun River. Armed incidents led the then-Commissioner of Police, Duncan MacIntosh, to erect a chain of strong police posts across the border hilltops at strategic points, each within sight of one another. These 'MacIntosh Cathedrals' were imposing concrete structures with a distinctive appearance and outline against the skyline.[97] Built on military lines, they were organised as panoptical towers:

> Centrally, there is a round, two storied, tower, and jutting from its sides are two long, one storied arms ... The upper storey of the tower is the Control room, equipped with radio and telephone, which is manned continuously. In the wall, at head height around the circumference, windows afford a 360 degree arc of vision ... [It] is manned throughout the twenty four hours of the day ... The whole building is surrounded by a barbed wire perimeter of some depth ... All the posts are well-armed, having automatic weapons and grenades as well as ... rifles and revolvers ... and there is a plentiful supply of ammunition.[98]

Later additions included concrete bunkers, barbed-wire-topped chain-linked fences, barbed-wire entanglements and slit trenches.[99] These gave the police 'a strong visible presence along the colony's first line

[96] H. van Houtum, 'The Geopolitics of Border and Boundaries', *Geopolitics*, 10 (2005), pp. 672–9.

[97] M. E. Davis, *Police Magazine*, December 1953, cited in R. G. Horsnell, 'The Macintosh Cathedrals, *Journal of the Hong Kong Branch of the Royal Asiatic Society*, 35 (1995), pp. 173–4.

[98] Horsnell, 'The Macintosh Cathedrals'.

[99] Horsnell, 'The Macintosh Cathedrals'.

of defence'.[100] In the lead up to 1997, the 'Towers' were equipped with more sophisticated equipment, such as thermal imagers and sensors to enable night vision detection, as well as electronic surveillance equipment capable of seeing into buildings on the mainland side. This physical border between Hong Kong and mainland China remained intact after 1997. Though officially renamed 'the boundary', as one Hong Kong resident put it, 'I went to see the border. What can I say? It's still there.'[101]

BOUNDARY-MAKING: THE SYMBOLIC (RE)CONSTRUCTION OF COMMUNITY

State borders hold different meanings for people. They signify 'the point at which something becomes something else, at which the way things are done changes, at which "we" end and "they" begin, at which certain rules of behaviour no longer obtain and others take hold'.[102] Some of these borders can be found on the map, others are symbolic dividing lines 'that cannot be found on any map at all … they are social constructions'.[103] They are made and remade through social interaction in what Gieryn calls 'boundary work'.[104] It is at such borders that value systems meet, and with the increased porosity of the Hong Kong/mainland border, the differences between them have become more apparent. Modern border studies examines borders as differentiators of socially-constructed mindscapes and meaning.[105] A border is:

> a mutable and culturally constructed mixture of representation and physical form. Spaces mean different things to different people at

[100] Horsnell, 'The Macintosh Cathedrals'.

[101] W. Wei, 'A Hong Kong diary: June 22–1 July 1997', *Asia Week*, 4–10 July 1997.

[102] J. S. Migdal, 'Mental maps and virtual checkpoints: struggles to construct and maintain state and social boundaries', in J. S. Migdal (ed.), *Boundaries and Belonging: States and Societies in the Struggle to Shape Identities and Local Practices* (Cambridge: Cambridge University Press, 2004), pp. 3–26.

[103] Migdal, *Mental Maps*, pp. 5–6.

[104] T. F. Geryn, 'Boundary-work and the demarcation of science from non-science', *American Sociological Review*, 48, no. 6, 1983, pp. 781–95, cited in A. Wimmer, *Ethnic boundary making: institutions, power, networks* (Oxford: Oxford University Press, 2013).

[105] van Houtem, 'The geopolitics of borders and boundaries', pp. 672–79.

> different times and represent, reinforce, idealise and naturalise socio-cultural power relations ... Spaces and places ... are not fixed but are in a constant state of transition as a result of continuous, dialectical struggles of power and resistance among and between a diversity of stakeholders ... The "meanings" of any space ... draw on the cultural codes of the society that constructed it. These meanings ... are thus embedded in and permeated by a society's social and cultural norms and symbols.[106]

Boundary-making practices include modes of speaking, bodily markers (such as scars) and dress, all of which allow identification of one's own group members and the identification of outsiders.[107] Magdal terms the scrutiny of such markers 'virtual checkpoints' and 'mental maps' that divide 'home' from alien territory. Boundaries are 'more than simple dividers of spaces occupied by states. Multiple sets of boundaries can exist, beyond those associated with state borders. Social groupings have their own boundaries, virtual checkpoints and mental maps marking them off from other groupings'.[108]

According to Magdal, people's feelings of security depend upon these virtual checkpoints; they are 'constantly navigating' and searching for signs of the unfamiliar, ways of acting that make a place feel dangerous. Those who seek to set themselves apart reinforce their boundaries by adding what Wimmer calls new cultural diacritics in order to show how culturally different they are. These symbolic boundary markers mark out, amongst other things, safe places where the rules of conduct, dress, behaviour and values are familiar. The law is one of the clearest means of marking such a boundary:

> Not only does law set out the ways of doing things, it also projects an essential image of the state, as when it denotes a whole body of rules, institutions (such as courts) associated with them, and their affective component (as in 'respect for the law'). People are classified by whether they stay within state law (law abiding) or step outside them (law breakers). State law, then, both prescribes behaviour within the boundaries of the state and symbolically demarks those boundaries by signifying the realm and limits of the state's law.[109]

[106] A. Pritchard and N. Morgan, 'Hotel Babylon? Exploring hotels as liminal sites of transition and transgression', *Tourism Management*, 27 (2007), pp. 762–72.

[107] Wimmer, *Ethnic Boundary Making*, p. 11. [108] Migdal, *Mental Maps*, p. 7.

[109] Migdal, *Mental Maps*, p. 13.

Struggles over the construction of boundaries are 'the most fundamental personal and social processes. They construct a personal sense of belonging and identity ... binding their members in communities of belonging'.[110] Attempts to erode a boundary or change its meaning through reclassification or assimilation are likely to provoke a counteraction by members of the disappearing group.[111] The 1997 government's renaming of the 'border' as the 'boundary' was just such an attempt to reclassify the border, a semiotic step in the process of mainlandisation. But it was also a step towards the creation of an economic power-house in the Pearl River Delta. In his writings on regional economies, Ohmae identified the Hong Kong/Guangzhou nexus as a 'natural economic zone'.[112]

There is, however, little 'natural' about it. As Luke and O'Tuathail argue, such 'natural' units are more likely to be 'cartographical illusions' and 'neoliberal fantasies', created by the flow of industry, investment, individuals and information and intended to function as ports of entry into a global economy.[113] Whilst the dominance of the commercial elite post-1997 means that this plan has government backing, Hong Kong people view talk of 'the boundary' as fuzzy and suspicious. However, as senior Chinese official Lu Ping made clear in 1995, the mainland sees the value of Hong Kong as essentially economic, providing China with access to management skills, advanced technology and worldwide financial links.[114] Lu argued that:

> the value of Hong Kong to China has been and will be its economic value ... Of course, there are always a handful who are so naïve [as] to think that they can turn Hong Kong into a political city in order to influence the mainland in the sense of politics. If that were the case, Hong Kong would be of negative value instead of positive value to China. This [would be] disastrous for Hong Kong.[115]

110 Migdal, *Mental Maps*, p. 15. 111 Wimmer, *Ethnic Boundary Making*, p. 60.

112 See K. Ohmae, *The End of the Nation State: The Rise of Regional Economies* (New York: Free Press, 1995).

113 T. W. Luke and G. O'Tuathail, 'Global flowmations, local fundamentalisms, and fast geopolitics' in A. Herod, A. G. O'Tuathail, and S. M. Roberts, *Unruly World? Globalization, Governance and Geography* (London: Routledge, 1998), pp.72–94.

114 L. Choy and C. Law, 'Lu vows to snub Patten on HK visit', *SCMP*, 18 April 1995.

115 'Lu Ping's speech on Hong Kong's future', *SCMP*, 7 May 1994, cited in A. J. Nathan, China's *Transition: The Struggle for Hong Kong's Future* (New York: Columbia University Press, 1999).

In the run-up to 1997, leading Hong Kong businesses entered into collaboration with China as part of a strategy to increase their regional competitiveness.[116] China's pre-1997 discourse, Sum says, depicted Hong Kong predominantly as an economy, a 'prosperous and stable gateway for the modernization of the PRC'.[117] With the emergence of global capital: 'the older narratives of British colonialism, U.S. imperialism and Chinese nationalism no longer suffice to account for what is operating as a fluid, transnational, collaborationist structure of financial interests that, despite the ideological divergences of the parties involved, have as their mutually self-serving goal the prosperity and stability of the "Pearl of the Orient"'.[118]

Collusion between Hong Kong and mainland business interests, as well as political elites, aimed at keeping things the same and 'allowing institutional capitalism to reach new heights'.[119] However, as the foregoing suggests, since 1997, Hong Kong has become a highly political city and the reintegration project has become more problematic. The counteraction to mainlandisation in particular has produced a picture of a more unified (or over-unified) community solidarity. This apparently homogenous identity masks internal variations, disputes and differences, but as Cohen explains, symbolisations of community are 'umbrellas under which diversity can flourish, masks behind which a considerable degree of heterogeneity is possible'.[120] However, the symbolic construction of a sense of belonging that started life as a defence against 'outsiders' may, under repeated attacks, harden into an over-unified sense of community. Over time, this may produce a conception of identity as essentialist as the identity it originally sought to contest. This begins to capture what has been happening in Hong Kong since 1997 and perhaps explains the appeal of rule of law as an ideology.

On the face of it, a culture based on rule of law should be an integrative mechanism in Hong Kong life. But, as Schudson argues, 'culture is paradoxically both the most visible and most problematic of

[116] Sum, 'War of Words', pp. 76–7. [117] Sum, 'War of Words'.

[118] R. Chow, *King Kong in Hong Kong: Watching the "Handover" from the USA*', *Social Text*, 55 (1998), p. 224.

[119] A. Chun, *Unstructuring Chinese Society: The Fictions of Colonial Practice and the Changing Realities of "Land" in the New Territories of Hong Kong* (New York: Routledge, 2002), p. 20.

[120] R. Jenkins, *Social Identity* (London: Routledge, 1996), p. 111.

forces for societal integration'.[121] Whilst nation-states frequently try to use a common language, common education and collective rituals to integrate citizens and ensure their loyalty, culture 'does not necessarily call forth integration'.[122] A sociocultural community comes together around common, sacred symbols, often in moments of 'collective effervescence,' which energise the members of a community at that time, and later through memories of that time. In this way, ritual objects and practices contribute to social cohesion and solidarity.[123]

The 'rituals' which have provided cohesion in post-1997 Hong Kong have been public demonstrations against the erosion of the rule of law by the state, whose actions are seen as disintegrative and destabilising. Legitimacy has, as a result, shifted away from formal institutions to what Priban calls 'a narrative of justice'.[124] This new social solidarity is multifaceted and has its own norms, beliefs and values,[125] symbolised in the 2004 'Hong Kong Core Values Declaration'. This listed Hongkongers' core values as liberty, democracy, human rights, rule of law, fairness, social justice, peace and compassion, integrity and transparency, plurality, respect for individuals and upholding professionalism. The declaration's organisers said they were:

> greatly disturbed by the increasing erosion of Hong Kong's core values. The goals pursued by our community seem [to be] becoming more distant. The community is filled with a strong sense of helplessness and rising frustrations . . . Our core values are being shaken. Our city's governance and business environment have deteriorated. Our society's institutional rationality and social cohesion are being weakened. We have come to the critical moment. The alarm has rung to defend Hong Kong's core values.[126]

Protests in defence of core values have 'the emotional power to generate a sense of community' – they act like batteries recharging a sense of community and firing the style in which they are imagined.[127]

[121] M. Schudson, 'Culture and the integration of national societies', in Crane, *Sociology of Culture*, pp. 22–3.
[122] Schudson, 'Culture and the integration of national societies'.
[123] See E. Durkheim, *The Elementary Forms of Religious Life* (New York: Macmillan, 1915).
[124] Priban, *Beyond Procedural Legitimation*, p. 342.
[125] See C. Geertz, *The Interpretation of Culture* (Princeton: Basic Books, 1973).
[126] A. Leung, 'Push to defend city's Core Values', *SCMP*, 7 September 2004.
[127] M. Featherstone, *Undoing Culture: Globalization, Postmodernism and Identity* (London: Sage, 1995), p.108, referring to B. Anderson, *Imagined Communities* (London: Verso, 1991), p. 6.

Demonstrations, such as those on 4 June and 1 July, and Hong Kong's own 'Goddess of Democracy' are emblems of the kind which, during the early days of Maoist rule, the Communist Party regarded as 'a serious barrier to their efforts at political integration and transformation'.[128] That remains the mainland's attitude today. But for Hongkongers, such rituals are often a means of making some sense or order out of a situation of uncertainty and social change. They bring a cognitive structure to a territory involved in an 'elimination contest' with the mainland, sharpening local beliefs, practices and relationships.[129] In such situations, the particularity of a place's own identity is emphasised: 'The shifts in the interdependencies and power balances increase the local people's consciousness of the symbolic boundary between themselves and others which is aided by the mobilisation and reconstitution of symbolic repertoires with which the community can think and formulate a unified image of its difference from the opposite party'.[130] As I hope to show, communal symbols such as law have been mobilised in these ways to reconstitute a more unified sense of Hong Kong identity. Other markers of this identity include a growing concern with protecting the environment, recycling of goods, conservation, the preservation of local landmarks, concerns about discrimination, social welfare and the rights of minority and vulnerable groups and demands for greater respect for public opinion in policy-making.[131] Where once consumption, capitalism and development were taken as core Hong Kong values, now these face vocal opposition. Kwong and Yu argue that this 'post-materialistic' local identity is one way Hongkongers use to distinguish themselves from mainlanders.[132] In effect, these are new symbolic borders, and they thwart the mainland's efforts to persuade Hongkongers to ditch their cultural heritage, art, architecture, literature, music and all the other symbols, norms, beliefs and values of their collective life – including the rule of law.

[128] Schudson, 'The integration of national societies', p. 34.

[129] N. J. Smelser, 'Culture: coherent or incoherent', in R. Munch and N. J. Smelser (eds.), *Theory of Culture* (Berkeley: University of California Press, 1992), p. 11.

[130] Featherstone, *Undoing Culture*, p. 110, referring to A. Cohen, *The Symbolic Construction of Community* (London: Tavistock 1995).

[131] See M. Sing, 'Hong Kong at the crossroads: public pressure for democratic reform', in M. Sing (ed.), *Government and Politics in Hong Kong: Crisis under Chinese Sovereignty* (London: Routledge, 2009), pp. 122–3.

[132] Kwong and Yu, 'Identity Politics', p. 129.

As one elderly resident told a news reporter, 'Of course we are Chinese too ... but after all, Hongkongers are very different from mainlanders. We have developed our own culture and have become accustomed to living under the rule of law.'[133]

As indicated above, these boundaries can be constructed using a variety of means, often employing what Scott (in another context) terms the 'arts of resistance' and the 'weapons of the weak'.[134] Instead of producing compliant subjects, then, Beijing's attempt to displace the local with state-sponsored cultural forms has only encouraged the production of a new semiotics of dissent. In constructing cultural, linguistic and artistic borders, Hongkongers attempt to keep mainlandisation out. The boundaries they produce delineate the self from the 'other', the 'strangers' necessary for formulating an identity.[135] They encapsulate the identity of the community and mark the difference 'with entities from which they are, or wish to be, distinguished'.[136] Boundaries focus attention on differences and similarities: 'The sense of difference ... lies at the heart of people's awareness of their culture and, indeed, makes it appropriate for ethnographers to designate as "cultures" such arenas of distinctiveness ... [P]eople become aware of their culture when they stand at its boundaries.'[137]

Many of the boundaries that Hongkongers have made are marked by law; some are expressed in racial, linguistic or religious ways, whilst others exist 'in the minds of their beholders ... This is the *symbolic* aspect of community boundary'.[138] These are the (b)ordering practices that differentiate between 'us and them',[139] where 'they' are perceived as a threatening presence.[140] This is largely underpinned

[133] Leung Shing-hong, 'Elderly Hongkongers see only trouble ahead for their hometown', interview by Emily Tsang, *SCMP*, 25 July 2014.

[134] J. C. Scott, *Domination and the Arts of Resistance* (New Haven: Yale University Press, 1995); J. C. Scott, *Weapons of the Weak: Everyday Forms of Peasant Resistance* (New Haven: Yale University Press, 1985).

[135] S. McIver, 'Contextualising national identity', in B. Petersson and E. Clark (eds.), *Identity Dynamics and the Construction of Boundaries* (Lund: Nordic Academic Press, 2003), pp. 43–60.

[136] Cohen, *Symbolic Construction of Community*, p. 12.

[137] Cohen, *Symbolic Construction of Community*, pp. 2–3.

[138] Cohen, *Symbolic Construction of Community*, p. 12.

[139] H. van Houtum and T. Van Naerssen, 'Bordering, Ordering and Othering', *Tijdschrift voor Economische en Sociale Geografie* 93, no. 2 (2002), pp. 125–36.

[140] McIver, *Contextualising national identity*, p. 49, citing A. Triandafyllidou, 'National Identity and the "Other"', *Ethnic and Racial Studies*, 21, no. 4 (1998).

by, and confirms, the conception of Hong Kong as a 'city of law' and China as a 'law-less' place.

Some of what I document in the following pages is, I argue, the consequence of a weakening of the physical and legal borders between Hong Kong and the mainland. This has led to the creation of alternative, symbolic, boundary-markers. The 'Other' for Hongkongers is the mainlander and mainland ways of doing things. Mainlanders herald the 'looming disorderliness' of mainland China with which Hongkongers are familiar from the media, rumours and travelers' tales. Though the border between Hong Kong and mainland China appears as an emphatic physical presence, since 1997 it has become permeable and porous. The 'walls of law' around the territory have also proved an unreliable defence. They provide space for interpretation but also spaces into which people disappear, where mainland ways 'sneak in' under the radar. The act of crossing the border with the mainland is itself depicted in stories and rumours as a moment of dangerous 'in-betweeness' or liminality.[141] Towns along the mainland-side of the border are zones of transgression, pleasure and decadence for Hongkongers seeking escape, but they are also zones of crime and danger, frontier, 'Wild West' towns where the Hong Kong way of doing things is reversed.

Recognition of culture and community stems from the awareness 'that things are done differently *there*, and the sense of threat which that poses for how things are done *here*'.[142] A major marker of difference between mainland China and Hong Kong is the rule of law, with Hongkongers having a deep foreboding that the 'law-less' way things are done *there* will pollute the 'law-full' way things are done *here*.

What I suggest is happening in Hong Kong is that, with the diminution of the geographical base of community boundaries and the weakening of the legal border between Hong Kong and the mainland, other symbolic and cultural boundaries have emerged and become more emphatic.[143] The symbolic expression of community and its boundaries 'increases in importance as the actual geo-social boundaries of the community are undermined, blurred or otherwise weakened ... [P]eople resort increasingly to symbolic behaviour to reconstitute the

[141] R. Shields, *Places on the Margin: Alternative Geographies of Modernity* (London: Routledge, 1991), p. 191.

[142] Jenkins, *Social Identity*, pp. 106–7.

[143] Cohen, cited in Jenkins, *Social Identity*, p. 109.

boundary'.[144] This leads to their renewed assertion in symbolic terms. The border between 'them' and 'us' is remade 'in terms of its symbols, signs . . . and stories [with] much emphasis on the form and the story by which borders are represented and symbolised'.[145] The more pressure there is to change, the more vigorously boundaries will be symbolised: 'Difference will be constructed and emphasised and we-ness asserted in opposition to them. A symbolically contrived sense of local similarity may be the only available symbolic defence'.[146] Communities fight to keep boundaries alive by the manipulation of their symbols. In doing so, they socially reconstruct the boundary as well as the community to which they belong.

What I try to document here are some of the ways in which this reconstitutive 'boundary-making' is occurring in Hong Kong. Sometimes it occurs in the law courts, sometimes in official narratives and discourse, sometimes in culture and sometimes in fleeting metaphors and parables, insubstantial myths and rumours. All contribute to what Cohen calls the symbolic construction of a community.[147] Paradoxically, however, I argue that though law and lawyers play their part in this construction, by elevating the rule of law to such a dominant cultural position, they may contribute to the disarming of democracy.

[144] Cohen, *Construction of Community*, pp. 55, 70.
[145] van Houtem et al., *B/ordering Space*, p. 676.
[146] Jenkins, *Social Identity*, p. 109.
[147] Jenkins, *Social Identity*.

2

Walls of law

In their exploration of the fetishisation of law in former colonies,[1] John and Jean Comaroff describe how the disjuncture of the postcolonial is often associated in the collective consciousness with 'transgression, liminality and lawlessness'.[2] Keeping this lawlessness at bay in post-1997 Hong Kong are walls of law. This *mondo juralis* is a 'walled space of legality', creating order against what is imagined to be the 'looming chaos' of life at an uncertain time in an uncertain place, a place and time of transition on the edge of China.[3] It is life in 'a universe represented, archetypically, as at once ordered and unruly. And always just one step away from implosion.'[4]

The antecedents of this *mondo juralis* can be traced back to a time when Hong Kong's tradition of 'British rule of law' was invented.[5] At the founding of the colony, Hong Kong was represented in orthodox British history as a lawless place. The British, according to this narrative, brought order out of chaos, establishing legal institutions and the

[1] J. Comaroff and J. L. Comaroff (eds.),'Introduction', in *Law and Disorder in the PostColony* (Chicago: University of Chicago Press, 2006), pp. 1–56.

[2] Comaroff and Comaroff, 'Introduction', p. 2.

[3] Comaroff and Comaroff, 'Introduction', p. 35.

[4] Comaroff and Comaroff, 'Introduction'.

[5] On the invention of tradition, see E. Hobsbawn and T. Ranger, *The Invention of Tradition* (Cambridge: Cambridge University Press, 1983); M. Chanock, *Law, Custom and Social Order: The Colonial Experience in Malawi and Zambia* (Cambridge: Cambridge University Press, 1985).

rule of law, vanquishing corruption and containing the shadowy netherworld of triads and organised crime. The re-settlement of the millions of refugees who fled China in the 1950s and Hong Kong's economic success were both taken as further proof that 'British rule of law' could bring order out of chaos. The juxtaposition of Hong Kong and Communist China in the Cold War secured the association between rule of law, order and the free world and Communism, chaos and authoritarianism.

The last British governor, Chris Patten, strengthened the *mondo juralis* narrative by stressing that the rule of law stood at the heart of Hong Kong. Under Patten, rule of law came into its full ideological glory. In his inaugural speech, Patten laid out what was to become the leading motif of his administration. The 'bedrock' of Hong Kong's way of life was:

> the rule of law that guarantees fair and equitable treatment for everyone. It governs all your dealing, personal and financial. You have an independent Judiciary in which every individual can have confidence. Because no one is above the law. No politician, no business leader, no citizen, no Governor. Because no one is above the law, the law serves everyone ... You enjoy freedom of worship and freedom of speech.[6]

Similarly, in his farewell speech in 1997, Patten described the rule of law as one of Hong Kong's key pieces of 'scaffolding', along with 'clean, light-handed government', 'the values of a free society' and 'decent values' which are universal.[7] His characterisation of Hong Kong as 'free', 'open', 'fair', a 'level playing field' and 'open to all on the basis of merit' made an immense and long-lasting impact, so much so that rule of law is now seen as the territory's core value. Thus, the rule of law had become part of Hong Kong's social imaginary.[8]

As one commentator observed, Patten had placed 'plates of glass' around Hong Kong on the understanding that, if China shattered them, at least the world would hear.[9] Their shattering has been most audible in the courts of law. Legal cases have galvanised fears about

[6] Chris Patten, 'Inaugural Policy Address to the Legislative Council', 7 October 1992.
[7] Chris Patten, 'Speech at Farewell Ceremony of the Hong Kong Handover', 30 June 1997.
[8] Shields, *Places on the Margin*, p. 23.
[9] Nathan, *China's Transition*. Patten himself called them 'glass windows'.

the resilience of law, rights and freedoms in the face of mainland pressure. Some cases – notably the 'Big Spender' and 'Telford Gardens' cases – left Hongkongers in little doubt that the HKSAR government would not protect them should they fall foul of law across the border. Others, such as Emily Lau's attempt to call Xinhua to account and the non-prosecution of newspaper proprietor Sally Aw, raised important questions about whether, after 1997, some people were above the law. Other cases (e.g., concerning the presence of the Falun Gong and the defiling of the national flag) raised questions about fundamental freedoms. A string of civil cases concerning the status of mainland-born children of Hong Kong residents provoked the first constitutional crisis of the new regime in 1999. Thanks to WikiLeaks, we now know that the CFA judges considered resigning *en masse* when they were forced to 'clarify' their judgment by the NPCSC, a blow inflicted by the HKSAR government itself. Mass demonstrations against anti-subversion laws (Article 23) in 2003 also marked a significant point in citizens' mobilisation against the restrictions of rights and freedoms. Another commentator, observing the extent to which the law courts have become a premier Hong Kong/mainland battleground, described the situation thus:

> If you stand in the main square in the middle of Hong Kong and look up the narrow street between the metal and glass headquarters of the Hongkong Shanghai Bank and the old stone premises of the Bank of China, you see, neatly framed by the two high building, a red brick edifice on a promontory . . . Since 1 July 1997, it has housed Hong Kong's top judicial body, the Court of Final Appeal . . . Sitting up there above Central, with the Anglican Cathedral to its left and the main government office behind it, the building looks like a fortress. As things are turning out, that's exactly what it is becoming.[10]

Some of the legal battles were predicted before 1997; others have surprised both Hong Kong and mainland legal experts and developed the law in new directions. This chapter introduces the principal laws upon which Hong Kong's *mondo juralis* is founded. Subsequent chapters examine how the 'law wars' have been fought around them.

[10] J. Fenby, *Dealing with the Dragon: A Year in the New Hong Kong* (London: Little Brown, 2007), p. 78.

THE JOINT DECLARATION

The Joint Sino-British Declaration of 1984 was an international treaty signed by two sovereign powers.[11] It provided the scaffolding for the walls of law, the single most important of which was the Basic Law which would become Hong Kong's 'mini-constitution' after 1997. Being a treaty drawn up by diplomats and without Hong Kong representation, it glosses over awkward-to-negotiate issues, leaving them unresolved for the future. For Hung, the change of sovereignty itself left Hongkongers facing a crisis.[12] Critics of the Joint Declaration likened it to a gang rape, jointly carried out by Britain and China whilst the victim (Hong Kong) silently screamed.[13] Without being consulted, Hongkongers found themselves 'sutured under a mask of unity'[14] into a nation state from which they had been separated for some 155 years. As a result, separation had produced 'many instances of distrust'.[15] In 1992, for example, Emily Lau stated that: 'Nobody knows what the Hong Kong people want because nobody ever wanted to find out . . . It's tragic that six million people have no say on the discussion of their future. Our future was discussed in the early 1980s behind closed doors, and that has continued up until now'.[16]

But, Chan observes, talking about Hong Kong as a battleground between the two superpowers from which Hong Kong was absent denies Hongkongers a collective will of their own. Hong Kong is 'always trapped between the vise of super-power politics . . . perpetually a character in somebody else's movie . . . still curiously absent from discussions supposed to be about it'.[17] It is a discourse, Chan argues, which reduces Hong Kong to 'at best a ghostly presence', a place which, after its brief international stardom in 1997[18] disappeared back into the fold of the Motherland.[19]

11 *Joint Declaration of the Government of Great Britain and Northern Ireland and the Government of the People's Republic of China on the Question of Hong Kong*, 19 December 1984.
12 *Joint Declaration of the Government*.
13 Ha Gong, cited in Chow, *Writing Diaspora*, p. 184.
14 J. Wolch and M. Dear, *The Power of Geography: How Territory Shapes Social Life* (Winchester, MA: Unwin Hyman, 1989), p. 278.
15 Abbas, *Culture and the Politics of Disappearance*, p. 2.
16 Abbas, *Culture and the Politics of Disappearance*.
17 E. Chan, 'Postmodernism and Hong Kong cinema', in Arif Dirlik and Zhang Xudon (eds.), *Postmodernism in China* (Durham, NC: Duke University Press, 2000).
18 Chan, 'Postmodernism and Hong Kong cinema' in Dirlik and Xudon, *Postmodernism in China*.
19 Chan, 'Postmodernism and Hong Kong cinema', citing S. Tea, *Hong Kong Cinema: The Extra Dimensions* (London: British Film Institute, 1997).

Annex I of the Joint Declaration did state that Hong Kong's previous capitalist system and 'life-style' would remain unchanged for fifty years, that the HKSAR would 'enjoy a high degree of autonomy' except for foreign and defence affairs (which are the responsibilities of the Central People's Government). Furthermore:

- The HKSAR would be 'be vested with executive, legislative and independent judicial power, including that of final adjudication'.
- the laws previously in force in Hong Kong (i.e., the common law, rules of equity, ordinances, subordinate legislation and customary law) would be maintained, save for any that contravene the Basic Law and subject to any amendment by the HKSAR legislature'.
- the HKSAR Government was to maintain the rights and freedoms as provided for by the laws previously in force in Hong Kong, including freedom of the person, of speech, of the press, of assembly, of association, to form and join trade unions, of correspondence, of travel, of movement, of strike, of demonstration, of choice of occupation, of academic research, of belief, inviolability of the home, the freedom to marry and the right to raise a family freely;
- The judicial system previously practised in Hong Kong would be maintained; judicial power would be 'vested in the courts' and was to be exercised 'independently and free from any interference';
- The courts were to continue to decide cases in accordance with the laws of the HKSAR and the precedents of other common law jurisdictions;
- Judges could be recruited from other common law jurisdictions. The power of final judgment of the HKSAR was to be vested in the court of final appeal, which could also 'as required' invite judges from other common law jurisdictions to sit on it;
- Judges would be appointed by the chief executive of the HKSAR acting in accordance with the recommendation of an independent commission composed of local judges, persons from the legal profession and other eminent persons. Getting rid of a judge was to remain difficult: a judge could only be removed for 'inability to discharge the functions of his office, or for misbehaviour, by the chief executive of the HKSAR acting in accordance with the recommendation of a tribunal appointed by the chief judge of the court of final appeal, consisting of not fewer than three local judges'. The appointment or removal of principal judges (i.e., those of the highest rank) could only be made by the chief executive with the endorsement of the HKSAR legislature and had to be reported to the NPCSC;

- Every person was to have the right to challenge the actions of the executive in the courts, the right to confidential legal advice, access to the courts, representation in the courts by lawyers of his choice and to obtain judicial remedies;
- The provisions of the International Covenant on Civil and Political Rights (ICCPR) and the International Covenant on Economic, Social and Cultural Rights (ICESC) as applied to Hong Kong were to remain in force.

Hong Kong was reassured by this document. It seemed to promise a future very like the past. It would retain the common law and its courts would be able to continue to refer to precedents set in the rest of the common law world. The judiciary could also be drawn from this common law world and was to remain independent of the executive and legislative arms of the government. This was a very different legal architecture from mainland China, where the judiciary did not operate independently of political organs but was closely aligned to them at local and national levels, where senior judges were required to be Communist Party members and where decisions in sensitive cases were delivered by trial judges instructed by a politico-judicial Adjudication Committee. Before the 1996 revision to the PRC's Criminal Law and Criminal Procedure Law, mainland trials could not begin until the verdict was known ('verdict first, trial second'), and numerous matters not considered offences in Hong Kong were subject to prosecution. Hongkongers knew that mainland justice was much more summary, arbitrary and lacking in due process protections than their own. The Joint Declaration was intended to assuage fears that their system would in the future be tainted by these mainland features.

Though the Joint Declaration seemed to promise little change, one major alteration to the legal system was the introduction of a 'mini-constitution' (the Basic Law). Moreover, ten years after the Joint Declaration in mid-1994, the Vice President of the Supreme People's Court and former Basic Law drafter, Duanmu Zheng, predicted that the common law system would not survive Hong Kong's return to China.[20] The mainland system was, he argued, simpler. As the *SCMP* argued at the time:

> Coming from a man of such influence, the remarks were seen as a threat. The subtext read into his statement was that the independence of the

[20] Editorial, *SCMP*, 12 April 1994.

> judiciary enshrined in the British legal system (as well as the Joint Declaration and the Basic Law) would be phased out with it . . . What matters is not the English legal system *per se*, but judicial independence, the presumption of innocence, and the maintenance of the rule of law over the arbitrary 'rule of man'.[21]

Writing in 2007, Carroll also returned to the problem of the areas left vague in the Joint Declaration due to the failure of the Sino-British negotiators to agree.[22] These vague areas, Carroll says, enabled the British and Chinese sides to interpret the treaty's terms in their own ways. Carried forward into the drafting of the Basic Law, they stored up trouble, which the Hong Kong courts have been grappling with ever since. Formulations of the Basic Law are, Ghai says, frequently vague; there are different understandings of its provisions, and its relationship to the PRC Constitution is unclear.[23] The CFA has frequently had to arrive at decisions on matters left unclear by both the Joint Declaration and the Basic Law. Like all common law courts (but unlike mainland courts), it has had to do this in public, setting out the reasons and justifications for its decisions. Unlike secret political negotiations, Ghai says, in a court of law 'awkward issues cannot so easily be ducked or fudged'.[24] Many of them have had to be dealt with head-on in a series of 'law wars' since 1997.

The Joint Declaration has proved less of a guarantee than expected. When, in 2014, Beijing issued its White Paper on Hong Kong, it claimed that it alone exercised control over the HKSAR, raising questions about Britain's superintendence of the treaty. Britain remained silent, though a Parliamentary Select Committee was prevailed upon by Martin Lee and Anson Chan to undertake a visit to the territory to see for itself how the 'one country, two systems' formula was working. In its regular reports on Hong Kong, however, Britain has singularly failed to live up to its role as joint author of the treaty, remaining quiescent about any breaches or politically controversial issues. For the British government, Hong Kong is – as it originally was – a stepping stone for trade with China. Moreover, there are no

21 Editorial, *SCMP*, 12 April 1994.

22 Carroll, *Concise History of Hong Kong*.

23 Y. Ghai, 'Final appeals: setting and context', in S. N. M. Young and Y. Ghai (eds.), *Hong Kong's Court of Final Appeal* (Cambridge: Cambridge University Press, 2013), p. 58.

24 Y. Ghai, 'Themes and arguments' in Young and Ghai, *Hong Kong's Court of Final Appeal*, p. 3.

provisions in the Joint Declaration for dealing with breaches of the treaty. This meant that the British government stayed silent when, in 2014, an editorial in *Ming Pao* described the situation as 'worrying' and others warned of 'blood on the streets', of a watershed, that the 'one country, two systems' formula was now an 'empty shell',[25] and that Hong Kong could 'kiss goodbye' to judicial independence. The Joint Declaration, it seemed, was less a wall of law than a plate of glass. In 2014, defiant demonstrators publicly burnt copies of Beijing's White Paper.[26]

THE BASIC LAW

The 'walls of law' around Hong Kong include, of course, its 'mini-constitution', the Basic Law. Jayawickrama points out that it was drafted by a committee appointed by the NPC, in which the Hong Kong nominees were in a minority, meaning that none of the nominees were elected by the people of Hong Kong and that they did not, therefore, 'function in a representative capacity'. The law was enacted by the NPC, a legislature in which Hong Kong people were not represented, and the authority of the NPC to enact the Basic Law was 'derived from the Joint Declaration, which was a treaty negotiated between the colonial power and another sovereign state without any prior consultation with the people of Hong Kong'.[27] Given this, Jaywickrama asked, how could a law imposed without the consent of the people achieve legitimacy?

The Basic Law legally instantiates what was, in the Joint Declaration, a political agreement. Article 1 states that the Hong Kong Special Administrative Region is an inalienable part of the People's Republic of China. Article 2 makes it clear that the National People's Congress authorizes the HKSAR to exercise a high degree of autonomy and enjoy executive, legislative and independent judicial power, including that of final adjudication. Article 22 also draws a line between the mainland and Hong Kong by stating that no department

[25] 'White Paper on Hong Kong', *Ming Pao*, 11 June 2014.

[26] T. Cheung, 'Protesters burn Beijing's white paper on "one country, two systems"', *SCMP*, 11 June 2014.

[27] N. Jayawickrama, 'The right of self-determination', in *The Basic Law: Problems and Perspectives* (Hong Kong: The University of Hong Kong Faculty of Law, University of Hong Kong, 1990), pp. 95–6.

of the Central People's Government may interfere in the affairs that the HKSAR administers on its own. Article 5 further promises that the socialist system and policies will not be practised in Hong Kong and that the previous capitalist system and way of life will remain unchanged for fifty years, until 2047.

As to the continuation of the common law in the HKSAR, Article 8 promises that the laws previously in force in Hong Kong (the common law, rules of equity, ordinances, subordinate legislation and customary law) shall be maintained, except for any that contravene the Basic Law, and subject to any amendment by LEGCO. Article 11 also says that Hong Kong will retain its previous systems and policies, including the social and economic systems; the system for safeguarding the fundamental rights and freedoms of its residents; the executive, legislative and judicial systems; and the relevant policies. Article 12 guarantees that Hong Kong shall enjoy a high degree of autonomy. Article 19 specifies that the HKSAR shall be vested with independent judicial power, including that of final adjudication. Article 81 deals with the judicial structure and states that the judicial system previously practised in Hong Kong shall be maintained. Article 82 says that the power of final adjudication shall be vested in the Court of Final Appeal, which may as required invite judges from other common law jurisdictions to sit on the Court of Final Appeal. Article 86 maintains the principle of trial by jury; Article 85 stipulates that the courts of shall exercise judicial power independently, 'free from any interference'. Article 87 preserves the right to fair trial and presumption of innocence. Article 17 states that the HKSAR shall be vested with legislative power, that laws enacted by the legislature must be reported to the NPCSC for the record. However, it goes on:

> If the Standing Committee of the National People's Congress, after consulting the Committee for the Basic Law of the Hong Kong Special Administrative Region under it, considers that any law enacted by the legislature of the Region is not in conformity with the provisions of this Law regarding affairs within the responsibility of the Central Authorities or regarding the relationship between the Central Authorities and the Region, the Standing Committee may return the law in question but shall not amend it. Any law returned by the Standing Committee of the National People's Congress shall immediately be invalidated. This invalidation shall not have retroactive effect, unless otherwise provided for in the laws of the Region.

Article 18 stipulates that national laws will not apply in Hong Kong (with the exception of those listed in Annex III) but adds that, in the event of war or turmoil in Hong Kong that endangers national unity or security and is beyond the control of the government of the HKSAR, or the HKSAR is in a state of emergency, the Central People's Government 'may issue an order applying the relevant national laws in the Region'. Article 24 defines who qualifies as a Hong Kong resident and was to become central to a protracted 'law war' about interpretation of the Basic Law.

Hong Kong residents are, according to Article 25, equal before the law whilst Article 27 entitles them to freedom of speech, of the press and of publication; freedom of association, of assembly, of procession and of demonstration; and the right and freedom to form and join trade unions and to strike. Under Article 28, they are also protected against arbitrary or unlawful arrest, detention or imprisonment; arbitrary or unlawful search of the body; deprivation or restriction of freedom, torture; or arbitrary or unlawful deprivation of life. Articles 30–34 guarantee freedom and privacy of communication; freedom of movement; freedom to travel; freedom of conscience; freedom of religious belief and freedom to preach and to conduct and participate in religious activities in public; freedom of choice of occupation; and freedom to engage in academic research, literary and artistic creation, and other cultural activities. Article 39 also states that the provisions of the International Covenant on Civil and Political Rights, the International Covenant on Economic, Social and Cultural Rights, and international labour conventions as applied to Hong Kong 'shall remain in force'.

Cumulatively, then, the Basic Law looks like a surprisingly resilient wall of law. Chen points out that the Hong Kong courts have, for example, interpreted Article 39 to mean that the relevant provisions of the ICCPR 'have the same constitutional force as the Basic Law itself, thus overriding laws that are inconsistent with these provisions'.[28] The Bill of Rights introduced in 1991 incorporated the ICCPR into domestic law, and after 1991 Hong Kong courts were able to strike down any existing law which did not comply with the ICCPR and the Bill of Rights. Nonetheless, doubt arose as to whether this situation would

[28] A. H. Y. Chen, 'The rule of law under "one country, two systems": the case of Hong Kong 1997–2009', Social Science Research Network, http://ssrn.com/abstract ±1474748

continue after 1997 because the NPCSC took the view that the Basic Law was the superior law and no other law could override it. As Chen notes, however, in a case concerning the desecration of the national flag, the CFA effectively confirmed 'the operative force of the Bill of Rights and the ICCPR', and the power of the courts 'to review the constitutionality of Hong Kong legislation on human rights grounds, and, if necessary, to strike down such legislation'.[29] This decision, Chen concludes, had 'far-reaching positive implications for the regime of rights protection in post-1997 Hong Kong'. However, the Basic Law contains no protections for Hong Kong's own language, culture or traditions. It also contains some critical obstacles to democracy in the formula laid down for the appointment of the chief executive, what Ghai terms 'the restricted power of Hong Kong people in the selection of the CE, the CE's extensive powers and lack of accountability within the HKSAR'.[30]

Interpretations of the Basic Law have, moreover, proved highly controversial. The line it draws between the mainland and Hong Kong has turned out to be more ambiguous than originally suggested. Most problematic is Article 158, which stipulates that the power of interpretation of the Basic Law shall be vested in the NPCSC. It allows that the NPCSC shall authorize the HKSAR courts to interpret on their own, in adjudicating cases, the provisions of the Basic Law that are within the limits of the HKSAR's autonomy and that they may also interpret other provisions of the Basic Law in adjudicating cases. However, it adds that:

> if the courts of the Region, in adjudicating cases, need to interpret the provisions of this [l]aw concerning affairs which are the responsibility of the Central People's Government, or concerning the relationship between the Central Authorities and the Region, and if such interpretation will affect the judgments on the cases, the courts of the Region shall, before making their final judgments which are not appealable, seek an interpretation of the relevant provisions from the Standing Committee of the National People's Congress through the Court of Final Appeal of the Region. When the Standing Committee makes an interpretation of the provisions concerned, the courts of the Region, in applying those provisions, shall follow the

[29] Chen, 'The rule of law'.
[30] Y. Ghai, 'The Basic Law: a comparative analysis', in *The Basic Law: Problems and Perspectives*.

> interpretation of the Standing Committee. However, judgments previously rendered shall not be affected.

As Chen points out, the NPCSC's power to issue an interpretation of the Basic Law is built into the new legal order of Hong Kong, and 'once the NPCSC has spoken, the Hong Kong courts must comply.'[31] It may issue an interpretation on its own initiative or upon a reference from the CFA, but once an interpretation is issued, it is binding on the Hong Kong courts. Only in the absence of any binding interpretation by the NPCSC are the courts free to interpret the provisions of the Basic Law on their own.[32] This understanding of the HKSAR courts' position was reached at the conclusion of its first 'law war' concerning the right of abode (see Chapter 7).

Writing in 1990, Yash Ghai had already identified as problematic the fact that the power of interpretation of the Basic Law is vested in the NPCSC, a political rather than a judicial body.[33] The final say on any amendment to the Basic Law lies, he pointed out, with Beijing; the right to propose an amendment is vested in the NPCSC, the State Council and the SAR, but if the first two propose an amendment, there is no requirement that it be referred to any HKSAR institution.[34] If a proposal to amend the Basic Law comes from the HKSAR, on the other hand, it has to secure the two-thirds support of Hong Kong deputies to the NPC, two-thirds of LEGCO members and the consent of the CE, a task which, because of the government's built-in majority in LEGCO, is virtually impossible for any group apart from pro-Beijing loyalists. It is therefore perfectly possible, Ghai observes, for Beijing to amend the Basic Law 'without any formal consultation with, much less the consent of, the SAR'.[35]

What has proved to be more crucial, perhaps, is the ambiguity of the 'one country, two systems' formula, which, Ghai says, means that the autonomy of the 'two systems' is always threatened by the doctrine of sovereignty inherent in 'one country'.[36] The threat lies with 'the overarching political authority of the Chinese government implicit, as viewed by the Chinese, in sovereignty'. The issuance of the 2014 White Paper was clearly intended to remind Hongkongers of this.

[31] Chen, 'Rule of law'. [32] Chen, 'Rule of law'.
[33] Ghai, 'The Basic Law: comparative analysis'.
[34] Ghai, 'The Basic Law: comparative analysis'.
[35] Ghai, 'The Basic Law: comparative analysis'.
[36] Ghai, 'The Basic Law: comparative analysis', p. 14.

Moreover, the White Paper also suggested that judges were 'administrators' of the HKSAR and must be 'patriots'. This was the first indication that Beijing thought judges should demonstrate 'patriotism' when making their decisions.

The exclusion of 'non-patriots' from positions of power has been a long-running theme of Beijing's post-1997 governance of Hong Kong. As Leung, Tam and Chu point out, the Basic Law was amended after 4 June precisely to exclude pro-democracy supporters deemed 'unpatriotic' in the eyes of Beijing. In addition, to ensure that those considered 'unpatriotic' could not be elected as CE, 'preventative measures were designed into the Basic Law not to allow any one from the "unpatriotic" cohort to get a seat in the office of Chief Executive of the Hong Kong SAR'. Articles 43, 44, 45, 46 and 52, as well as Appendix 1 and 2 and the Chief Executive Election Ordinance ensure this exclusion of 'undesirables' by insisting that 'any person who is a candidate in the election for chief executive needs at least 100 members' nominations from the Election Committee, which is composed of a majority of leftists. It is then extremely difficult for the "unpatriotic candidate" to overcome this obstacle.'[37]

The composition of the Nomination Committee is a mechanism for screening out 'undesirables' from election as CE. Packed with Beijing loyalists, since 1997 this committee has ensured that Beijing's chosen person always gets the job. The result has been a series of incompetent administrations devoid of public legitimacy. But with the rise of the pro-democracy movement in Hong Kong, demands have been made to change the composition of the Nomination Committee to remove this blockage. This has been part of the campaign led by the Occupy Central movement since 2012. In June 2014, a series of proposals to change the composition of the Nomination Committee was put to the vote in an informal referendum, which Beijing classified as 'illegal'. Eight hundred thousand Hongkongers voted, with the majority favouring public nomination of the candidates for the 2017 chief executive election, an idea repeatedly dismissed by Beijing as inconsistent with the Basic Law. Eighty-eight per cent of voters also agreed that the Legislative Council should veto any reform proposal put

[37] B. Leung, C. Tam and M. Chu, 'The Catholic role in Hong Kong SAR's governance: past and present' in Cheng, *The Hong Kong Special Administrative Region*, p. 872.

forward by the government if it failed to meet international standards allowing genuine choice for electors.

Faced with demands for a change to this system, pro-democracy supporters have been told that any other system is contrary to the Basic Law.[38] In March 2014, for example, Basic Law Committee member Rao Geping insisted that democratic demands 'cannot deviate from the law' and that the International Covenant on Civil and Political Rights might not apply to Hong Kong after all. This implied that constitutional reform might not have to comply with international standards.[39] Officials of the Central Government's Liaison Office in Hong Kong repeatedly made it clear that candidates considered 'unpatriotic' would not be allowed to stand for election. The war which surrounded this issue was, then, a political war being fought on legal territory. Beijing's opposition to universal suffrage – a political issue – was represented as a legal question, a matter of sticking strictly to the letter of the Basic Law.

To common law and constitutional law experts around the world, this insistence upon the literal interpretation of a constitutional document is at odds with accepted international practice. The mainland's insistence on literal interpretation of the Basic Law would, for example, see Hongkongers' hopes for democracy dashed, since mainland legal experts claim that the manner and form of democratisation is laid down in precise terms in various articles and annexes of the Basic Law. The idea of public nomination of candidates was held to be 'Basic Law compliant' by the Bar Association, which argued that it did not want to see *political* objections presented as *legal* objections, 'thereby shutting the public out from debating the political merits and demerits of legally permissible proposals. Hong Kong people's long standing respect for the Rule of Law should not be used ... to deal with non-legal matters.'[40] In China, the *People's Daily* reminded Hongkongers of the need for 'patriotism to the country', and the *Global Times* stated that Beijing would not allow 'chaos' in Hong Kong, warning Hongkongers not to think they could turn the HKSAR into Ukraine or Thailand.

[38] Article 45 of the Basic Law stipulates that the CE should be nominated by a 'broadly representative' nomination committee 'in accordance with democratic procedures'.

[39] T. Chong, 'Top Chinese law scholar rules out any public nomination of chief executive candidates', *SCMP*, 23 March 2014.

[40] Paul Shieh, speech at the opening of the 2014 legal year.

THE BILL OF RIGHTS

The Bill of Rights owes its existence to the events of 4 June 1989 in mainland China, when pro-democracy demonstrations in Beijing and other mainland cities were suppressed by armed force. This had a profound impact on Hongkongers, and a million of them demonstrated in support of the pro-democracy movement in China. The colonial government adopted a tolerant, low-profile approach, heightening the contrast with Beijing and providing an otherwise unlooked for propaganda coup. Numerous commentators identify Tiananmen as a watershed in the consolidation of the Hong Kong identity. 'Chineseness' was crystallised as identifying with the culture and people of mainland China but not with the Communist regime. In this pivotal moment, the Hong Kong identity also became inextricably tied to the rule of law, for it was this which was seen to differentiate Hong Kong so markedly from Beijing, 'city of tanks'. It was also law – the Bill of Rights – which was in this moment offered to Hongkongers as their salvation in the face of oppression.

In the immediate aftermath of 1989, Hong Kong experienced both an 'explosion of civil society'[41] and a shoring up of its legal defences. With the transfer of sovereignty only eight years away, 4 June was seen as an ominous portent of life under mainland rule. Even if there was no outright crackdown on post-1997 Hong Kong, the sense was that through insidious corruption and misgovernment, the mainland would 'destroy that which made Hong Kong prosperous and stable'.[42] This feeling was so strong that majorities rejected mainland sovereignty up until just six months before the handover.[43] Those in Hong Kong who had provided financial, moral and logistical support to the demonstrators found themselves castigated by the pro-Beijing media as 'subversives' and subject to prohibitions. A hasty amendment to the Basic Law prevented anyone deemed 'unpatriotic' from ever being eligible to stand for election as CE. Two of the founding members of the Alliance in Support of the Patriotic Democratic Movement in China, lawyer

[41] A. Y. So, *Hong Kong's Embattled Democracy: A Societal Analysis* (Baltimore: John Hopkins University Press, 1999), cited in Carroll, *A Concise History of Hong Kong*, p. 197.

[42] The Hong Kong Transition Project survey, Baptist University of Hong Kong, April 2002.

[43] The Hong Kong Transition Project survey.

Martin Lee and teachers' union leader Szeto Wah, were excluded from the Basic Law Drafting Committee.[44]

Following a flight of capital and people post-Tiananmen, the Hong Kong government attempted to calm nerves and restore confidence in the future by reassuring the population that their rights and freedoms would endure beyond 1997. To this end, in 1991 the British administration introduced a Bill of Rights (BOR).[45] This 'wall of law' incorporated many of the rights contained in the International Covenant on Civil and Political Rights.[46] Several articles specifically addressed the liberty of the person. Article 5, for example, stated that:

(1) Everyone has the right to liberty and security of person. No one shall be subjected to arbitrary arrest or detention. No one shall be deprived of his liberty except on such grounds and in accordance with such procedure as are established by law.
(2) Anyone who is arrested shall be informed, at the time of arrest, of the reasons for his arrest and shall be promptly informed of any charges against him.
(3) Anyone arrested or detained on a criminal charge shall be brought promptly before a judge or other officer authorized by law to exercise judicial power and shall be entitled to trial within a reasonable time or to release. It shall not be the general rule that persons awaiting trial shall be detained in custody, but release may be subject to guarantees to appear for trial, at any other stage of the judicial proceedings, and, should occasion arise, for execution of the judgment.
(4) Anyone who is deprived of his liberty by arrest or detention shall be entitled to take proceedings before a court, in order that that court may decide without delay on the lawfulness of his detention and order his release if the detention is not lawful.
(5) Anyone who has been the victim of unlawful arrest or detention shall have an enforceable right to compensation.

Article 6 specified that '(1) All persons deprived of their liberty shall be treated with humanity and with respect for the inherent dignity of

[44] Carroll, *A Concise History of Hong Kong*, p. 193.
[45] Cap 383 of the Laws of Hong Kong, enacted 8 June 1991.
[46] The Joint Sino-British Declaration, signed in 1984, promised that existing provisions of the International Covenant on Civil & Political Rights, and the Covenant on Economic, Social & Cultural Rights would remain in force after 1997. Article 39 of the Basic Law confirmed this position.

the human person'. Article 10 guaranteed equality before the courts and the right to fair and public hearing. Article 11 laid down the due process rights of those accused of a crime:

(1) Everyone charged with a criminal offence shall have the right to be presumed innocent until proved guilty according to law.
(2) In the determination of any criminal charge against him, everyone shall be entitled to the following minimum guarantees, in full equality-
    (a) to be informed promptly and in detail in a language which he understands of the nature and cause of the charge against him;
    (b) to have adequate time and facilities for the preparation of his defence and to communicate with counsel of his own choosing;
    (c) to be tried without undue delay;
    (d) to be tried in his presence, and to defend himself in person or through legal assistance of his own choosing; to be informed, if he does not have legal assistance, of this right; and to have legal assistance assigned to him, in any case where the interests of justice so require, and without payment by him in any such case if he does not have sufficient means to pay for it;
    (e) to examine, or have examined, the witnesses against him and to obtain the attendance and examination of witnesses on his behalf under the same conditions as witnesses against him;
    (f) to have the free assistance of an interpreter if he cannot understand or speak the language used in court;
    (g) not to be compelled to testify against himself or to confess guilt ...
(4) Everyone convicted of a crime shall have the right to his conviction and sentence being reviewed by a higher tribunal according to law ...
(6) No one shall be liable to be tried or punished again for an offence for which he has already been finally convicted or acquitted in accordance with the law and penal procedure of Hong Kong.

Article 12 specifically prohibited retrospective criminal offences or penalties. In addition – and important in light of incidents in mainland China – Article 7 prohibited imprisonment for breach of contract. Article 8 addressed the issue of liberty of movement:

(1) Everyone lawfully within Hong Kong shall, within Hong Kong, have the right to liberty of movement and freedom to choose his residence.
(2) Everyone shall be free to leave Hong Kong.
(3) The above-mentioned rights shall not be subject to any restrictions except those which are provided by law, are necessary to protect national

security, public order *(ordre public)*, public health or morals or the rights and freedoms of others, and are consistent with the other rights recognized in this Bill of Rights.

(4) No one who has the right of abode in Hong Kong shall be arbitrarily deprived of the right to enter Hong Kong.

On other civil liberties, Article 15 of the BOR protected freedom of thought, conscience and religion:

(1) Everyone shall have the right to freedom of thought, conscience and religion. This right shall include freedom to have or to adopt a religion or belief of his choice, and freedom, either individually or in community with others and in public or private, to manifest his religion or belief in worship, observance, practice and teaching.

(2) No one shall be subject to coercion which would impair his freedom to have or to adopt a religion or belief of his choice.

(3) Freedom to manifest one's religion or beliefs may be subject only to such limitations as are prescribed by law and are necessary to protect public safety, order, health, or morals or the fundamental rights and freedoms of others.

Article 16 guaranteed freedom of opinion and expression and states that everyone shall have the right to hold opinions without interference and the right to freedom of expression. It adds as a proviso, 'The exercise of the rights provided for in paragraph (2) of this article carries with it special duties and responsibilities. It may therefore be subject to certain restrictions, but these shall only be such as are provided by law and are necessary (a) for respect of the rights or reputations of others; or (b) for the protection of national security or of public order *(ordre public)*, or of public health or morals.'

Article 17 guaranteed the right of peaceful assembly and specified that 'No restrictions may be placed on the exercise of this right other than those imposed in conformity with the law and which are necessary in a democratic society in the interests of national security or public safety, public order *(ordre public)*, the protection of public health or morals or the protection of the rights and freedoms of others'. Article 18 addressed freedom of association and gave everyone the right to freedom of association with others, including the right to form and join trade unions. No restrictions were to be placed on the exercise of this right 'other than those which are prescribed by law and which are necessary in a democratic society in the interest of national security or public safety, public order *(ordre public)*, the protection of public health or morals or the protection of the rights and freedoms of others'.[47]

In sum, the BOR constructed an indomitable 'wall of law' around Hong Kong. A short 'freeze period' was permitted, during which government lawyers audited the laws of Hong Kong to bring them into line with the BOR. This meant, amongst other things, removing the presumption of guilt extant in several ordinances. As Carroll notes, Beijing opposed the Bill of Rights from the start, arguing that it violated the Joint Declaration and that the Basic Law already provided sufficient protections of these rights.[48] China's reaction was to claim the right to review and repeal all Hong Kong laws, including the Bill of Rights, if they violated the Basic Law.[49] Further irritated by the reforms introduced by the British between 1992 and 1997, China issued the same threat when it replaced what should have been the Legislative Council throughout the 1997 transition with its own Provisional LEGCO. A legal sub-group of Provisional LEGCO announced in January 1997 that it proposed to repeal or amend more than 10 per cent of Hong Kong's laws.[50] This established the tenor of Beijing's future reaction to laws it did not like.

Arguably, over the next six years, human rights discourse assumed a prominence it had never before enjoyed. Between 1991 and 1997, the BOR proved a formidable weapon, used repeatedly to bring the government and its agencies to account. Chen argues that, since 1991, the courts have exercised their power of judicial review of legislation to develop human rights norms and 'a solid body of case law on the protection of human rights'.[51] The outgoing colonial administration also took steps to embed rights discourse by issuing 'human rights kits' to schoolchildren aged between seven and fourteen as part of their civic education. In addition, the administration was obliged to present regular reports to the United Nations Human Rights Committee on the human rights situation in Hong Kong; local NGOs were also able to submit their reports. This meant that British rule in Hong Kong was

[47] For a discussion of Mainland reassurances on press freedom see J. Hong, 'Hong Kong's press freedom: a comparative sociology of Western and Hong Kong views' in Shi-Xu, M. Kienpointer and J. Servaes (eds.), *Read the Cultural Other: Forms of Otherness in the Discourses of Hong Kong's Decolonisation* (Berlin: Mouton de Gruyter, 2005), pp. 103–18.

[48] Carroll, *Concise History of Hong Kong*, p. 193.

[49] Carroll, *Concise History of Hong Kong*.

[50] Carroll, *Concise History of Hong Kong*, p. 212.

[51] Chen, 'Rule of law'.

open to critique in international fora. The government was also required to report to the British Parliament where, in the past, members had raised uncomfortable questions about the Hong Kong administration, a mechanism of scrutiny that disappeared in 1997. Together these measures meant that, between 1991 and 1997, the government of Hong Kong was probably made more accountable than at any other time before or since.

THE COURT OF FINAL APPEAL

Apart from the laws themselves, the wall of law constructed around Hong Kong after 1997 included an independent judiciary and a Court of Final Appeal (CFA). During colonial rule, the final court of appeal for Hong Kong litigants was the Privy Council, sitting in London. The Joint Declaration provided for its replacement, the CFA, after 1997. The establishment of the court had been agreed by the Joint Liaison Group (JLG) in 1991, subsequent to secret negotiations between London and Beijing. By the mid-1990s, however, no steps had been taken to form the CFA. Prolonged negotiations as to the CFA's powers, jurisdiction and the composition of its judges delayed its establishment. Indeed, the arguments over the CFA caused Democratic Party leader and barrister, Martin Lee, to conclude that things looked bleaker for Hong Kong than at any time since the 1989 pro-democracy crackdown in China.[52]

The appointment of foreign judges to the CFA was seen as essential to guarantee its stature, independence and connection with the common law world. Article 82 of the Basic Law permitted the CFA to invite overseas judges (in the plural) to sit on the court. During Sino-British negotiations, however, the Chinese side insisted that only *one* foreign judge would be permitted to sit on the CFA at any given time. The original bill to establish the CFA was thrown out by LEGCO in 1991.[53] The Bar called the subsequent 1994 draft of the CFA proposals unacceptable, saying they would establish a third-rate court in Hong Kong.[54] The bill was eventually passed in 1995 after bitter debate.

[52] M. Lee, 'The sell-out that has to stop', *SCMP*, 1 July 1995.

[53] See C. Yeung and L. F. So, 'Third rate court attack', *SCMP*, 7 December 1994.

[54] D. Gittings, 'Changing expectations: how the rule of law fared in the first decade of the Hong Kong SAR', *Hong Kong Journal, The Quarterly Online Journal*, no. 7, 1 July 2007. http://hdl.handle.net/10722/193250.

RULE OF LAW: THE IDEOLOGY AND THE RHETORIC

Words constructed another kind of wall of law around Hong Kong. On 1 July 1995, two years exactly to the handover deadline, Hong Kong's last colonial governor, Chris Patten, published a speech in which he set out his agenda for the remaining two years of British rule. Key to this was the completion of work to preserve and enhance civil liberties so 'the community gets what the Bill of Rights promises'.[55] This included legislation to secure press freedom, women's rights and the rights of the disabled, more open and accountable government and easier citizen redress of grievances. According to Patten,

> A question I'm asked more and more frequently is: 'Will it all be ok?' And my answer – a resounding yes, provided people want it to be ok, that they want Hong Kong to go on like it is today. Decent. Prosperous. Stable. Free. The 1997 change-over will come and go. But Hong Kong will remain, an open and plural society, a working model of values both universal and inextinguishable.[56]

In what local media characterised as his 'swan song' address to LEGCO on 2 October 1996, Patten listed a series of benchmarks for vigilance in the post-transition years. These included maintenance of a free press, a judiciary unfettered by mainland influence, freedom of assembly and religion, a move towards democracy and a continued role for democratic politicians. At the handover ceremony, Patten argued that Britain's contribution to Hong Kong's success was:

> the rule of law. Clean and light-handed government. The values of a free society. The beginnings of representative government and democratic accountability. This is a Chinese city, a very Chinese city, with British characteristics. No dependent territory has been left more prosperous, none with such a rich texture and fabric of civil society, professions, churches, newspapers, charities, civil servants of the highest probity and the most steadfast commitment to the public good.[57]

Reviewing his governorship in 1999, Patten again reiterated his belief in what he termed the 'set of institutional arrangements' that comprised 'the rule of law, representative government, freedom of speech,

[55] 'Change-over will come and go, Hong Kong's here to stay', *SCMP*, 1 July1995.

[56] A. Ho, *More Quotations from Chris Patten* (Hong Kong: Sub-culture, 1997).

[57] Cited in Vines, *Hong Kong: China's New Colony*, p. 11.

independent courts, clean police, and free trade'.[58] Part of his task in Hong Kong was, he said, to encourage the Hong Kong people to believe that if they stood up for the things they were promised in the Joint Declaration, there was more chance of Hong Kong surviving as a free society: 'I saw an important part of my job as being, as it were, a bully pulpit for the liberties, the values, that go with civil society.'[59] A year after the handover, Patten argued that the 'rule of law' and 'free society' put Hong Kong in a good position.[60]

In her analysis of the war of words that broke out between Patten and the Chinese authorities after his arrival in 1992, Sum argues that Patten's appeal to certain universalising values – such as democracy, equality and the rule of law – formed part of a strategy to capture support across class and racial divides 'by framing new codes of meaning and creat[ing] a new collective identity'.[61] Central to this identity were the rule of law and the accountability of government. Patten signalled what would become the leading trope of his administration:

> Democracy is more than just a philosophical ideal. It is, for instance, an essential element in the pursuit of economic progress . . . Without the rule of law buttressed by democratic institutions, investors are left unprotected. Without an independent judiciary enforcing laws democratically enacted, businesses will be vulnerable to arbitrary political decisions taken on a whim – a sure recipe for a collapse of confidence and a powerful deterrent to investors from overseas.[62]

When the business elites suddenly switched their allegiance from Britain to Beijing in the wake of China's hostility to his reform proposals, Patten was driven by what Sum calls a 'hollowing out' of old colonial economic and political power to cultivate grassroots support for his administration. His top-down strategy promoted an 'imagined autonomous identity' for Hong Kong that contrasted with the collective national identity proposed by the PRC.

[58] Chris Patten, 'Conversations with History', interview by Harry Kreisler, Institute of International Studies, University of California, Berkeley, 1999. http://globetrotter.berkeley.edu/conversations/Patten.

[59] Patten, 'Conversations with History'.

[60] 'Chris Patten: reflections on Hong Kong', *RTHK*, 30 June 1998.

[61] Sum, 'War of words', p. 88.

[62] C. Patten, 7 October 1992, cited in *Public Statements, House of Lords*, 9 December 1992, HL 541/207–12.

Patten's electoral reforms expanded the compass of the functional constituencies, enfranchising over two million people. In provoking the wrath of China and the business community by these proposals, he came to be seen as standing up for Hong Kong and its ordinary citizens.[63] His personal style of government was more open than anything that went before or came after. It included, for example, town hall appearances at which he answered questions from the public, something no other Hong Kong governor had ever attempted. This cultivation of 'grassroots' democracy may have been a political strategy designed to restore some honour to the last days of colonial rule, but it nevertheless established the notion that the ordinary people were entitled to direct dealings with those in power, to openly challenge what they had to say, and to have their voice heard.

At the time, Martin Lee supported Patten's view that the rule of law was Hong Kong's most important defence against any attempts by Beijing to erode Hong Kong's way of life. History, he argued, 'has taught us that without democratic and accountable government, we will never be able to maintain the rule of law, and without the rule of law, Hong Kong will experience a surge in the corruption and *guanxi* (politics based on personal contacts) endemic in China'.[64] In his policy address to LEGCO in 1993, Patten argued that the rule of law was essential to Hong Kong's continued prosperity, stability and freedom,[65] and in a series of speeches between 1992 and 1997, he continually linked the rule of law with Hong Kong's capitalist system, its freedoms, its values, 'this way of life'. It was the rule of law upon which Hong Kong's success was said to depend; the rule of law which guaranteed 'stability and our fundamental freedoms'; the rule of law was the 'glue by which millions of people of different ambitions, abilities and temperament may be joined together'; the rule of law 'championed the rights of the individual against the collective, the rights of the weak against the mighty, the individual against the state, the vulnerable against the powerful'. Rule of law went 'hand in hand with clean and competent government'; it was the 'bedrock of your way of life'; it guaranteed fair and equitable treatment for everyone, kept crime and corruption under 'unremitting attack' and produced 'a safe and secure

[63] 'Reform plan attacked by big business', *Eastern Express*, 24 May 1994.
[64] M. Lee, 'Tide of democracy', *Far Eastern Economic Review*, 22 November 1992.
[65] C. Patten, 'Today's success, tomorrow's challenges', address to LEGCO on the opening of the 1993/4 legislative year.

environment for the individual, for families and for businesses to flourish', a 'decent, open, plural society living in freedom under the rule of law'. Rule of law was the community's 'most prized possession'. Everyone could have confidence in the law because no one was above the law, 'no politician, no business leader, no Governor'; the law served everyone. Hong Kong was:

> A success story almost without parallel. A community with a pretty good government, run by an excellent largely Chinese civil service. Low crime. Excellent police. Competitive businesses. The rule of law. It's argumentative and free. Open and responsible. Moderate and fair.[66]

Interviewed in September 1996, Patten was asked what values he would like to see the British leave behind in Hong Kong. He answered:

> Those with which de Tocqueville would have been comfortable with: the rule of law, the institutions of civil society, a meritocratic politically neutral civil service, the restraint and responsibility which go with those institutional arrangements in a successful plural society. I think one of the reasons for Hong Kong's moderation and for Hong Kong's stability is the interplay between those values, those institutions and the people who live here.[67]

Asked whether this amounted to 'cultural imperialism', Patten responded that, 'It's interesting that some people should regard Leninism or Marxism as inherent to Asia but not de Tocqueville'.[68] He reiterated his view that Hongkongers would lose their freedoms under the rule of law unless they themselves were prepared to stand up for their rights.

Hong Kong academics, Sin Wai Man and Chu Yiu Wai, subsequently asked why the law become so 'normalised' in Hong Kong. Why had it 'never enjoyed a higher status than in recent years'?[69] Why was it 'more and more frequently hailed as the secret of the present success of the economy and the key to Hong Hong's future

[66] Ho, *Quotations from Chris Patten*; J. Flowerdew, *The Final Years of British Hong Kong: The Discourse of Colonial Withdrawal* (Basingstoke: Palgrave, 1997).

[67] Chris Patten, 'An interview with Chris Patten, Governor of Hong Kong', interview by J. Flowerdew. 16 September 1996, Government House, Hong Kong. Unpublished paper, City University of Hong Kong.

[68] Flowerdew, 'An interview with Chris Patten'.

[69] W. M. Sin and Y. W. Chu, 'Whose rule of law? Rethinking (post-)colonial legal culture in Hong Kong', *Social & Legal Studies*, 7, no. 2 (1998), pp. 47–169.

prosperity', the 'bulwark for the protection of human rights' against both the pre- and post-1997 governments?[70] The answer, they concluded, was that the rule of law had by the 1990s acquired the status of a grand narrative. Hong Kong was not alone in this, of course. By the 1990s, the rule of law had become *the* grand narrative around the world, achieving global hegemony. Even China officially subscribed. Although the 'Washington Consensus' doctrines of unfettered free markets and democracy eventually lost credit, the rule of law retained near-global support as a universal 'good'. The ascent of rule of law discourse in Hong Kong owed something to this trend, as well as to the rule of law mantra chanted by the outgoing colonial power. By 1997, hearts and minds *had* been won; belief in the rule of law *had* been internalised; it *was* part of the Hong Kong 'way of life', a 'core value'. A survey conducted after 1997 concluded that 'worry about the ruler of law is . . . strongly associated with satisfaction with life here'.[71] By 1997, law such as the Basic Law and the Bill of Rights, coupled with the rhetoric of the rule of law, had constructed a highly effective wall of law around the HKSAR. Together, they formed a guarantee that people in post-1997 Hong Kong would still be able to claim their rights. 'True believers' were created amongst public and academia alike, partly by China's use of the military against its own people in 1989, making the rule of law a kind of talisman and symbol of the community.

The strength of the rule of law as a symbol would endure in spite – or perhaps because – of China's attacks upon it after 1997. As Ho points out, Beijing did not keep things the same: the NPCSC attempted to scrap the BOR; the Public Order Ordinance was amended to restrict civil liberties; and, in 2002, the HKSAR administration introduced national security legislation, as required by Article 23 of the Basic Law.[72] These steps, together with NPCSC interventions in the legal system, provoked claims that the rule of law in Hong Kong 'was dead', killed by what was seen as examples of the HKSAR government's tendency 'to exert authoritarian regulation over civil society in the name of legality, order, and patriotism'.[73] What China wished to see was an end to citizen movements for freedom and rights and a return to

70 Sin and Chu, 'Whose rule of law?'

71 The Hong Kong Transition Project report, Baptist University of Hong Kong, 2006, p. 32.

72 Ho, *Quotations from Chris Patten.*

73 Ku and Pun, *Remaking Citizenship*, p. 11.

the old-style Hong Kong colonial citizen, *homo economicus*, the apolitical, self-starting, self-helping, entrepreneur of neo-liberalism, content with the political status quo and preferably patriotic. Paradoxically, it was China's insistence on these qualities that produced amongst Hongkongers the very opposition it sought to erase. Its interventions in the legal system also helped to mould a judiciary far more active and committed to upholding the rule of law and expert in human rights protections than it had been in the last years of colonialism.[74]

GENERAL ZHOU CROSSES THE BORDER

Before 1997, pundits in the international media had speculated as to how China would make her presence felt in the new HKSAR. Some argued that tanks would soon be rolling down the streets in a full-scale display of power; others that China would leave Hong Kong alone, because it was the goose that laid the golden eggs. A third view was that China's inability to fully comprehend how Hong Kong worked meant that its leaders would simply 'screw things up'.[75] The tanks are not visible, but the presence of the PLA serves as a reminder of the new sovereign's power to punish. PLA manoeuvres in Victoria Harbour in 2013 and 2014 were certainly interpreted as warning shots, reminding the public who held the monopoly on coercive power. Local figures have also been summoned to the Central Government's Liaison Office for 'reminders' of the need to uphold the party line. Such background manoeuvres escaped international attention.

One incident in the months preceding 1 July 1997 exemplifies how much Hongkongers had taken the rule of law to heart as their principal defence against China. A PLA General, Major General Zhou Borong, attempted to enter the restricted zone along the Hong Kong border without the necessary permit. He was prevented from doing so by a border official. In the ensuing row, General Zhou demanded that the officer show more respect for the PLA and allow him to pass. After a series of phone calls in high places, the general was allowed to cross without the proper permit. The indignant front-line officer subsequently

[74] See Y. Ghai, 'Sentinels of liberty or sheep in wolf's clothing? Judicial politics and the Hong Kong Bill of Rights', *The Modern Law Review*, 60, no. 4 (July 1997), pp. 459–80.

[75] See R. Jacob, 'Hong Kong's threatened Rule of Law', *The Financial Times*, 24 February 1999.

telephoned a local radio phone-in programme to complain, arguing that 'no-one in Hong Kong is supposed to be above the law'. 'Even the Governor', he insisted, was required to produce the proper papers when he wished to cross the border. This was 'the beginning of the end' for the rule of law in Hong Kong.[76]

General Zhou's insistence that the rules did not apply to him were widely taken as an indication of things to come: after 1997, Chinese officials would think they should get special treatment and be exempt from the law, as was often the case in the mainland. As LEGCO member James To put it, 'That's what Hong Kong people are worried about'. Pro-Beijing critics responded to public outcries about the General Zhao incident by denouncing supporters of the rule of law as 'running dogs' of the outgoing colonial masters. Rule of law rhetoric was, they insisted, simply a means by which the British sought to prolong their influence over a subjugated people.

The episode carried greater significance because the Chinese official in this instance was a member of the PLA. The events of 4 June 1989 had left Hongkongers with a suspicion of the PLA, and there was a lack of clarity about its post-1997 role in the territory. China's plan to send 4,000 PLA troops across the border in 400 vehicles (including armoured personnel carriers) at dawn on 1 July 1997 was already seen as provocative by pro-democracy groups in Hong Kong. Others simply saw it as an attempt to publicly humiliate the British and stamp China's authority on the territory. The border crossing ceremony by armed PLA officers provided the international media gathered in Hong Kong for the handover with one of its most widely-used images. It embodied the apocalyptic version of the handover, with serried ranks of unsmiling, uniformed guards driving into Hong Kong as an invading army. Would the walls of law stand?

[76] See C. K. Lau, 'Voices above the crowd', *SCMP*, 6 Jul 1995.

3

Transitional fears and fantasies

The walls of law were put in place chiefly to assuage the fear that 1997 would precipitate an exodus of people and capital, followed by an 'invasion' of Hong Kong's way of life. The lyrics of a hit song of the early 1990s spoke of 1997 not as a 're-union' but a 'take-over'. The video accompanying the song, 'Queen's Road East', showed PLA soldiers marching along Queen's Road into the heart of Central Hong Kong.[1] The 1992 film 'Wicked City' depicted 'reptilian humanoids plotting to take over the city' on 1 July 1997.[2] In the twilight zone between the two worlds of Hong Kong and mainland China, strange happenings were reported. In reality as in the film, those who transited through to the 'other side' entered a lawless world full of danger, whilst disease, crime and corruption were seen as creeping across the border to infect Hong Kong.

Disorder and chaos always threatened, either from within (a reported resurgence of crime and corruption) or from without (crime and disease spilled over from China). Constant vigilance and high investment in the forces of law and order were seen as necessary prerequisites for the continuance of an orderly daily life. Hong Kong in the run-up to 1997 adopted a kind of fortress mentality. China was the bogeyman, an ever-present threat to Hong Kong's political stability.

[1] Music Factory, *Huanghou da dao dong (Queen's Road East)*, catalogue no. MFCR91012, Hong Kong, 1991.

[2] A. Abbas, *Hong Kong: Culture and the Politics of Disappearance* (Hong Kong: Hong Kong University Press, 1997).

WEAK POINTS IN THE DEFENCES

Despite the 'walls of law', in the run-up to 1997, Hongkongers remained sceptical that their rights and freedoms would survive the handover. Of particular concern was what exactly would constitute legitimate political criticism after 1997:

> In Hong Kong, there are very few instances when people are told what they can and cannot say. But in the Chinese context this freedom is limited and such restrictions extend even to the political field without clear demarcations, so the restrictions are dependent on subjective judgments and not on the basis of law, as here. This is extremely dangerous and in no way benefits Hong Kong. Right now, there are no clear assurances that the current freedoms which allow us to talk and express opinions freely even on non-political matters will continue ... Law in China is an instrument of policy. The rule of law as a concept does not exist ... [W]ith sovereignty just four years away, there is an increasing urgency to set up institutions to preserve and strengthen the rule of law and protect the Bill of Rights Ordinance ... A Human Rights, Freedom of Information and a Legal Aid Commission are vitally necessary to protect human rights and safeguard Hong Kong's way of life.[3]

A 1996 survey showed that fears about freedom of the press and freedom of speech topped Hongkongers' concerns about the transition. This fear was reflected in press interviews. As one interviewee said, 'Before, we liked to speak loudly ... After the handover, I think you will have to beware of your speech'. Another stated that, 'Even under the British we could express our opinions. Now you've got a question mark in your mind'.[4] A 'test run' of the 'human rights kit' developed for schoolchildren found that, though they had little clear idea of human rights in the abstract, on closer examination, they knew their rights and feared the future:

> Buddhist Tracy Chan Kwan-yu, 10 ... felt she was entitled to worship freely. Kenneth Lam Wai-yuen, 12 ... said all people should be equal in the eyes of the law: 'We all want to leave before '97. The mainlanders are different. I have been to Shenzhen and it is easy to get kidnapped or

[3] N. De Silva, 'Territory's rights hang in the balance', The *Sunday Standard*, 14 February 1993.

[4] Chris Wood, 'Hong Kong Handover', *The Canadian Encyclopaedia*, www.thecanadaianencyclopedia.com (accessed 16 March 2006).

> pushed around by rude people' ... Dorothy said: 'What if I say something wrong or offensive? They might take me and send me to another part of the country. Even worse, I could be executed'.[5]

The survival of the BOR was also doubted. China had made it clear that the Basic Law – not the BOR – would be the supreme law governing Hong Kong after 1997. The NPCSC also retained the right to interpret the Basic Law. If the provisions of the BOR were found to violate the Basic Law (or the NPCSC's interpretations of the BL), it was clearly understood which legal instrument would prevail. The creation of the CFA also failed to assuage anxieties. By 1995 no overseas judges had been approached to sit on the court. Time was running out. At a ceremony to mark the opening of the 1995 Legal Year, Chief Justice Sir Ti Liang Yang warned of the possibility of a 'vacuum' should the court fail to be established by 1997. It would detrimentally affect Hong Kong's prosperity, stability and the credibility of its judicial system.[6] To avoid this prospect, the government framed a contingency plan – Patten was thought to have obtained Britain's secret agreement to unilaterally establish the court if no agreement with China was forthcoming. Eventually, in June 1995, the Chinese side agreed to the establishment of a CFA but not until the 1997 transition itself. Moreover:

> The price was a high one. Mr Patten was forced to go back on his repeated pledges to establish the court before the handover ... By leaving China to establish the court, with the Hong Kong Government's role reduced to rendering such assistance to the Beijing team-designate deemed necessary, Britain finally acknowledged it had lost the initiative in governing the territory.[7]

As a LEGCO member, Emily Lau later observed that Hongkongers were not 'told all the facts' about this agreement.[8] The term 'team-designate' included the SAR chief executive designate, all the principal officials designate, and others involved in setting up the SAR government.[9] This, she argued, amounted to an agreement between China

[5] 'Pupils want freedom of speech', *SCMP*, 2 March 1996.
[6] 'Plea for top level of redress', *SCMP*, 14 January 1995.
[7] D. Gittings, 'The year we held our breath', *SCMP International Weekly*, 6 January 1996.
[8] E. Lau, 'Shadow legislature will sow confusion', *SCMP International Weekly*, 2 December 1995.
[9] Lau, 'Shadow legislature'.

and Britain that a 'shadow legislature' would be established in 1996.[10] This 'team-designate' would nominate judges, based on recommendations from an independent commission set up before 1997. The CFA agreement meant that 'China now called the shots' in major decisions. Martin Lee called it a 'bad deal', arguing that 'China was not supposed to take over in 1995, or even in 1997. Hong Kong people were to be masters of our own house, and in the now empty phrase of the Joint Declaration, Hong Kong people were to rule Hong Kong with a high degree of autonomy.'[11] Lee argued that China had 'got everything it wanted on the court'.[12] Delaying the CFA's establishment until 1997 meant that China would control the process. This meant that China would be able to limit 'the discretion and independence of the CFA in inviting overseas judges, and restricting the jurisdiction through acts of state so that there could be no challenge by Hong Kong people to Beijing's decisions . . . The only 'certainty' provided by the Sino-British CFA agreement is the certainty that the rule of law is finished in Hong Kong'.[13]

Hong Kong people, Lee argued, 'know only too well the value of our rule of law and way of life', but the British government and the governor had 'now compromised what would have been their greatest legacy to Hong Kong'.[14] In a 1992 interview, Lau also raised the spectre of Hong Kong's legal system becoming subordinate to that of the mainland:

> The British legacy in Hong Kong is the rule of law, we hope. Will it last? I don't know. Maybe it will be swept away. It will be one of the good things that the British leave behind, if it survives. If. It's something very valuable, even in Asian contexts. Respect for the rule of law, equality before the law, fair arbitration of disputes and so on. We hope that can be preserved.[15]

Upholding the rule of law was a stated objective of both branches of the legal profession. But despite the plethora of laws now 'on the books',

[10] Lau, 'Shadow legislature'.
[11] M. Lee, 'The sell-out that has to stop', *SCMP*, 1 July 1995.
[12] Lee, 'The sell-out that has to stop'. [13] Lee, 'The sell-out that has to stop'.
[14] Lee, 'The sell-out that has to stop'.
[15] Chris Patten, 'Hong Kong beyond 1997: Interview with Governor Chris Patten and three LEGCO members', interview by J. A. Gordon and C. Wong, The *Harvard Journal of World Affairs*, 1994. www.ontheissues.org/spectrum/beyond97.htm (accessed 16 March 2006).

they, together with pro-democracy activists and a large swathe of public opinion, feared that there was still time for China to put in place measures that would undermine the rule of law before 1997. In this mood, Hongkongers vigilantly scrutinised social, political and legal events for signs of such measures.

CORRUPTION

Writing in 1995, journalist Kevin Sinclair called upon Sino-British negotiators to address the concerns of the ordinary men and women of Hong Kong, uppermost of which, he argued, was the fear that 'the widespread corruption which flourishes along with increasing prosperity over the border may seep into Hong Kong as our economies become more entwined'.[16] In 1996, The Better Hong Kong Foundation (a group of leading Hong Kong businessmen including Li Ka-shing) presented a report to the Chinese leadership that raised the business sector's concerns of the prospect of rising corruption after 1997.[17] Concerns about corruption had been growing since 1993 when official statistics indicated a rise in reports. Between 1991 and 1996, corruption complaints increased at more than seven times the rate of staffing in the operations department of the ICAC, prompting the biggest intake of new investigative staff in the history of the commission.[18] ICAC statistics for 1993 showed a 44 per cent increase in complaints, followed by another increase in 1994. The rise was blamed on election-related graft, police malpractice and an increase in criminal 'get rich quick' schemes before 1997.[19] ICAC concerns about corruption within the police force were confirmed by a report by the Police Force Anti-Corruption Strategy Committee, which questioned levels of integrity within the police and the willingness of senior officers to tackle the problem.[20]

Fears about 'mainland-style' corruption creeping over the border after 1997 intensified after a mainland initiative to remove the word 'independent' from the title of the Independent Commission Against

16 K. Sinclair, 'A vital dialogue that's good for all', *SCMP*, 24 July 1995.
17 C. Ng and C. Yeung, 'No China overlord for HK, says Lu', *SCMP*, 27 January 1996.
18 J. Hill, 'Anti-graft chief ready for hard fight', *SCMP*, 27 January 1996.
19 D. Goodsir, 'Corruption reports up after polls', *SCMP* 14 January 1995.
20 D. Goodsir, 'Tainted officers shielded', *SCMP International Weekly*, 2 December 1995.

Corruption. Founded in 1974, the ICAC had been a central plank in the colonial government's claim to legitimacy. It is credited with making Hong Kong one of the least corrupt societies in the world and enjoyed legendary status. In the 1970s, a soap opera based on the ICAC ran weekly on Hong Kong television which, Chan recalls, 'riveted' the whole community: 'half of Hong Kong stayed home to follow one episode after another for weeks'.[21] The suggestion that the word 'independent' was to be deleted was seen, therefore, as a sign that even one of Hong Kong's key institutions was not safe from interference. The suggested change of title also provoked anxieties about the ICAC's ability to prosecute corruption without fear of favour after 1997, especially when investigating mainland-owned organisations, or those with close connections to powerful mainland figures. Hongkongers were familiar with reports of widespread corruption in the mainland; some had directly experienced corruption as part of their business dealings with China. China was seen as a corrupt polity – a major complaint of the 4 June protestors had been the extent of corruption, especially amongst the children of the party leaders (the 'Red Princes and Princesses'):

> [T]he Communist Party tends to operate along the lines of 'rule by personality' rather than 'rule of law' ... The fact that the bulk of the mainland executives who have established anything from footholds to empires in Hong Kong are either members of Beijing's power elite – or their offspring – gives even more cause for concern over Beijing's apparent reluctance to put the law before individuals.[22]

Pre-1997, there was a fear that a resurgence of corruption in Hong Kong could undermine the rule of law and trigger political, social as well as criminal consequences. Those familiar with mainland politics also knew that allegations of corruption in China often served as a proxy for tests of political strength. The accuracy of such an accusation was less important than one's ability to successfully make it stick – or to resist it. Related to concerns about the removal of the word 'independent' from the ICAC's title, therefore, symbolised fears about the infiltration of this kind of politics and tactics into Hong Kong's political and commercial life.

[21] Chan, 'Postmodernism and Hong Kong cinema', in Dirlik and Xudon, *Postmodernism in China.*

[22] J. Braude, 'Graft guide a start', *SCMP*, 6 May 1993.

TRIADS AND ORGANISED CRIME

Triads, their history, organisation and activities are the stuff of myth and hyperbole. In popular culture, academic narratives, and in law, triads are associated with the swearing of secret oaths, secret organisations, secret signs and secret activities. They belong to an underworld that Hong Kong's forces of law and order have long striven to keep in check. Triads typically trace their history back to their support for the efforts of the Qing regime to resist the incursions of the British and other imperial nations into China during the nineteenth century. Though tolerated by a number of British colonial administrations in East Asia, in Hong Kong such secret societies were proscribed from the first years of British rule. Triads were a threat because of their clandestine cross-border activities. In the nineteenth century, triads had mobilised Hongkongers around mainland political struggles. In the 1950s, they were blamed for helping to organise support for Nationalist riots. To weaken such particularistic ties, in the 1970s long-standing anti-triad measures were supplemented by a raft of measures designed to bind Hong Kong people to universalistic values and institutions, such as the rule of law and the courts.

In the early 1990s, however, Hong Kong was astonished when a 1984 speech by Deng Xiaoping was re-released in which he described triad societies as 'patriotic'. In the fervid atmosphere of these years, such a speech by the paramount leader himself generated widespread speculation. It was released at the height of the row between Beijing and Patten over the future political landscape of Hong Kong. Central to the Patten rhetoric was the characterisation of Hong Kong as an open, fair and stable society, at the cornerstone of which lay the rule of law. Triad affiliation and its associated clandestine order represented the polar opposite. Deng also implied that triads could play a part in resisting the coloniser by demonstrating their loyalty to mainland leaders.[23] This was understood as a call for triads and other 'patriotic' groups to resist British attempts to retain influence on Chinese soil after 1997. Triad proximity to the post-1997 regime would pose serious questions for the ability of law enforcement agencies to prosecute triad and organised crime after 1997. Deng's speech called into question the *raison d'etre* of their existence, generating uncertainty about how the

[23] See 'Assignment: dealing with the triads', BBC2, 4 November 1995.

post-1997 regime would view law enforcement against 'patriotic' (possibly CCP) but criminal associations. It seemed to the police that they were being asked to regard triads as aides to postcolonial governance. There was another undercurrent to society's reaction, one which seemed to be borne out by events after 1997. This was the notion that Beijing could readily mobilise triads against those it did not consider 'patriots' after 1997.

CRIME AND DISORDER

The susceptibility of Hong Kong to 'contamination' by mainland crime and disorder was a recurrent theme of 1990s culture. Films often depicted a police force penetrated by gangsters posing undercover as cops. As one commentator observes, these 'undercover films' are a special genre in Hong Kong and have huge popular resonance.[24] Janet Ng argues that the debates and discussions surrounding such films as *Infernal Affairs* are in fact a vehicle for the 'non-existent public venue for political discussions in Hong Kong'.[25] A common theme is that of divided loyalties, of the 'good guys' with family members or best friends in the criminal underworld. Traditional ties of blood and kinship vie with loyalty to the police, law and the state, an ambivalence that is seldom satisfactorily resolved. The struggle against destiny, 'undercover' existence and loss of identity are all themes which serve as reminders of the need to disguise one's true identity – or shuttle between identities – to survive, much as Hong Kong was required to do in the transitional years.[26]

According to one dominant narrative in these years of transition, for the city to survive and thrive, the boundary between law and lawlessness had to be policed to prevent contamination of the 'good' by the 'bad'; the 'clean' by the 'dirty'; and the rational and fair by the irrational, capricious and arbitrary. In the run-up to 1997, contamination by 'bad guys across the border' (e.g., criminals and corrupt officials) was the main threat. A rise in spectacular shoot-outs and armed, gold shop robberies in the early 1990s was blamed on mainland gangsters 'sneaking' across the border or hiring Hong Kong criminals to

[24] The post analyses two films: *Infernal Affairs*, *City on Fire* and *Man on the Brink*. hegelchong, 'Post-colonizing Hong Kong', 11 March 2006. www.pageinsider.com/narratinghk.blogspot.com.

[25] Ng, *Paradigm City*, pp. 20–1. [26] Ng, *Paradigm City*.

commit crimes at their behest. An increase in vice-related activities was similarly blamed on an influx of mainland prostitutes, smuggled in by cross-border criminal gangs. Ng argues that fears about the invasion by an evil presence were reflected in films like *PTU*, in which a mainland gang is 'unambiguously depicted as a foreign invasion ... Through the metaphor of the gangsters, China's strategy of rule in Hong Kong is represented as a combination of insensitive stampede, ignorant aggressiveness, and ruthless rampage'.[27]

OTHER MAINLAND INCURSIONS

Anxiety about the rule of law increased when, in the mid-1990s, reports appeared in the local press of a series of incursions by mainland security forces into Hong Kong territory. On 18 March 1995, for example, mainland authorities seized two Hong Kong men, took them to Zhuhai and charged them with smuggling, an offence that carried the death sentence in mainland China. They were arrested by mainland forces despite the fact that the men were operating in local waters off Sai Kung.[28] The Hong Kong Marine Police had tried to prevent the abduction but were confronted by mainland security personnel. The mainland security vessel was itself in Hong Kong waters; the security officers on board were armed with sub-machine guns. According to an *SCMP* report, the police were threatened at gunpoint when they tried to board the Chinese vessel. Witnesses reported hearing shots fired; some mainland security guards wore hoods over their heads to protect their identity, whilst others refused to provide proof of their identity.[29] The Hong Kong Government officials ordered the Marine Police not to open fire and also told the navy not to intervene. Later reports claimed that 'Senior British naval officers in Hong Kong apparently by-passed the Governor to seek endorsement directly from Whitehall to intervene ... [N]aval officers were said to be upset when told by the Hong Kong government not to get involved in the incident'.[30] This 'lame' response prompted criticism of the government for having emasculated its own security forces and abdicated responsibility for border security.

[27] Ng, *Paradigm City*, 29.
[28] The men were scheduled to appear before a Zhuhai court on 16 April 1995.
[29] D. Goodsir and A. Gilbert, 'Get tough, Patten tells Navy', *SCMP*, 1 April 1995.
[30] A. Ho, 'Calling the Troops in', *SCMP*, 6 July 1995.

The incident had wider ramifications. It occurred against the background of ongoing Sino-British talks about the role of the PLA after 1997. One concern was that, although Article 14 of the Basic Law provided some reassurance, there was a complete lack of clarity regarding the actual interaction between local law enforcement agencies and Chinese security personnel, should they be called upon to intervene in Hong Kong matters. The incident was also seen as the latest example of the Hong Kong administration effectively 'handing over' to China before the 1997 retrocession. One newspaper asked, 'What faith can be placed in the Basic Law's guarantees of administrative autonomy after 1997 if the Government connives at Chinese breaches of Hong Kong's territorial integrity while Britain is still the sovereign power? … It is craven and short-sighted to be condoning blatant PSB [Public Security Bureau] encroachment more than two years in advance of the transfer of sovereignty.'[31] In its editorial, the newspaper observed that:

> China maintains that the vessels were being followed on suspicion of smuggling and that mainland security forces had already boarded before strong winds pushed them back into Hong Kong waters. Therefore they were entirely within their right to abduct the men in Hong Kong and bring them to the mainland to face charges. However, this overlooks a crucial point. Chinese forces have no jurisdiction in Hong Kong, yet feel no hesitation in making arrests if their pursuit of suspicious vessels strays into local waters. It would be less worrying if this incident were isolated, yet the growing number of incursions into territorial waters by Chinese security forces suggests a total disregard for Hong Kong law … Britain should strenuously make its objections known over this incident. It is a test of how serious Britain and the Hong Kong government are about upholding the rule of law and ensuring that it is respected by others.[32]

Concern increased when it was learned that another Hong Kong vessel had also been boarded earlier in March by mainland security forces. They forced the crew at gunpoint to sail to an island in Chinese waters (Dangan Lidao), where the ship was searched and the crew detained at a Chinese military base before being released.[33] The incident badly affected local confidence in the autonomy of the Hong Kong police exercising their jurisdiction within the territory's borders. Local

[31] 'Breach of Borders', *SCMP*, 25 March 1995. [32] *SCMP*, 15 April 1995.
[33] 'Sea Row deepens over new hijacking', *SCMP*, 8 April 1995.

politician Christine Loh argued that rising crime, and the ability of Hong Kong criminals to recruit well-armed and well-trained gangsters from the mainland to carry out robberies in the territory, meant that Hong Kong people wanted to see *some* cooperation between the Hong Kong and mainland law enforcement agencies in the run-up to 1997. Somewhat presciently given events after 1997, she cautioned:

> [Whilst they] might say that what they want to see is criminals caught, and that where they are tried is not so important . . . we should think more deeply about this. Procedures for arrest and detention, the right to independent counsel and a defence, the right to an open trial, the determination of guilt and sentencing and the right of appeal are very different in China.[34]

The governor ordered the police and the Royal Navy to review their rules of engagement to prevent Chinese security vessels illegally entering Hong Kong waters.[35] Local police sent a report to Whitehall arguing that the local police force may have 'already lost control [of the border] to PRC authorities'.[36] An official protest was lodged with the mainland authorities but received no response; a top-level police delegation prepared to visit China to secure the men's release.[37] Though diplomatic protests eventually produced an apology from the Chinese authorities, the two Hong Kong citizens remained under detention in China, the Chinese authorities insisting that they had every right to put them on trial in the mainland. Chinese officials accused Britain of 'politiking' and 'making a mountain out of a mole hill' by raising the issue in the Joint Liaison Group. The issue of a cross-border agreement for handing over suspects, however, was left unresolved. When it recurred in 1998, in the case of Cheung Tze-keung and his gang,[38] pre-handover fears turned out to have been justified.

In the years leading up to 1997, the government continued to turn a blind eye to such matters. Security Branch statistics for 1996, for example, failed to count all of the incursions into Hong Kong territory.

[34] C. Loh, 'We must team up to fight crime', *SCMP*, 15 April 1995.

[35] Goodsir and Gilbert, 'Get tough'. [36] Goodsir and Gilbert, 'Get tough'.

[37] Goodsir and Gilbert, 'Get tough'.

[38] Cheung Tze-keung ('Big Spender') and four members of his gang were executed in Guangzhou in 1998 following a trial in a mainland court under mainland China's Criminal Law for kidnapping Victor Li Tzar-kuoi and Walter Kwok Ping-sheung in Hong Kong. Li Yuhui was tried and executed in Shantou for five murders at Telford Gardens, Hong Kong.

The 1995 figures put incursions at a record low (three incidents compared with seven in 1994 and fifteen in 1993), but these did not include the incident near Waglan Island in March 1995, in which the crew of a Panamanian cargo vessel were taken at gunpoint to a Chinese military base at Dangan Liadao, south of Hong Kong. In a second incident, on 22 December 1995, a suspected Chinese security vessel was said to have fired two shots at a Hong Kong vessel off Waglan Island. According to the local press, with 1997 approaching:

> [T]he police are becoming more lenient towards incursions by security vessels ... 'Under internal directions, there is a line we will not cross', said a senior Marine Police officer. 'You will find it in Cap 242'. Cap 242 ... the Smuggling into China (Control) Ordinance 1948, which gives China certain anti-smuggling powers in an area near its coast in Mirs Bay and Deep Bay, of which the high-water mark is the actual border.' 'However, the ordinance specifically states it should not limit Hong Kong's jurisdiction in the areas ...' Another police source said the Cap 242 line had become a virtual border with China in Mirs Bay ... But while Security Branch insists the police and navy stay away from the Chinese coast, Chinese security forces are allowed to regularly operate in Hong Kong waters, well beyond the Cap 242 line ... 'It's a question of not wanting to rock the boat', one source said.[39]

The police also said they had 'delicate arrangements with the Chinese which no-one wants to disturb ... The last thing anyone wants is to make a big issue out of incursions so soon before the handover'.[40] The government ordered the police not to cross a line up to five kilometres from the border, allowing Chinese security forces to push forward the frontiers of their jurisdiction in Mirs Bay.[41] The implication was that the border no longer existed and that the Hong Kong government had already surrendered jurisdiction over part of the territory.

POLITICAL TUNNELS

These incidents occurred at a time of heightened tension, when talks between Britain and China over Hong Kong (in the Joint Liaison Group) had all but ceased. After announcing that it would dismantle

[39] *SCMP*, 2 March 1996.

[40] 'Figures fail to show true extent of China border encroachment', *SCMP*, 2 March 1996.

[41] A. Gilbert, 'HK turning blind eye to incursions', *SCMP*, 2 March 1996.

Patten's reforms,[42] China installed its own, parallel LEGCO, Provisional LEGCO.[43] This 'shadow' legislature met in Shenzhen. It consisted of China-appointed members and was set to replace Hong Kong's LEGCO on 1 July 1997. However, it was already passing laws before the handover. A survey conducted in the mid-1990s indicated that only seven per cent of Hongkongers trusted this body to protect their interests, whilst over 50 per cent supported the existing LEGCO.[44] The existence of the Provisional LEGCO served as a reminder of China's hostility to democratic reform in Hong Kong. There was also the question of who was to run Hong Kong in the years preceding the handover. Even during the negotiations over the Joint Declaration, China had proposed the creation of a Sino-British body to oversee the transition period, with Beijing holding a veto on all major decisions.[45] This proposal was eventually dropped following British opposition, but in 1985, China proposed a policy of 'convergence' whereby Britain's proposals for political reform in Hong Kong had to converge with China's plans for the territory after 1997. Beijing 'used every opportunity to press [its] demand for greater control over Hong Kong matters in the remaining years of British sovereignty'.[46] Plans were already in train to dismantle the system of local government, advisory committees and other community bodies. Highly diffuse, this system of 'consultative government' (what A. Y. C. King calls the 'administrative absorption of politics')[47] had acted as a conduit between government and community. The reception of policy at the local level was moved through such channels; grievances were communicated upwards to the government. From 1995 onwards, *Xinhua* (China's unofficial embassy in the territory) relied on newly-appointed advisers at the district level and upwards. These added to scores of other Beijing-appointed Hong Kong affairs advisers, and the Preliminary Working Committee (PWC) making, as one observer put it, 'the shadow of the incoming power ... more visible'.[48] Despite their success at local elections, the

[42] The NPC Standing Committee unanimously voted to end Hong Kong's political structure on 31 August 1994.
[43] See Editorial, *Far Eastern Economic Review*, 17 December 1992.
[44] *SCMP*, 1 July 1995.
[45] F. Ching, 'Boxed in a corner', *Far Eastern Economic Review*, 17 December 1992.
[46] Ching, 'Boxed in a corner'.
[47] A. Y. C. King, 'The administrative absorption of politics in Hong Kong', *Asian Survey*, 15 (1975).
[48] F. Wong, 'Talking at cross purposes', *SCMP*, 15 January 1995.

Democrats were generally excluded. In late 1995, the PWC legal subgroup unsettled the Hong Kong public by proposing to reinstate six 'Draconian' laws which could threaten freedom of speech and assembly after 1997; it also suggested diluting the Bill of Rights (BOR).[49] These included measures which, after 1997, would allow the police to ban demonstrations considered a threat to 'national security', prompting speculation that events such as the 4 June commemoration might be banned. Other anti-subversion measures would, it was thought, outlaw support for Tibetan or Taiwanese independence, forbid political groups from receiving foreign support and allow the government to prohibit organisations it considered subversive. At the same time, comments made by the then chief justice, Sir Ti Liang (made public by the Vice Director of *Xinhua*) suggesting that the BOR overrode all other statutes prompted a formal correction by the attorney general, but not before they were interpreted by Chinese officials as confirmation that Britain was seeking to undermine the post-1997 administration.

According to Lau Siu-kai, bodies such as the PWC were inevitably out of touch with local people since they were the product of elitist politics on either side of the border.[50] PWC members were said to have adopted a 'crisis mentality', taking the view that they could never win popular support.[51] The Preparatory Committee to oversee the handover was also overwhelmingly pro-China in its membership. This was the committee that would select the 400-member body responsible for electing the new CE of the HKSAR. Its unrepresentative nature – and the exclusion of the Democrats – was interpreted as a sign that Beijing was not interested in local opinion and issues. Leading members of the PWC and JLG had already alienated many Hong Kong social groups by attacking the Patten government's spending on welfare for the poor. Chen Zuo'er argued that welfare spending had increased by 66 per cent in real terms since Patten's appointment. A Hong Kong government official responded that 'to be denounced for socialism by communists borders on the absurd'.[52] The attempt by Beijing to control the Hong Kong budget before the handover was seen as an attack on Hong Kong's autonomy, a fear compounded by PWC member Sir Sze-yuen

[49] S. K. Lau, 'Preparing territory for the handover', *SCMP*, 17 December 1995.
[50] Lau, 'Preparing territory for the handover'.
[51] Lau, 'Preparing territory for the handover'.
[52] C. Yeung, 'Beijing attacks rising social welfare spending', *SCMP International Weekly*, 2 December 1995.

Chung's comment that a shadow government would be established in the six months preceding the handover. His remarks were attacked in London as likely to produce a fall in confidence.[53] Establishing an alternative centre of power before 1997 would, Lau argued, 'sow unease, apprehension and even chaos ... [It] would undermine the authority of and effectiveness of the Hong Kong government; lead to confusion and instability within the community; and damage the morale of the civil service ... [It] is a recipe for disaster and could make the colony ungovernable'.[54]

The fear that Hong Kong's rights, freedoms and rule of law were already under threat before the handover prompted local activists and legislators to form a new political alliance (Frontier) which would 'dare to speak out on sensitive issues like democracy and the rule of law'.[55] The call coincided with renewed anxiety over China's handling of dissidents.[56] In 1996, the colonial government also announced an amendment to Hong Kong law to ensure that the Habeas Corpus Acts of 1679 and 1816 would still apply to the territory after its reversion to Chinese sovereignty.

According to one observer, Chinese and Hong Kong politicians and officials all anticipated that 1996 would be a crucial year, 'a year of change, uncertainty, confusion, confrontation and conflict'.[57] With eighteen months to go until the handover, it was anticipated that China would now marginalise both the British and Hong Kong administrations in decisions about the future of the territory. China's constant insistence on sovereignty in all matters discussed by the JLG was said by one British official to be 'in danger of suffocating autonomy ... The fundamental point of the Joint Declaration is the high degree of autonomy. Just leaving Hong Kong as it is today. Lots of people are now wondering whether that's achievable'.[58] A former senior British government official lauded Patten for exposing what he described as the

[53] D. Wallen, 'Sir S. Y. wrong, Commons told', *SCMP International Weekly*, 2 December 1995.

[54] E. Lau, 'Shadow legislature will sow confusion', *SCMP International Weekly*, 2 December 1995.

[55] L. Choy, 'Alliance formed to defend democracy', *SCMP*, 31 August 1996.

[56] Chinese dissident Wei Jingsheng was detained incommunicado for nineteen months. At trial in 1995, he was sentenced to a further fourteen years in prison.

[57] C. Yeung, 'Stepping into the era of uncertainty', *SCMP International Weekly*, 6 January 1996.

[58] 'UK pessimism on Hurd talks', *SCMP*, 15 April 1995.

'duplicity of both the British and Chinese governments' in their high-handed treatment of Hong Kong in the Joint Declaration.[59] Neither the Basic Law nor the Joint Declaration, the official said, really protected civil and political rights in post-1997 Hong Kong.

FREEDOM OF THE PRESS

Public opinion polls in 1995 and 1996 showing rising mistrust of the future HKSAR administration were partly fuelled by the hard-line approach adopted by the Provisional LEGCO. The outgoing British administration was under pressure to amend existing colonial laws, which gave the government wide powers to control the media in an emergency situation. Given the Provisional LEGCO's approach, it was feared that it would use these laws to stifle press freedom after 1997. Remarks made by former British Ambassador Sir Robin McLaren in 1994 also sowed doubts as to how far Hongkongers could rely on Britain to 'stand up' for their freedoms after 1997. In a lecture at the University of Hong Kong, he argued that:

> You sometimes need to be prepared to compromise three per cent of the freedoms you enjoy in order to be able to ensure you keep the other 97 per cent ... The interests of Hong Kong people lie in ensuring that, after 1997, the issue of Hong Kong appears as infrequently as possible on the agenda of the State Council [of the Chinese Government].[60]

In December 1995, Hong Kong reporters had already been warned to 'love their mother country', be patriotic and obey mainland laws when reporting in China.[61] A Hong Kong reporter for *Ming Pao* was imprisoned in China for 'stealing state secrets', an offence open to a wide degree of interpretation. The Vice Director of Xinhua reassured Hong Kong journalists that freedom of the press was protected under the Basic Law but added, 'Regarding the self-censorship issue ... I think because of the law, ethics and social environment, a certain degree of discipline is necessary. Anybody who objects [to] this discipline is being unreasonable'.[62] Hong Kong publisher and known anti-communist

59 J. Walden, letter to the editor, *SCMP*, 28 September 1996.
60 D. Gittings, 'Lie low after 1997, McLaren tells HK', *SCMP*, 20 November 1994.
61 C. P. L. Lee, 'Press warned on China laws', *SCMP International Weekly*, 2 December 1995.
62 Lee, 'Press warned on China laws'.

Jimmy Lai suffered aggressive retaliation for allowing his magazine *Next* to publish detrimental comments about Li Peng. China refused Lai's journalists permission to attend and report on official Sino-British and PWC meetings. Another of Lai's publications, *Apple Daily*, became the target of triad intimidation and official suppression on the mainland soon after its launch in June 1995. Internal Chinese documents labelled the paper as 'anti-China and stirring up trouble in Hong Kong'.[63]

These attacks raised questions about press freedom after 1997. At the same time, *Ming Pao* reporter Xi Yang was serving eighteen months of a twelve-year sentence for 'stealing state secrets', for a story he wrote concerning the Chinese central bank's plans to sell gold reserves on the international markets. In 1996, in an interview with *Le Figaro*, Chinese President Jiang Zemin argued that an independent judiciary and free press were not necessary, adding that, 'There is no press in the world that is not subject to laws and there is no absolute freedom to operate outside the law'.[64] To reassure Hongkongers that all would be well after 1997, the then-director of the Hong Kong and Macau Affairs Office, Lu Ping, promised that whilst the Hong Kong media would not be allowed to advocate Taiwanese independence, it would be allowed to report if someone else supported it.[65] This statement occurred during rising tension in the region, prompted by a US/China standoff following Chinese war games in the Taiwan Strait.[66]

In December 1995, the Hong Kong press reported that China had plans to invade Taiwan if Lee Teng-hui was re-elected as President.[67] The sweeping swing against pro-China candidates in the 1995 LEGCO elections was interpreted as a consequence of China's 'sabre rattling' over Taiwan.[68] The 'sweeping victory' at the polls for the 'vociferous

[63] C. K. Lau, 'Increased price could upset the Apple cart', *SCMP*, 20 July 1995.

[64] W. W. L. Lam and C. Yeung, 'Jiang plays down role of judiciary and press', *SCMP*, 14 September 1996.

[65] F. Ching, 'When silence speaks louder than words', *SCMP*, 19 June 2007.

[66] The University of Hong Kong Public Opinion Programme (POP) Surveys, 1995 and 1996, administered by Dr. Robert Ting-Yiu Chung. http://hkupop.hku.hk/english.

[67] W. W. L. Lam, 'Chinese set plans to invade Taiwan', *SCMP International Weekly*, 2 December 1995.

[68] S. Holberton, 'Hong Kong voters face question of loyalty', *The Financial Times*, 11 September 1995.

foes of China' was denounced by Beijing.[69] This 'humiliating rebuff' of China strengthened Beijing's resolve to 'redraw the political map in Hong Kong' after the handover.[70] As a defeated member of the Democratic Alliance for the Betterment of Hong Kong (DAB) put it, 'Hong Kong people have to pay for this'.[71] The Beijing-controlled *Ta Kung Pao* reminded its readers that Deng Xiaoping had disapproved of democracy in Hong Kong because direct elections did not always result in the right candidates being elected ('people who love the Motherland and love Hong Kong').

Throughout the pre-handover period, Hong Kong journalists worried whether and how China would place restraints on press freedom. In a 1995 report, they described Beijing's strategies to control the Hong Kong media, including sending 'undercover agents' to Hong Kong to work as rank-and-file reporters.[72] The report pointed to the operation of an 'invisible hand' – 80 per cent of respondents said self-censorship was occurring in the local news media; 84 per cent believed that press freedom would shrink in the remaining years before the handover.[73]

Censorship occurred in various guises. In 1995, a local theatre group, Zuni Icosahedron, attempted to stage a play entitled *Two or Three Events . . . of No Significance*, prompting the Urban Council to disassociate itself from the production which, it thought, might offend China. In the previous year, it had also withdrawn from a film festival two films banned in the mainland.[74] One journalist warned readers that if they wanted to take a glimpse of Hong Kong's future, they should take a closer look at the small print in the programme notes of plays and concerts funded by the Urban Council.[75] From January 1995, he pointed out, these now included a disclaimer stating that the council did not take responsibility for the productions it funded. The local arts community saw this as a move to appease Beijing. Many interpreted the disclaimer as a 'no confidence' vote in the future of freedom of expression'.[76] One local theatre critic asked, 'Why is the Urban Council

[69] A. Higgins, 'Hong Kong Democrats sweep vote', *The Financial Times*, 19 September 1995.
[70] S. Holberton, 'HK voters set to rebuff China', *The Financial Times*, 18 September 1995.
[71] A. Higgins, 'The Vanishing Trick', *The Financial Times*, 19 September 1995.
[72] K. C. Ng, 'Fears for press freedom', *SCMP*, 1 July 1995.
[73] Ng, 'Fears for press freedom'.
[74] See J. Kohut, 'The creeping art of self-censorship', *SCMP*, 1 April 1995.
[75] Kohut, 'The creeping art of self-censorship'.
[76] Kohut, 'The creeping art of self-censorship'.

kicking up such a fuss? ... It's this line of being afraid even before there's a threat ... They appear to be afraid that after Hong Kong reverts to Chinese rule, there will be a McCarthy-like witch-hunt so, "you don't want your name on the list" ... It's a way of saying "we're not going to put our necks on the block"'.[77] Though the Basic Law guaranteed freedom of artistic expression, this suggested those responsible for the arts in Hong Kong were already 'second-guessing' what China might find offensive in order to avoid incurring its future wrath. Hong points out that, whilst Article 27 of the Basic Law guaranteed press freedom, Article 23 also gave the government wide powers to curb free expression.[78]

It might be thought that the walls of law would assuage such fears. However, although the ICCPR had been signed by the British government, it had never been ratified by or acceded to the mainland government. For this reason, some local lawyers and legislators doubted whether the protections provided in the BOR would survive the handover.[79] There was also a fear that, because of the bitter tenor of Sino-British relations in the early 1990s, Beijing would not only eradicate those elements of democracy put in place by the British before 1997 but also overturn the BOR itself.[80]

Christine Loh urged Hongkongers to resist any attempts to stifle debate. It was, she said, 'unfortunate that any criticism of the Chinese leadership is viewed as calling for the downfall of the [p]arty. This is legitimate political criticism but because of the fear of being identified as being critical of the leadership, there is self-censorship ... At this time, there is good reason to worry about the freedom of expression and about the extent of self-censorship'.[81] Also cautioning against self-censorship, Martin Lee argued that, 'If you assume that a bamboo curtain is coming down ... you will restrict your freedoms yourself. People should be brave enough and courageous enough to carry on as before'.[82]

[77] Kohut, 'The creeping art of self-censorship'.
[78] Hong, 'Hong Kong's press freedom' in Shi-Xu, Kienpointer and Servaes, *Read the Cultural Other*.
[79] 'Protocols for protection unlikely to be signed by China', The *Sunday Standard*, 14 February 1993.
[80] De Silva, 'Territory's rights hang in the balance'.
[81] De Silva, 'Territory's rights hang in the balance'.
[82] Wood, 'Hong Kong Handover'.

In the climate of the times, however, those who criticised China risked being labelled 'unpatriotic'. To avoid such accusations by the local party faithful, critics (including academics) tailored their observations so as to omit or avoid anything that could be construed as a criticism. In 1996, for example, the Department of Education decided to have textbooks omit certain events over the previous 20 years, including the 4 June Massacre.[83] The use of the phrase 'democratic return' as a substitute for 'transfer of sovereignty' was also lambasted as an example of how political correctness resulted in self-censorship.[84] Chinese reporters sent to cover Hong Kong were said to be under central government orders to ignore demonstrations; a 1996 survey of over 553 local journalists found that over half agreed that journalists were being careful not to criticize China for fear of reprisals or being fired.[85]

These fears were well-founded. Early targets were the hosts of outspoken popular radio phone-in programmes, which played a critical role in forming public opinion before and after 1997.[86] So and Lee note that, in 1992, three celebrities (Albert Cheng, Yuk-man Wong and Allen Lee, known as 'the three famous mouths') started a television talk show, *Dragon Gate Forum*. They used a new format of openly political, outspoken talk to discuss public affairs, including the 1997 handover. All three became targets of pro-Beijing loyalists. When ATV's *News Tease* was taken off the air in 1994, its host, Wong Yukman, started a paper, *Mad Dog Daily*, publishing outspoken jibes at Beijing. Another host, Albert Cheng, started a radio phone-in talk show, *Teacup in a Storm* in 1995, a hugely popular programme that allowed lay persons with no particular expertise or little education to air their views. The fact that callers could remain anonymous encouraged free criticism of the authorities without the threat of retribution. As the shows were aired live, their comments were also uncensored. The success of this programme 'turned these shows into powerful formulators of public opinion and even an influential political force'.[87] It was a phone call to such a show (*The Nineties*) by a frustrated customs official in 1997 that alerted the public to the fact that a PLA general insisted

[83] K. Young, letter to the editor, *SCMP*, 14 September 1996.
[84] Young, letter to the editor. [85] Wood, 'Hong Kong Handover'.
[86] Y. K. So and A. Y. L. Lee, 'The radio phone-in talk show as the people's council in postcolonial Hong Kong', in Cheng, *The Hong Kong Special Administrative Region*, p. 828.
[87] So and Lee, 'Radio phone-in talk show', p. 830.

on crossing the border without the requisite papers. The on-air complaint sparked criticisms from other callers, who decried as a breach of the principle that no one, however powerful, was above the law.[88]

CROSS-BORDER DISAPPEARANCES AND DEATHS

The fate of Hongkongers and overseas Chinese – including journalists – detained on the mainland brought further proof that neither the border itself nor the law could offer much protection against such 'mainland ways of doing things'. This first became apparent in the 1990s, but its continuation long after the retrocession has raised fears about the ability of the SAR (or any other government) to protect its citizens inside mainland China. In 1995, for example, businessman, James Peng Jiandong, an Australian Chinese citizen, was sentenced to sixteen years imprisonment in China on an embezzlement charge following the retrospective application of mainland law. Peng had been detained in China since 1993, when he was abducted from his hotel room in Macau (then a Portuguese colony) by PSB officers. Despite official calls from Australia for his release, a Guangdong court upheld Peng's sentence in December 1995. A Chinese Foreign Ministry official pointed out that foreigners who violated China's laws could be sentenced to substantial prison terms.[89] In July 1995, American citizen, Harry Wu Hongda, was also arrested when he made a return visit to the mainland; US consular access was denied and his whereabouts were unknown. Such cases prompted calls for the Hong Kong government to 'ring fence' Hong Kong citizens:

> So far there has been no known case of a foreign citizen arrested – or kidnapped in Hong Kong and spirited across the border to face punishment in China. But the fact that it has happened in Macau should be warning enough. Unless the territory is vigilant in maintaining the legal and operational ring-fencing promised by 'one country, two systems', the danger is that we may see consular officials chasing false trials round China searching for citizens arrested in Hong Kong.[90]

[88] 'PLA must not get privileges: General Zhou's customs check scene sparks calls for reassurance', *SCMP*, 18 June 1997.
[89] S. Hutcheon, 'Australia to appeal for clemency', *SCMP International Weekly*, 2 December 1995.
[90] Editorial, *SCMP*, 5 July 1995.

The safety of Hongkongers in China was already a matter of public concern. As one journalist claimed, 'a spate of recent blackmail, extortion and murder cases in Guangdong has caused enormous worry amongst the tens of thousands of Hongkongers who regularly visit China'.[91] By January 1996, six Hong Kong business people were being held by the mainland Public Security Bureau (PSB) because of business disputes with mainland associates,[92] despite an official policy that forbade the arrest of people for business disputes. The six were amongst twelve Hong Kong business people detained on similar grounds. The matter was raised in LEGCO. Families of the detained sought assistance from the government, and the matter was raised through diplomatic channels. However, China responded to only one of the cases.[93] The families of Hongkongers detained in China found it almost impossible to secure assistance.

The detention of Hong Kong film director Au Fook-hung also stemmed from a dispute connected with his father's business in China. The arrest of the son by the PSB prompted an editorial in the *SCMP* entitled 'Justice held hostage'. Au's case raised more general questions about the safety of local people doing legitimate business in China:

> If China is serious about developing commercial law and a sound judicial system, it should ensure that family and friends can no longer be held ransom for others' alleged wrongdoing ... The proper way to recover an alleged debt is through a civil action in the courts, not by kidnapping or bringing charges against a third party who happens to be within reach.[94]

Hongkongers faced many similar problems in mainland China. There was a widespread belief that mainlanders regarded them as easy targets, their dress and accents marking them out for robbers and pickpockets. On vacation trips to China, Hongkongers 'found themselves treated as future wards by scruffy mainlanders'. Hongkongers responded with a mix of 'fear, hostility, condescension and aversion.'[95] Precautions were

[91] K. Sinclair, 'A vital dialogue that's good for all', *SCMP*, 24 July 1995.
[92] W. Szeto, 'Six held over China business disputes', *SCMP International Weekly*, 6 January 1996.
[93] Szeto, 'Six held over China business disputes'.
[94] 'Justice held hostage', *SCMP*, 29 December 1995.
[95] S. K. Lau, quoted in Z. Lin and T.W. Robinson (eds.), *The Chinese and their Future: Beijing, Taipei, Hong Kong* (Washington: AEI Press, 1994), p. 301.

necessary to avoid falling victim to such crimes. There were also rumours of male children being snatched by child traffickers from their Hong Kong parents at busy tourist venues, the one-child policy having made boys a valuable commodity on the mainland.

Hong Kong's business community was further unsettled by incidents that revealed the close connection between power and commerce in mainland China. In early 1995, *The Wall Street Journal* reported that 'As Hong Kong Looks North, Its Mood Darkens', a report which analysed the impact of the arrest in Beijing of businessman Zhou Beifang, son of a powerful mainland family with connections to Deng Xiaoping. According to the article, 'The Zhou arrest signalled that the privatisation of the state's huge and moribund industrial holdings ... has been suspended. That suggests that the development of a powerful class of private businessmen with an important interest in promoting the rule of law has been retarded as well.'[96]

Fears that the powerful Chinese politico-business elite might squeeze Hong Kong business after 1997 partly explained the continued out-migration of entrepreneurs, 'and why Hong Kong is coming to seem more and more like a Chinese city ... It may also explain the ... continuing sense of unease that afflicts this private enterprise jewel of the Orient'.[97] The numbers emigrating before 1997 rose from 43,000 in 1995 to 53,000 in 1996.[98] In 1995, more than 40 per cent of young people wished to emigrate.[99] Those with negative views about the handover expressed concerns about loss of freedom and human rights, deteriorating law and order and corruption.[100] Fears for Hong Kong's future stemmed from the spread of the mainland's rampant corruption, social unrest and runaway inflation.[101] If China's proto-capitalism developed along the lines of Eastern Europe's transition to capitalism, Hong Kong might be swallowed up in black markets and gangsterism.[102]

96 G. Melloan, 'Global view', *The Wall Street Journal*, 27 February 1995.
97 Melloan, 'Global view'.
98 G. Schloss, 'Exodus expected as 1997 nears', *SCMP*, 14 September 1996.
99 Poll by Sha Tin District Board and the Telephone Survey Research Programme, Asia-Pacific Institute, Chinese University of Hong Kong, 15 and 24 October, 1995, *SCMP International Weekly*, 6 January 1996.
100 Poll by Sha Tin District Board and the Telephone Survery Research Programme.
101 'Another hazard of the handover', *The Times*, 2 July 1993.
102 'Another hazard of the handover'.

The Chinese leadership was known to fear a popular uprising of the kind that had toppled Polish Communism. The end of the Cold War had fostered a belief that the West would try to use democratisation in Hong Kong to defeat communism in China.[103] Hong Kong needed to be kept under PRC control to prevent it becoming a base for subversion. There was, however, confusion about the mainland's policy for Hong Kong due to the ongoing jostling for power within the CCP leadership prior to the anticipated death of Deng Xiaoping. According to one observer, between 1995 and 1996, China entered a 'political freeze' and, despite growing economic and diplomatic success, still presented itself 'as a country deeply wronged by the world and surrounded by smiling enemies'.[104] In its handling of Hong Kong, Taiwan and Tibet, 'the [p]arty seemed determined to show that even in victory it is vindictive'.[105] Contenders for leadership positions were all trying to demonstrate their patriotic credentials by appearing tough and loyal to the Communist cause. As Martin Lee pointed out in 1992:

> When the Communists are uncertain, the Golden Rule ... is that if you must err, err on the side of the left, not the right, meaning you take the hard line ... [U]nless there is consensus in Beijing over Hong Kong, nobody would dare to take responsibility, because he would lose his job ... Even the top Chinese officials don't know what will happen to them when the great day comes for Deng Xiaoping to see God in Heaven.[106]

In this climate of uncertainty, stories about Hongkongers facing detention and death on the mainland stoked anxiety. Early in 1996, Hong Kong media carried the story of a former Shenzhen planning official, Wang Jianye, who had been executed despite having been promised that he would not face the death penalty if he agreed to be extradited from Thailand.[107] Wang's extradition from Thailand was conducted in secret between the Thai and Guangdong police. Because there was no official written record of the process, mainland courts decided that there was no evidence of any such promise. The press carried

[103] Ching, 'Boxed in a corner'.
[104] J. Becker, 'Beijing remains out in the cold', *SCMP International Weekly*, 6 January 1996.
[105] Becker, 'Beijing remains out in the cold'.
[106] Chris Patten, 'Interview with Chris Patten', interview by Gordon and Wong.
[107] 'Case raises many questions. Fears remain over extradition', *SCMP International Weekly*, 6 January 1996.

photographs of Wang and his co-defendants being driven to the execution ground on the back of a lorry. Alongside, a table showed that nineteen cadres had been sentenced for corruption-related charges between 28 November and 28 December 1995 – of the eight sentenced to death, five were executed and three given suspended death penalties. Only a month earlier, the press had carried reports of twenty-seven people being executed in a crackdown in Hainan and of mass sentencing rallies in Zhanzhou, Qiongshan and Dengmai.[108] Though the Chinese authorities tried to prevent the use of telephoto lenses at the execution ground, colour photographs appeared in Hong Kong's daily papers. Like Hainan and Zhuhai, Shenzhen was a favoured destination for Hong Kong tourists. Outwardly, it resembled Hong Kong with its high-rise buildings, modern shopping malls and expensive cars. However, these executions reminded Hongkongers that things were done very differently there.

The idea that Hong Kong was being invaded by the mainland seemed to be borne out shortly after the handover when Hong Kong was hit by the SARS (atypical pneumonia) and bird-flu epidemics. The outbreak of SARS on the mainland was covered up by mainland officials. Such incidents, Lee argues, meant that despite all the advantages the mainland offered, even if Hongkongers were offered full Chinese citizenship in lieu of the Hong Kong Identity Card and SAR passport, 'he or she would probably say no'.[109] At the time, Patten argued that such incidents were a good example of why one 'is supportive of the rule of law'.[110] On 30 June 1997, Hong Kong's pro-democracy groups tied a yellow ribbon around the LEGCO Building 'to symbolize peoples' loss of freedom'.[111] At that point, no one was completely sure how this loss would be manifested, or to what degree. As subsequent chapters demonstrate, it was to occur on many levels, ranging from attacks on the rule of law, language and culture to the disappearance of persons who stepped over the threshold onto the mainland itself.

[108] 'Hainan executes 27 in purge', *SCMP International Weekly*, 2 December 1995.
[109] L. O. Lee, *City Between Worlds: My Hong Kong* (Cambridge, MA: The Belknap Press, 2008).
[110] O. Hughes and J. Becker, 'HK pair face death penalty', *SCMP*, 15 April 1995.
[111] Wei, 'A Hong Kong diary'.

4

Danger, death and disappearance

The fate of Hong Kong after 1997 has frequently been associated with the word 'disappearance'; the Hong Kong identity is often described as fleeting, hyper-modern, unfixed and insubstantial. The place has a reputation for being 'in between', and visitors are invited to explore 'the land in between'. Hong Kong, Rey Chow writes, is a port, a place which everyone, regardless of identification and social status, passes through.[1] Portals transport people to another world. They are liminal sites associated with 'out of body' experiences and disappearances,[2] death and decomposition,[3] invisibility and hauntings by ghosts. The marginalized and liminal live betwixt and between but with 'no cultural assurance of a final stable resolution of their ambiguity',[4] often failing to re-emerge from their 'rite of passage' with a clear, unambiguous self.[5]

[1] R. Chow, 'Things common/places, passages of the Port City: on Hong Kong and Hong Kong author Leung Ping-kwan', *differences: a journal of feminist cultural studies* 5, no. 3 (1993), pp. 179–204.

[2] V. Turner, *The Ritual Process: Structure and Anti-Structure* (Chicago: Aldine, 1969); A. Van Gennep, *The Rites of Passage* (1909; Chicago: University of Chicago Press, 1960). Leung Ping-kwan, 'Homeless' in 'Homeless Poems and Photographs', *NuNa-HeDuo (Dislocation)* 2.2, Public Vs Image Issue, pp. 1–2 cited in Chow, 'Things/Commonplaces', p. 194.

[3] V. Turner, *The Forest of Symbols: Aspects of Ndembu Ritual* (Ithaca: Cornell University Press, 1967).

[4] V. Turner, *Dramas, Fields and Metaphors* (Ithaca: Cornell University Press, 1974), p. 233.

[5] R. Dobson, 'Beaches and breaches: articulations and negotiations of identity, ethnicity and cosmopolitanism in Mauritius – 'The most cosmopolitan island under the sun'', *Limina*, http://limina.arts.uswa.edu.au.

In pre-handover Hong Kong, these images were a kind of rebus, projecting the city's desires and fears that it would become a 'space of disappearance'.[6] Luo Dayou argues that Hong Kong needs to know itself as 'a bastard and orphan ... [s]truggling for a compromised survival in the gap between East and West'.[7] For others, Hong Kong was just a stepping stone between East and West 'with no existence of its own except as a convenient passage between these two cultures'.[8] Abbas argued that the place had even developed a set of techniques for 'working with disappearance ... using disappearance to deal with disappearance'.[9] Poet Louise Ho writes of Hong Kong as 'a floating island / We have no site / Nowhere to land / No domicile / Come July this year / We may begin to hover in situ'.[10] For Ho, this 'collective sense of ambivalence, unease, anguish and security' stems from what is seen as a virtue in Hong Kong, i.e., an 'open and accommodative culture',[11] often depicted as the ability of Hongkongers 'to accommodate, absorb, adopt, manipulate and transform anything that can help resolve our problems and enrich our life'.[12] The culture is permanently liminal, a culture of anomaly, loss, uncertainty and in-betweeness.[13] It is in this unstable space that Hong Kong identity has developed.[14]

[6] Dobson, 'Beaches and breaches'.

[7] Luo Dayou, cited in R. Chow, 'Between colonizers: post-colonial Hong Kong's self-writing in the 1990s', *Diaspora*, 2, no. 2 (1992), p. 157.

[8] O. Ho, 'Hong Kong: a curatorial journey for an identity', *Art Journal*, 57, no. 4 (1998), pp. 39–43, cited in H. Cheng and G. Wan, 'Identity and interactive media: a discourse analysis of web diaries', in Shi-xu et al., *Read the Cultural Other*, pp. 180–1.

[9] A. Abbas, *Culture and the Politics of Disappearance* (Hong Kong: Hong Kong University Press, 1997), p. 8.

[10] L. Ho, 'Island' in L. Ho (ed.), *New Ends, Old Beginnings* (Hong Kong: Asia 2000, 1997).

[11] S. L. Wong, 'Changing Hong Kong identities', in G. Wang and J. Wong (eds.), *Hong Kong in China: The Challenges of Transition* (Singapore: Times Academic Press), pp. 181–202, cited in Cheng and Wan, 'Identity and Interactive Media', p. 191.

[12] Wong, 'Changing Hong Kong identities'.

[13] K. K. Tam, 'Voices of missing identity: a study of contemporary Hong Kong literary writings', in Shi-xu et al., *Read the Cultural Other*, pp. 165–76. The metaphor of the bridge is from Homi Bhabha, *The Location of Culture* (London: Routledge, 1994), p. 174.

[14] F. O'Toole, 'A singular territory', *London Review of Books*, 3 July 1998, pp. 18–19, cited in Tam, 'Missing identity' in Shi-xu et al., *Read the Cultural Other*, p. 167.

> Hong Kong doesn't have much of a history . . . and what it has is largely invisible: the city is in a state of relentless flux, its historical buildings torn down, its street-scapes altered, so that no accumulation of resonances is possible. Even the map of the physical territory is utterly unstable: small islands have been annexed to the larger one by filling in the harbour; frantic reclamation has remoulded the shape of the surrounding seas.[15]

In his book of short stories, *The Last Train to Lo Wu*, Jess Row likens Hong Kong to a mirage, 'hovering above the ground: skyscrapers built on mountainsides, islands swallowed in fog for days'.[16] Tam, too, sees Hong Kong as a sort of modern-day 'Brigadoon', a city 'where everything floats and nothing seems to have been built on solid ground', a place where 'identities are not something fixed but something that appears, disappears and re-appears'.[17] However, post-1997 Hong Kong is no longer a 'floating city' but a 'home', and 'the boundary itself' has become 'the place from which something begins its presencing . . . Hong Kong . . . is a bridge that gathers, and not just crosses. That is, Hong Kong has also become a place to form an identity of its own'.[18] Whereas before 1997 Hong Kong people saw themselves as passengers on a 'bridge' over which they would cross into China, Tam argues that by post-1997 they choose to 'stay on the bridge' rather than making their way to 'either end',[19] echoing what Bhabha describes as the colonised subject's attempts to elude the subject positions ascribed to it.[20]

This firming up of identity is partly a result of skirmishes with the mainland; however, this is not the whole story. Many Hongkongers – including those who disdain mainlandisation – regularly visit the mainland for leisure and business. Indeed, Shenzhen's freedom *from* Hong Kong law and conventions makes it attractive. Borderlands are 'locations of desire',[21] synonymous with transgressive behaviour.

15 O'Toole, 'A singluar territory'.
16 J. Row, 'The secret of bats' in *The Last Train to Lo Wu* (New York. The Dial Press, Random House, 2006).
17 Tam, 'Missing identity' in Shi-xu et al., *Read the Cultural Other*, pp. 168–73.
18 Tam, 'Missing identity'. See also Bhabha, *The Location of Culture*, p. 1, citing M. Heidegger, 'Building, dwelling, thinking', *Poetry, Language, Thought* (New York: Harper & Row, 1971).
19 Tam, 'Missing identity' in Shi-xu et al., *Read the Cultural Other*, pp. 165–76.
20 Bhabha, *The Location of Culture*.
21 R. Preston-Whyte, 'The beach as a liminal space' in A. Lew, C. M. Hall and A. Williams (eds.), *The Blackwell's Tourism Companion* (Oxford: Blackwell, 2006).

A 2007 study revealed that young adults from Hong Kong found it easier to obtain drugs such as ecstasy, heroin, cannabis and ketamine at raves and discos in Shenzhen, where they were also cheaper and arrest less likely:[22]

> Shenzhen, China: Flash-lit by synchronized lasers, a nightclub heaving with Hong Kong teenagers vibrates to the latest dance hit as a pair cavort on the stage in the skimpiest of outfits ... It's a typical Friday night but while many of the clubbers hail from Hong Kong the venue itself is not in their home city. Welcome to Shenzhen. Shenzhen is cheap, it's vibrant and it's close – and crucially for many of those who regularly make the weekend trip, it's a good source of recreational drugs ... Club owners here target the Hong Kong market because they can afford higher entrance fees than local people and drinks that cost three times more ... They also appear to appreciate easier access to illegal drugs ... With police in Hong Kong frequently checking the clubs there, Shenzhen has become a better choice.[23]

The 'heyday' of Shazuicun was 1996 and 1997, when many Hong Kong people made overnight fortunes on the property and stock markets: 'They all loved to come here looking for pleasure and relaxation ... I bumped into friends in Shazuicun who I hadn't seen for years in Hong Kong. It became a small colony for Hong Kong men'.[24] Some men find prostitutes and wives in Shenzhen, 'because they believed that women in China are more affordable than those in Hong Kong'.[25] In 1996, a total of 2,484 cross-border marriages were registered in Hong Kong; by 2010, the number had risen to 11,519.[26] In about 80 per cent of these marriages, a Hong Kong man married a mainland wife. Since children with right of abode also have the right to free education in Hong Kong, some families domiciled on the mainland send them to

[22] J. T. F. Lau, H. T. Tsui, L. T. Lam and M. Lau, 'Cross boundary substance uses among Hong Kong Chinese young adults', *Journal of Urban Health*, 84, no. 5 (2007), pp. 704–21.

[23] 'Drugs lure Hong Kong youth across the China border', *China Digital Times*, 7 June 2007. http://chinadigitaltimes.net/2007/06/drugs-lure-hong-kong-youth-across-china-border-afp/.

[24] C. Y. Chow, 'Lights dim on Shenzhen's streets of sin', *SCMP*, 22 August 2004.

[25] A. Y. So, 'Cross-border families in Hong Kong: the role of social class and politics', *Critical Asian Studies*, 35 (2003), pp. 515–34.

[26] N. L. S. Leung, 'A study of cross border students in Hong Kong: the new phenomenon of cross border students which arise from Cross Border Births', *World Academy of Science, Engineering and Technology*, 64 (2012), pp. 297–303.

school across the border.[27] Surveys suggest that those mainlanders who arrange to give birth in Hong Kong and send their children there for education do so because the territory provides better education, a comprehensive legal system and better quality of life.[28] For the same reasons, most Hongkongers have no desire to fully relocate.

Shenzhen offers opportunities and pleasures, but it is also a place of danger and a route of contagion. The prevalence of unsafe sex amongst cross-border pleasure seekers (and of HIV amongst mainland injecting drug users) have led to Shenzhen being identified as a 'bridge' for the transmission of HIV between the mainland and Hong Kong.[29] Reports also highlight the threat to life and limb. In September 2008, for example, a fire in a Shenzhen night club (the Wuwang) claimed the lives of five Hong Kong victims, including three teenagers, drawing attention to the dangers faced by Hongkongers visiting Shenzhen night clubs.[30] In 2007, the Hong Kong press carried a story about the discovery of the body of a newborn baby in the river at Sheung Shui, near the border crossing of Lok Ma Chau. The report claimed that the baby had been 'dumped' by her mother in Shenzhen shortly after she gave birth; the current carried the baby across the border into Hong Kong.[31] In 2007, the international media documented stories of the kidnapping of children and mentally impaired adults forced to work as labourers in Shanxi brick kilns. During the 2008 Sichuan earthquake, at least 5,000 students were killed when school buildings collapsed as a result of shoddy construction and corruption. Such stories fuel the image of the mainland as a desperate and predatory environment. Instead of nurturing her offspring, the Motherland killed them.

Disappearance affects the rich, too. Foreign and Hong Kong businessmen are especially vulnerable if they become involved in disputes with mainland partners. They are held as debt hostages, kidnapped to secure payment of some disputed debt, detained by state officials related to the mainland business, abducted illegally by police or triads, or, like many others, they fall through the cracks of the legal system. 'Debt hostages' worry the business community most. Business people 'disappear' on business trips; sometimes their family members are held

[27] Leung, 'A study of cross border students'.
[28] Leung, 'A study of cross border students'.
[29] Lau et al., 'Cross-boundary substance abuse'.
[30] He Huifeng, 'Birthday party turns into date with death', *SCMP*, 22 September 2008.
[31] F. Chan, 'New-born's body found in river', *SCMP*, 28 January 2008.

'hostage' as bargaining chips. Due to the direct or indirect involvement of powerful state players in mainland enterprises, as well as corrupt relations between enterprises, state officials and the police, some are detained in 'black jails' or police facilities, often incommunicado. The abduction by mainland police of Australian-Chinese businessman, James Peng, from his hotel room in Macau (then still a Portuguese colony) in 1994 was one of the first incidents to raise fears amongst the wider business community about the safety of doing business in China. The Hong Kong media described Peng's midnight abduction as 'Kafka-esque'. Detained for 10 months without trial, Peng was eventually tried on corruption and embezzlement charges arising out of a business dispute with the Champaign Industrial Company, owned partly by Chinese officials including Ding Peng, the niece of Deng Xiaoping. The law under which he was charged was not implemented until more than a year after his arrest. The charges carried the sentence of death. After his trial in 1995, Peng was imprisoned for 15 years. Requests by his wife to visit him were denied. As an Australian citizen, Peng was entitled to Australian Consular visits, but these were consistently denied, the Chinese government insisting that Peng was a Chinese citizen, even if he did hold an Australian passport.[32] His fate could befall any ethnic Chinese business person.[33] As a Hong Kong newspaper argued, Peng's fate did little to reassure foreign businessmen that they too would not face arbitrary detention and trial if their dealings led them to cross swords with China's powerful elite:

> if China is to be seen as a place to invest, the new laws have to be applied fairly and consistently, and also be transparent. And they must not normally be applied retrospectively to criminalise actions which were legal at the time of the alleged offence. They must certainly not be used to persecute an individual who someone influential wants sent down, but who cannot be proved to have committed any known crime.[34]

At the time, two American Chinese businessmen (Dr Philip Cheng Hui-ho and Chong Kwee-sung) were also being detained in China as a result of business disputes.[35] A 67-year-old HKSAR businessman, Lok Yuk-sing, was detained at gunpoint in a hotel restaurant in southern

[32] See 'Legal litmus test', *SCMP*, 15 June 1995.
[33] *SCMP*, 9 October 1994.
[34] *SCMP*, 9 October 1994.
[35] The US government successfully secured their release.

China in 1997; he was held in handcuffs and leg-chains for 487 days without charge or trial by the Dingsheng Public Security Bureau, firstly in prison then at a PSB guesthouse. His 'offence' was to represent a Hong Kong firm which owed HK$4 million to a mainland company:

> Lok remains locked up, suffering from ill health and extremes of climate, and subsisting on a mainland prison diet . . . [T]wo security officials tell his relatives that they will have to pay HK£4.7 million bail to get him out of prison. You people in Hong Kong are rich, the officials explain. They also denounce the family for telling the press about the case.[36]

The HKSAR government was said to be moving 'with extreme caution' in Lok's case:

> [T]he Secretary of Security says she has been assured by the Beijing authorities that no bail request was made, though Cynthia Wan [the *SCMP* reporter] witnessed the demand. On his return to Hong Kong, Lok's son-in-law, John Wong, sends me another e-mail saying 'at least HK SAR government now treats it more seriously than before . . . We need media who are able to speak out and fight for justice for the HK citizen, particularly post-handover'.[37]

In 1998, the government estimated that forty-five businessmen were being held (others put the total at eighty-five).[38] Later that year, another Hong Kong man, Peter Leung Wing-sum, also detained as a 'debt-hostage', was released:

> The assumption is that workers from the state-owned enterprise grabbed him. Leung says he was tortured, and fed once every two days as he was moved between different locations. 'It seemed like a movie', he adds. 'I thought I might be killed if the mainland police failed to arrest the person they wanted [the former mainland manager of the company].' After four months the manager was caught, and Leung was handed over to the local public security bureau, which held him for three months until an investigation cleared him, and a mainland businessman put up HK$100,000 bail.[39]

[36] The case was exposed by the *SCMP*. See Fenby, *Dealing with the Dragon*, pp. 201–2.
[37] Fenby, *Dealing with the Dragon*, pp. 201–2.
[38] Legislative Council of the HKSAR, Minutes of Council Meeting (Hansard), 18 November 1998.
[39] Fenby, *Dealing with the Dragon*, p. 283.

Yet another Hong Kong man, a partner in a mainland joint venture firm, was held, accused of deception. His wife was asked for HK$27 million for his release. She stated that, 'I phoned the government and the Chief Executive's office and asked for help . . . But they just told me there wasn't much they could do'.[40] Fenby documents the disappearance of another Hong Kong man accused of deception when an employment agency became bankrupt. He was held first in a town in Guangdong when police asked his family for HK$600,000 for his release. He was then moved to another location when the sum demanded increased by a further HK$1 million. According to an *SCMP* report, the mainland police insisted that they were acting within the law.[41] In 2000 (despite insisting two years earlier that it could not interfere in mainland legal affairs), the Hong Kong government appealed to the Beijing Procuratorate for the release of Yiu Yun-fai, a Hong Kong businessman held under 'residential surveillance' in a Cangzhou detention house since 1999, despite having been cleared of allegations of commercial fraud.

Between 1999 and 2001, more than 150 Hong Kong people detained on the mainland sought help from the HKSAR Office in Beijing. A further 300 complaints were received by the office dealing with malpractices among mainland government departments.[42] Ho Hei-wah, spokesman for the Hong Kong Society for Community Organisation, said that Yiu's plight should serve as a warning to other Hong Kong people:

> The problem is that in China they have laws that are very clear on how long they can detain a person and that they have the right to meet their relatives and a lawyer, but it's very simple – they don't follow them. There are no checks and balances . . . Also the Hong Kong Government does not make very strong protests when they receive these cases, so there is no strong message going to the Chinese government.[43]

The Security Bureau was said to be drawing up a plan for a notification system that would keep them informed of when Hong Kong people were being detained, but it was doubtful whether this would

[40] Fenby, *Dealing with the Dragon*, p. 283.
[41] Fenby, *Dealing with the Dragon*, p. 283.
[42] P. Moy and A. Lam, 'Security chief admits notification system excludes powerful agency and provides limited reach', *SCMP*, 1 April 2001.
[43] C. Wan, 'SAR man held "despite being cleared"', *SCMP*, 2 July 2000.

enable the Security Bureau to do anything to ensure such detainees were released or charged.[44]

The problem continued after 1997. In July 2009, another Australian Chinese businessman, Stern Hu, an employee of Rio Tinto Ltd., was detained, along with three Chinese colleagues, accused of obtaining information relating to the Chinese steel sector that could cause serious damage to China's national economic security. Charged eventually with stealing Chinese commercial secrets and receiving bribes, Hu was sentenced to ten years imprisonment. The incident assumed international diplomatic significance when the Chinese ambassador to Australia was summoned to discuss the matter with the Australian Prime Minister. Within Australia, the affair prompted high-level debate about the lack of legal protections for those engaged in the 'China business'. In January, 2012, yet another Australian Chinese businessman, Alan Wu, was detained 'for investigation' over allegations of smuggling. No charges were made at the time of his detention. The Australian Consulate General in Shanghai was permitted to provide limited assistance.[45]

The problem of 'debt hostages' assumed such proportions that, by June 2012, responding to the detention of another US businessman in China (Steve Fleischli), a *China Law Blog for Business* site posted advice on 'How Not to get Kidnapped in China: Part 3: resolve your debt problems before you go'.[46] Fleischli had flown to China to resolve his company's dispute personally, a move often advised by 'how to do business in China' books that emphasise face-to-face dealings and the importance of *guanxi*. Chinese authorities in Xiamen, however, decided to hold Fleischli personally liable for his company's debts and forced him to surrender his passport. The US State Department acknowledged that such cases could 'take years to resolve'.[47] Months into the dispute, Fleischli was dismissed by his company, thereby losing access to his company's lawyers in China. The *China Law Blog* noted that a 'high

[44] Wan, 'SAR man held'.

[45] 'Melbourne businessman has been detained by Chinese authorities', *Melbourne Leader*, 17 January 2012. In October 2008, the representative of a British scrap metal company was abducted from a Shanghai airport when he went to Ningbo to seek overdue payments from a Ningbo company. See M. Dickie, 'Kidnap alleged in China dispute', *The Financial Times*, 30 October 2008.

[46] Harris and Moure, plc., Chinalawblog.com, 22 June 2012. www.chinallawblog.com/.

[47] Harris and Moure, plc., Chinalawblog.com.

end China risk consultancy' had reported 'a massive increase' in such cases in 2012. It advised:

> If you are in a debt dispute with a Chinese company, think about not going to China at all. If you must go to China, think about using a bodyguard or two and think very carefully about where you stay and where you go. Most importantly, be very careful with whom you meet ... Consider pre-emptively suing the alleged creditor somewhere so that you can very plausibly claim that you have been seized not because you owe a debt, but out of retaliation for having sued someone. If you are going to sue, carry proof of your lawsuit with you at all times while you are in China.[48]

One US lawyer acknowledged that '[t]hese things only end by an agreement by the Chinese company to accept a certain payment and then that payment being made. Maybe these things can end some other way, but I am not aware of that ever having occurred. The Chinese company typically wants its money, not to physically harm anyone'.[49] This is, however, not always the case. The *China Law Blog* itself cautions that:

> one should not write off the possibility of violence in one's business dealings in China ... My law firm has been called in at least a half a dozen times where violence was either threatened or occurred. We tell our clients that if they owe money to a Chinese company or are involved in any sort of dispute with anyone in China ... they should avoid meeting to discuss the dispute/problem anywhere other than in a neutral, very public place in the day time. A high end hotel lobby in Shanghai or Beijing is a good choice.[50]

Even public places, however, are no guarantee of safety. In October 2005, a Hong Kong businessman was kidnapped in front of his wife and dozens of onlookers in a Shenzhen street:[51]

> The incident took place at about 4 P.M. in Shangbulu in the Futian district of Shenzhen. The Hong Kong businessman was in a car with his wife and a driver when they were intercepted by two cars outside a car-wash centre. Six crew-cut men in black jumped out and dragged the man from his car. At least three were armed with long knives, according

[48] Harris and Moure, plc., Chinalawblog.com.
[49] Harris and Moure, plc., Chinalawblog.com.
[50] Harris and Moure, plc., Chinalawblog.com.
[51] C. Y. Chow, 'No word from businessman's kidnappers', *SCMP*, 25 October 2005.

> to the wife ... [S]he said the men shouted in Putonghua with heavy north eastern accents ... Shenzhen is one of the richest cities on the [m] ainland but also suffers the highest crime rate. Honkongers have frequently been the target for criminals ... 178 [Hong Kong] residents had sought help after being kidnapped or illegally detained on the [m]-ainland in the first months of last year.[52]

In 2012, the fate of another Hong Kong permanent resident (and US national Wu Wai Sin) became the subject of an Amnesty International appeal when he was detained by the police in Guangdong, along with forty others. Wu, held on suspicion of being involved in triad activities, was detained incommunicado in three different places before he was taken to a detention centre in Huicheng district, Huizhou city. He told his lawyer that he had been tortured and beaten by the police, confessing to his crime under duress. According to Wu's family, the arrest was related to a legal action over a retail market business worth over 120 million yuan, which Wu sold to the former Deputy Director of the Public Security Bureau, Lin Qiang, in 2002. They were convinced that, as the former Deputy Director of the Public Security Bureau, Lin Qiang 'mobilised his connections within the local police in order to retaliate against Wu Wai Sing for the Supreme Court's decision earlier this year ... [and] deter Wu Wai Sing from pursuing his legal means of redress against Lin Qiang'.[53] In Shenzhen, a visiting Party Secretary told local officials that he 'felt ashamed of what I have seen ... Rule of law is the cornerstone of a stable society. If we do not punish those who break the law, it will lead to total anarchy'.[54]

The disappearance and death of businessmen assumed international prominence in 2012, following the murder of foreign business consultant, Neil Heywood, in a Chongqing hotel in 2011. Initially, officials claimed that Heywood had died of natural causes. However, in February 2012, local police chief and vice-mayor of Chongqing, Wang Lijun, sought refuge in first the British and then the American consulates, where he alleged that Heywood was murdered.[55] Charges were later laid against Gu Kailai, the wife of Chongqing Communist Party chief,

[52] Chow, 'No word from businessman's kidnappers'.

[53] Amnesty International, 'Businessman detained, tortured', UA: 231/12 Index ASA 17/026/2012 China, issued 6 August 2012.

[54] Zhang Dejiang, cited in C. Y. Chow, 'Police struggle to cope with Shenzhen crime wave', *SCMP*, 30 December 2005.

[55] 'The Chongqing scandal', *SCMP*, 28 September 2012.

Bo Xilai. Gu was tried and convicted in August 2012 for poisoning Heywood with cyanide after drinking with him in his hotel room. Heywood, a Mandarin-speaking consultant to foreign concerns seeking to invest in China, had business dealings with Gu and Bo Xilai, for whom he acted as a 'middleman'.[56] Bo Xilai was removed from his Chongqing position, suspended from the Politburo and Central Committee, and also disappeared from public view. In the extensive coverage of Wang Lijun's trial, his name was never mentioned. Although Bo's own trial took place in a blaze of publicity, rather than showcasing China's commitment to rule of law, the trial process confirmed the belief that the legal system was subject to direct political interference.

Hongkongers are very much attuned to these disappearances into criminal, administrative and private detention. Because many detainees are held incommunicado, the outside world knows little or nothing of their detention.[57] This in itself fuels speculation about their fate. Some become known through 'underground' channels and social media. They include, for example, those whose disappearance is linked to their petitioning of party leaders, labour activists, lawyers, environmental activists, campaigners for local justice and ordinary people involved in everyday matters relating to state/society relations.[58] Hongkongers are perhaps more aware of these lower-level disappearances because of their ties to their native places in China. Clashes with villagers opposing eviction and/or development of their land frequently become known to Hongkongers even where reporting restrictions and police cordons are imposed by the mainland authorities.

In 2012, the disappearance and subsequent suspicious death of Li Wangyang, a Tiananmen activist, provoked a public outcry in the territory. Since 4 June 1989, Hong Kong people have been particularly sensitive to the detention of political dissidents. Li was deaf, blind and in ill-health. Days before his death, he gave an interview to a Hong

[56] 'The Chongqing scandal', *SCMP*, 28 September 2012.

[57] In 1995, a Hong Kong woman was jailed secretly in Shenzhen for 'disrupting social order'. At trial she was not allowed to call witnesses; neither her family nor her lawyer were informed of her trial. For other examples, see Congressional Executive Commission on China, 2003 Annual Report on Rights of Criminal Suspects and Defendants.

[58] See M. Dutton, *Streetlife China* (Cambridge: Cambridge University Press, 1998); Human Rights Watch Bulletin, 'China: account for forcibly returned Uighurs', 2 September 2011. www.hrw.org/news/2011/09/02/china-account-forcibly-returned-uighurs.

Kong broadcaster to mark the twenty-third anniversary of the Tiananmen crackdown. The official verdict of 'suicide' was received with widespread scepticism in Hong Kong. Lawyers described the verdict as 'full of holes'; a group of local and mainland lawyers wrote an open letter to the NPC calling for a fresh inquiry.[59] LEGCO member Miriam Lau Kin-yee urged Beijing to launch a new enquiry since the existing verdict failed to explain how Li had overcome his disabilities to hang himself.[60] Large-scale protests about Li's death were predicted ahead of President Hu Jintao's visit to mark the fifteenth anniversary of the handover in July 2012. One senior government minister, Chow Yat-ngok, expressed his own reservations about the suicide verdict and stated that Beijing should listen to Hongkongers' petition for an investigation. The CE's popularity dropped due to his unwillingness to call for a re-investigation. During LEGCO questions on Li's death, Leung reiterated his 'determination to uphold Hong Kong's core values' but failed to 'stake out a strong position' on press freedom and freedom of expression when asked about police behaviour during Hu Jintao's visit.[61] As one local reporter observed:

> it seems that when people such as Vice-Premier Li Keqiang and President Hu Jintao set foot in Hong Kong, the police are suddenly transformed so that they are little different from their mainland counterparts ... During the Li visit, men in black suits took away Wong Kin, who was walking near his home in Laguna City and who had committed no known offence, except that he had the effrontery to wear a T-shirt condemning the crackdown in Tiananmen Square in 1989. The reason for his temporary 'disappearance' was that the vice-premier was in the vicinity ... [T]he police hustled away an *Apple Daily* reporter after he shouted a question at the president about Tiananmen Square ... a clear pattern has now emerged which is extremely worrisome.[62]

The report argued that, 'when the police start censoring the press and silencing protesters, things have gone too far'.[63] The police were 'undermining "one country, two systems" ... It is not the[ir] job to

[59] T. Ng, 'Call for fresh li Wangyang inquiry', *SCMP*, 24 June 2012.
[60] Y. K. Lai, 'Lau urges new probe into Li suicide', *SCMP*, 17 July 2012.
[61] F. Ching, 'In HK, gagging protests not police's job', *SCMP*, 18 July 2012.
[62] Ching, 'In HK, gagging protests not police's job'.
[63] Ching, 'In HK, gagging protests not police's job'. The *Apple Daily* reporter, Rex Hon Yiu-ting, was detained and questioned by police after shouting the question at Hu.

keep Chinese leaders from seeing or hearing Hong Kong protesters. It is certainly not the job of the police to decide which questions the press should be allowed to ask and which ones should be banned'.[64] Censorship in China meant that coverage of the mass protest that marked Hu's visit was blocked in the mainland media, which ran instead stories of how Hong Kong was 'thriving' under Chinese rule. Where they were mentioned, the protesters were described as 'mischief makers' who 'selfishly elevate local interests while ignoring national interests'.[65]

'DISRUPTIVE SUBJECTS'[66]

Anyone who opposes the government in Hong Kong knows that, though they might end up in prison for their activities, they will do so only after the due process of law. This is not the case on the mainland, and for many this encapsulates the difference between the 'two systems'. Following a mainland clampdown on Falun Gong members, for example, the *Xinhua* director in Hong Kong stated that the territory must not become a base from which Falun Gong could subvert China. When the former CE, Tung Chee-hwa, described the group in a LEGCO debate as an 'evil cult', he was criticised for 'looking North' because in Hong Kong, Falun Gong members routinely distribute literature and organise petitions. In 1999, 900 Falun Gong members from around the world arrived in the territory for a three-day meeting, during which they performed their exercises in front of the *Xinhua* news agency and demonstrated in the streets, flying large yellow banners,[67] activities for which they would be arrested across the border. Other religious leaders, such as Bishop Zen and Franco Mella, also regularly upset the mainland by their support for the pro-democracy movement.[68] Hong Kong Christians who smuggle bibles into China do so knowing they might disappear and/or be arrested.

Other 'mischief makers' liable to sanction should they step over the border include Hong Kong pro-democracy politicians. In 1999, LEGCO representative for the legal constituency, leading barrister

[64] F. Ching, 'Gagging protests'.
[65] C. Sebag-Montefiore, 'City scope: one country, two worlds', *SCMP*, 15 July 2012.
[66] The term comes from Barbara Yngvesson's book, *Virtuous Citizens, Disruptive Subjects* (New York: Routledge, 1993).
[67] Fenby, *Dealing with the Dragon*, p. 302.
[68] Franco Mella became the subject of the Hong Kong film, *Ordinary Heroes*.

Margaret Ng, was refused a visa to attend an international legal conference in Beijing to which she had been invited. Professor Jerome Cohen of New York University, leading China lawyer and participant in the conference, considered not giving his speech by way of protest and issued a statement to the media in Beijing criticising Ng's exclusion. Within the same decade, another leading legal figure, the Dean of the University of Hong Kong's Law Faculty, Johannes Chan, was refused entry to Macau to speak at a conference. Protesting about her exclusion, 'Ng said she was told by the Chief Executive's office that "he was 'too tired and too busy' to see her" ... She writes to him twice but is told by the private secretary to the Chief Executive's private secretary that he will not be available for at least three weeks'.[69] Ng was supported by 162 lawyers and legal academics who wrote an open letter to Tung calling the ban 'a blatant example of political persecution and the Central Government's intolerance of dissenting voices'.[70] They 'urged the Chief Executive to dispel fears that legitimate and lawful activity in Hong Kong could bring political retaliation from Beijing'.[71] Of her eventual interview with Tung Chee-hwa, Ng commented that she was left with the impression that 'he rather thought I should re-examine myself as to whether I could become a different person ... I found that rather chilling – an echo of the Cultural Revolution, when people were told not why they were being punished but were advised to reflect on their crimes themselves'.[72]

This 'chilling effect' affected other Hong Kong academics and journalists investigating stories on the mainland.[73] In 2001, a Hong Kong academic conducting research in the mainland, Li Shaomin, was detained, along with his wife and 5-year-old daughter. The mainland authorities convicted him in a secret trial of spying, a case seen in Hong Kong as 'part of a wider politically motivated crackdown on academics with connections to the United States'.[74] Though his wife and daughter were eventually released and allowed to return to Hong Kong, Li remained in detention. He was eventually released after a visit to Beijing by the US Secretary of State Colin Powell. Upon his release,

[69] Fenby, *Dealing with the Dragon*, pp. 226–7.

[70] Fenby, *Dealing with the Dragon*, , p. 238.

[71] Fenby, *Dealing with the Dragon*.

[72] Fenby, *Dealing with the Dragon*.

[73] A Hong Kong academic, Xu Zerong, was also detained by the state security police without notification being given.

[74] Carroll, *Concise History of Hong Kong*, p. 223.

he left Hong Kong for the United States. In 2008, the *SCMP* photographer Felix Wong Chi-keung was also detained by police in Beijing during the Olympics; in 2012, he was again beaten by police whilst covering anti-Japanese riots in Shenzhen.[75]

The fact that the mainland feels able to act in this fashion regarding articulate and educated professionals leaves the ordinary person in little doubt how they would fare if detained on the mainland. Experience has shown that the SAR government is unlikely to assist, especially where the detention is carried out by the Ministry of State Security, an institution which falls outside the normal notification system. In such circumstances, the HK SAR may not even be notified of the person's detention. A 2011 Human Rights Watch report claimed that 'disappeared' people are often at high risk of torture and are often detained outside official detention facilities in 'black jails'.[76]

Hong Kong is especially alert to clues of mainland-style practices occurring in Hong Kong itself. In 2013, for example, local activist, Yang Kuang, was detained on the mainland for 'provoking quarrels and making trouble' when he attempted to visit the wife of Liu Xiaobo, the imprisoned Nobel Prize winner. Other Hong Kong cameramen waiting in the vicinity of her house were also assaulted by unidentified men, raising fears in Hong Kong of 'gangster politics'. Local police were later criticised for using the same phrase 'provoking quarrels and making trouble' in respect to local protesters. In July 2012, mainlanders who participated in the 1 July annual protest march in Hong Kong were also detained upon their return to mainland China, an action interpreted locally as 'sending out a very strong message, threatening mainlanders not to learn the protest culture from Hong Kong people'.[77] A year later, mainland legal experts also warned that microbloggers posting *weibo* messages in Hong Kong could be imprisoned for up to three years on the mainland if they crossed the border having violated a new mainland law prohibiting the dissemination of false remarks with malicious intention.

[75] '*Post* Photographer Felix Wong beaten by Shenzhen police at protests', *SCMP*, 21 September 2012.

[76] 'China: enforced disappearances a growing threat', Human Rights Watch, 11 September 2011. www.hrw.org/news/2011/11/09/china-enforced-disappearances-growing-threat.

[77] S. Cheung, 'Activists sent to camp because of HK protests', *SCMP*, 26 July 2012.

DEATH

Shenzhen looks like Hong Kong; however, this sense of familiarity is jarred by the 'perp parades' that convey those sentenced to death through the streets on the backs of lorries and the 'big character' public posters of a red tick against photographs of the executed. Unlike most foreign tourists, Hongkongers see these signs of mainland life on a regular basis; their local media carry pictures of public sentencing rallies and blood-spattered execution grounds. They are reminded that thirty miles away, people are executed. In 1995, for example, the *Oriental Daily* carried a report entitled 'Shenzhen Tremendous Highway Hi-Jack Case: 13 Condemned prisoners are executed immediately', alongside a photograph of sixteen prisoners being paraded before 2,000 people in the Po On Province Town Gymnasium before being taken to the execution ground.[78] Photographs of the condemned prisoners showed them being held by PSB officers, with chains shackled around their waists and ropes around their necks. The report also showed 'blood filled holes' on the execution ground, 'the big pool of blood being caused by re-attempts to shoot the condemned prisoner'.[79] Other reports of the sentencing rally noted that the condemned prisoners were escorted to the execution ground on the back of a lorry, for all to see,[80] of the masses 'standing along both sides of the Ping Wu Road to watch the escorting of the criminal offenders to the execution ground'. Over twenty thousand people drawn from factories and work organisations, were summoned to attend the event.[81] An earlier report the same month stated that over a thousand people attended an 'adjudication process' of seafood market criminals at Shenzhen's East Gate Market.[82] The actual rate of execution can only be estimated, a lack of clarity that underscores the capricious nature of the mainland legal system, the unpredictability with which its laws are interpreted and the convicted despatched.

Since 1997, it has become clear that Hong Kong people cannot rely upon their government to rescue them from such a system. In 1995, Loh observed that those accused of crimes in the Chinese legal system enjoyed few of the rights and due process protections taken for granted by Hongkongers. The case of Cheung Tze-keung ('Big Spender')

78 *Oriental Daily*, 16 November 1995.
79 *Apple Daily*, 16 December 1995.
80 *Apple Daily*, 16 December 1995.
81 *Apple Daily*, 19 December 1995.
82 *Apple Daily*, 16 December 1995.

encapsulated her worst-case scenario. Cheung and his gang were known, high-profile criminals. In 1991, he was charged with a HK$167 million robbery from an airport security van. His conviction was later quashed; on retrial, he was acquitted. Other crimes in which he was believed to be involved included a series of spectacular, pre-handover, armed raids on gold shops in which the gang sprayed 'bullets from AK47 rifles'; the kidnaps of Hong Kong men visiting mainland China in which huge ransoms had been demanded; and robberies on the mainland. Cheung and his gang were depicted in the media as having all the hallmarks of 'psychopathic criminals ruthlessly attempting to make a fortune in this land of wealth and prosperity',[83] a theme explored in Johnny Mak's 1980s series of films, *Long Arm of the Law* in which the *Ah Charn* figure was said to mirror Hong Kong people's 'perception of threats from the mainland to their very way of life ... The contrast between "we" and "they" is brought out through dramatizing the ominous presence of the outsider'.[84] Paradoxically, however, it was Cheung, the Hong Kong 'insider' who brought this mainland menace to Hong Kong. Cheung and his gang were responsible for the 'spectacular kidnapping' of Victor Li Tzar-kuoi, the son of Hong Kong tycoon, Li Ka-shing and, later, of Walter Kwok Ping-sheung, chairman of the Sung Hung Kai group.[85] Neither of these kidnappings was reported to the police; both men were released on payment of a ransom of more than HK$1.3 billion. It was rumoured that Li Ka-shing by-passed law enforcement in the HKSAR by going straight to mainland officials in the hunt for Cheung. The gang was observed by the Hong Kong Police moving boxes of explosives smuggled from the mainland into the New Territories. Although most of the gang was later arrested, Cheung escaped across the border. He was eventually caught by the mainland police investigating the death of a Hong Kong police informer shot dead in Shenzhen. Cheung and thirty-five others were charged by the mainland Procurator with planning the Hong Kong kidnappings whilst on the mainland:

> Cheung stood trial in a closed court in Guangzhou with three dozen alleged accomplices, seventeen of them from Hong Kong. As the hearing opened, the first of two hastily-made films about Big Spender went

[83] B. Leung, *Perspectives on Hong Kong Society* (Hong Kong: Oxford University Press, 1996), p. 69.
[84] Leung, *Perspectives on Hong Kong Society*.
[85] See Fenby, *Dealing with the Dragon*, pp. 49–151.

> on show in Hong Kong. On the train to Guangzhou you could a buy a video on 'China's biggest criminal case in the twentieth century'. Armed paramilitaries surrounded the court. Snipers crouched on nearby roofs ... Big Spender was shot at an execution ground surrounded by hills and wild grass outside the city. The following day, ten police guarding the site turned away the pregnant widow of one of the gang members who had gone there to burn paper offerings to comfort her husband's soul in the beyond ... A reporter who visited the site wrote that it was littered with the shoes of the dead men, used cartridges, gloves discarded by the firing squad and cardboard signs hung around the convicts' necks recording their names and crimes.[86]

Secretary for Justice Elsie Leung refused to seek the return of the suspects for trial in Hong Kong. Since the crimes Cheung committed took place in Hong Kong, the Hong Kong courts should have heard the case against him. The case thus went to the heart of the 'one country, two systems' formula. The HKSAR government was accused of failing to adequately defend Hong Kong's jurisdiction. It replied that the lack of a rendition agreement between the two jurisdictions made it difficult to extract Cheung to stand trial in Hong Kong though, as critics pointed out, it had previously secured by negotiation the return of some 128 alleged criminals.[87]

The execution of Cheung allowed the mainland to appear as protector of Hong Kong against an arch-felon. However, Hongkongers were unconvinced, especially given the suggestion that powerful people had bypassed proper procedures in order to ensure Cheung's execution under a less stringent legal system. As Cullen and Fu point out, Hongkongers were already apprehensive about the mainland criminal justice system, and this trial did nothing to change their views.[88] They argue that the case highlighted a 'legal vacuum' in HKSAR/mainland relations since the Basic Law 'failed to provide any sort of comprehensive framework for arbitrating the association between the two jurisdictions'.[89] They called for a formal rendition agreement between Hong

86 Fenby, *Dealing with the Dragon*.
87 'Hong Kong's judicial autonomy undermined', *Hong Kong Voice of Democracy*, 28 November 1998.
88 R. Cullen and H. Fu, 'How the "Big Spender" case has exposed the limitations of the Basic Law', paper given at the French Centre for Research on Contemporary China, 27 November 1998.
89 Cullen and Fu, 'How the "Big Spender" case has exposed the limitations'.

Kong and mainland China, something which had still not been managed by 2014.

By executing Cheung, the mainland authorities were thought to have usurped the due process of law. The chairman of the Hong Kong Bar Association pointed out that:

> The issue is whether, putting aside the possible kidnapping charges, the fact that the Hong Kong government made no attempt to seek the return of some of the defendants in relation to possible robbery or forearms charges may give people the false impression that the judiciary and the rule of law of Hong Kong is somehow subordinate to that of the rest of China, and thus indirectly cast a question mark over the concept of 'one country, two systems'.[90]

In the same year, Li Yuhui (the 'Telford Gardens murderer') was tried and executed in Shantou for offences also committed in Hong Kong. Li was a mainlander who, whilst living in Hong Kong, poisoned three women and two girls. He was tried and executed in his home town, to which he had fled. Local papers covered his execution:

> Following the usual procedure, Li is driven in a convoy of vehicles to the shooting field immediately after the verdict has been read out. The Shantou City Intermediate People's Court formal execution ground is regarded as too public, given the crowd of Hong Kong journalists waiting there. So three policemen wearing white gloves take Li to an open space nearby. Two hold him. The third shoots him twice, at 10.15 A.M., three-quarters of an hour after he entered the court to hear the result of his appeal. 'Three pairs of white gloves donned by the security officers and another one worn by the pathologist were abandoned on the earth afterwards', writes *Post* reporter, Stella Lee. Blood stains the earth. The body is burned in the local crematorium. The ashes will be returned to his family. Local people in Shantou cannot understand the interest the Hong Kong media is showing in the case. After all, China executes at least 2,000 people each year.[91]

The executions of Li and Cheung underlined China's sovereign 'power to punish' not only those who offended within China's borders but also those who offended in the HKSAR. Neither the border nor the law prevented the 'two systems' from becoming 'one country'. In a 2014 report, Amnesty International pointed out that twenty-eight

[90] Fenby, *Dealing with the Dragon*, p. 155.
[91] Fenby, *Dealing with the Dragon*, pp. 147–8.

Hongkongers had been executed on the mainland since 2003, another twenty-eight faced suspended death sentences and the fate of another nineteen sentenced to death was unknown.[92]

It has been argued that violence of the kind used against the 'Big Spender' gang can be 'immensely productive' for the state,[93] authorizing 'war' against those who imperil the social order and justifying the state's monopoly over the means of coercion.[94] The figure of the arch-felon serves 'as the ground for on which a metaphysics of order, of the nation as a moral community guaranteed by the state, may be entertained, argued for, even demanded'.[95] The status of villains such as 'Big Spender' and his gang as 'outlaws' and the state's response to them 'underscores the fragility of order and gives focus to popular preoccupations with the threat of social meltdown . . . [This] comes to legitimise a physics of social order'.[96] However, the sense that at the hand-over Hong Kong hovered 'on the brink of dissolution' was due less to criminals like 'Big Spender' than the belief that state itself had circumvented the due process of law. Glad to be rid of the outlaw, the public remained fearful of the new sheriff.

[92] S. Chan, '28 Hongkongers executed on mainland in just over a decade, says Amnesty', *SCMP*, 27 March 2014.
[93] Comaroff and Comaroff, *Law and Disorder*, p. 279.
[94] Comaroff and Comaroff, *Law and Disorder*.
[95] Comaroff and Comaroff, *Law and Disorder*.
[96] Comaroff and Comaroff, *Law and Disorder*.

HKers anxious about Shenzhen — marginal location — inexpensive — dangerous — HKers do not want mainland laws . . .

5

The disappearance of Yu Man-hon

The executions of 'Big Spender' and the 'Telford Gardens murderer' occurred just after the handover when Hongkongers were hyper-sensitive to the differences between 'there' and 'here' and were becoming increasingly aware of the fact that their own government paid more attention to Beijing than to local voices. Anxieties were high about how Hongkongers would fare under mainland rule. This was the context in which, at 11.30 A.M. on 24 August 2000, Yu Man-hon, a fifteen-year-old autistic boy with a mental age of two, ran away from his mother at Yau Ma Tei MTR station in Hong Kong.[1] The family had just eaten dim sum in Yau Ma Tei and were returning home when Man-hon ran off. Somehow, he made his way to the Lo Wu checkpoint, crossed the border into the mainland and disappeared. Fourteen years later, his parents still search for him; a photograph of Man-hon and the details of his disappearance remains on the Hong Kong Police Missing Persons website. The failure to reunite mother and child made this a cautionary tale of the kind told to children to ensure they never stray. As one Hong Kong reporter wrote at the time,

> Everyone seems to have a theory about Yu Man-hon. On the day he ran away from his mother at Yau Ma Tei MTR, he disappeared into the world of speculation ... that he had fallen into the hands of gangsters who were forcing him to beg in another province (Hubei, Guangxi,

[1] The MTR and the KCRC took passengers across the Hong Kong/China Border at Lo Wu.

> Yunan, take your pick); that his organs were about to be taken from him and sold unless his family paid a ransom; that he was eking out an existence in various towns in Guangdong. Many people said with conviction, he must be dead, but that too is just a theory. There is no proof of anything about Man-hon's life beyond the moment when Hong Kong immigration officials sent him ... across the border to Shenzhen ... in the belief that the mainland was a place where a boy who couldn't speak, and who urinated in and threw food around an interrogation room belonged.[2]

Another wrote, 'As a result of this systematic laxity, Man-hon was handcuffed to prevent him hurting anyone and handed back to the Shenzhen Immigration Department, which assumed its duty was done when it dumped him in the street. In a city where street children are so common, that may not have been an unexpected response but it is hardly caring.'[3] Once on the mainland side, Man Hon was unable to retrace his steps. He became, instead, stranded in a twilight zone, known neither to be alive nor dead. His mother, however, still searches for him: 'In the dreams, he is with us, together and happy like we were in the past. But when we wake up and find it was just a dream, the pain is just unbearable ... We miss Man-hon very, very much. We miss him more whenever there's a typhoon or the weather is hot, worrying if he is sick, has a place to hide or food to eat'.[4]

YU MAN-HON DISAPPEARS

Despite his disabilities and the fact that he possessed no travel documents, Yu Man-hon managed to cross the Lo Wu border checkpoint. Mainland officers on the Chinese side intercepted him at 1.47 P.M. He seemed to them to be mentally disturbed. He was dressed like a Hong Kong resident, and he 'did not respond when their staff spoke Putonghua but made some response when they used Cantonese'.[5] Subsequently, they asked their Hong Kong counterparts to verify his identity and returned him to the Hong Kong side. HKSAR Immigration officers conducted a sixty-five-minute interview with him:

[2] Stella Lee, 'Officer in missing Yu Man-hon case quits', *SCMP*, 4 March 2001.

[3] 'Catalogue of errors', *SCMP*, 22 September 2000.

[4] BBC News, 'China widens search for missing boy', 31 August 2000. http://news.bbc.co.uk/1/hi/world/asia-pacific/904805.stm.

[5] BBC News, 'China widens search'.

> When an officer asked Man-hon in Cantonese and Putonghua his name, nickname and address, he got no response. A search was then conducted ... He noticed that the boy's wrists bore marks of being handcuffed before, apparently. His belly carried some rashes, the lower part of his legs bore some scars and his feet were dirty ... A senior officer then took off the boy's clothes and checked his shoes to see whether there was anything that might suggest the boy's identity. They found the boy was not wearing underwear and the trademark label on his T-shirt had been removed. His rubber shoes, according to the knowledge of the immigration officer and senior immigration officer, were of a well-known brand in the [m]ainland ... [O]fficers later changed their approach, praising the boy about his clothing and asking his favourite TV programmes and singers ... like Wah Chai [Andy Lau], Gi Gi and Kwok Fu-shing, etc. Again, the boy showed no response at all ... Man-hon was served with a lunch box and a can of coke. He became impatient and stood up, messed around and intended to rush out of the room ... [He] became emotional and impulsive when officers tried to stop him, swinging his hands around, kicking his legs and spitting at them ... The officers then handcuffed Man-hon to a chair and the boy was said to have calmed down. When the officers tried to get a response from him by using simple words such as 'dad', 'mum' and 'water', Man-hon did not follow and only uttered sounds like 'ah' and 'naughty' when he urinated on his chair'.[6]

The HKSAR Immigration officers concluded that Man-hon could not possibly be a Hong Konger, refused to allow him back into Hong Kong and, at 7.05 P.M., returned him to the mainland. A newspaper article reported on the last person to see him, a Mrs Chan, who later told an RTHK phone-in programme,

> He walked through the counter, an officer stood up and shouted at him and a few other officers were also alerted ... I could tell from his appearance that he was mentally disabled. I followed him to the Shenzhen border, thinking he must be lost and wanted to find his family.' Man-hon was finally stopped by a mainland official when he tried to pass through the Shenzhen immigration controls: 'They grabbed him and he struggled. I shouted in Putonghua, "He has problems, don't hit him!" Mrs Chan said the Shenzhen officials later asked her to leave. She said dozens of people must also have witnessed the drama ... 'My heart sank. I saw someone who badly needed help, but I didn't know how to save him'.[7]

6 'Catalogue of errors', *SCMP*, 22 September 2000.

7 'HKSARG makes every effort to locate Yu Man-hon', *SCMP*, 1 September 2000. See also HKSAR press release at www.info.gov.hk/gia/general/20009/01/0901344.htm.

An Immigration Department inquiry in the HKSAR subsequently revealed that both the Shenzhen officers and at least one of the HKSAR officers had suspected that Man-hon was 'mentally handicapped'.[8] Another inquiry, by the Ombudsman, identified four main blunders:

(i) The immigration channel supervisor at Lo Wu failed to report that a person had crossed the checkpoint illegally earlier in the day;
(ii) The immigration officer who interviewed Man-hon had failed to abide by departmental guidelines on the handling of mentally handicapped people;
(iii) Immigration officers had returned Man-hon to Shenzhen without paying adequate attention to the consequences of the fact that he was mentally handicapped;
(iv) Although Man-hon's mother had reported her son's disappearance to Kowloon East's Missing Persons Unit earlier in the day, a police inspector at the New Territories Regional Command and Control Centre had failed to circulate details of Man-hon's disappearance, despite being tasked to do so almost an hour before Man-hon was sent back to Shenzhen. As a result, no information about his disappearance was available to the immigration officers when they did seek police help in identifying Man-hon.[9]

At the end of their interview with Man-hon, one of the Immigration Officers stated that the boy 'was similar to a mentally handicapped person and could not communicate in a normal and clear way'.[10] Though Immigration Department guidelines required that professional help and/or an independent adult (e.g., parent, guardian) be employed when the interviewee appeared to be 'mentally impaired', no help was sought.

Crucial moments were lost in the initial days of the search for Man-hon. The boy disappeared on 24 August, but it was not until 28 August that the Immigration Department contacted the mainland authorities to try and relocate him. On 31 August, the Chief Executive contacted the Mayor of Shenzhen to seek assistance; on the same day, the Secretary for Security contacted the Director General of the

[8] *SCMP*, 22 September 2000.
[9] Hong Kong Immigration Department, 'Missing Person-Yu Man Hon-Summary of Investigation Report', Hong Kong. Hong Kong Government, September 2000.
[10] *SCMP*, 22 September 2000.

Guangdong Provincial Public Security Bureau (Liang Guoju) to ask for help in searching other mainland cities outside Shenzhen.[11]

Yu Man-hon's treatment by Hong Kong Immigration officials was not an isolated incident. Lawyers and human rights experts argued that the incidents were not just isolated blunders,

> but point to inherent problems in a department with too much authority ... A Human Rights Monitor report ... [noted] allegations of verbal abuse, threats, duress, improper pressure, unlawful isolation, denial of access to the telephone, misrepresentation of the options available, extraction of signatures by lies or mental pressure, having papers signed without letting the victims know the nature or content of the document, denial of bail and unnecessary or unjustified detention, discrimination towards certain minorities or nationals.[12]

Right of abode claimants also detained by immigration officials reported being woken in their cells in the middle of the night by having torches shone in their eyes, asked to sign unexplained documents and subject to strip-searches.[13] Such incidents indicated a culture of abuse of vulnerable people by powerful government officials, exactly the kind of problem that the rule of law was supposed to prevent.

Yu Man-hon was also a victim of prejudice. Frank Ching commented on the 'cold hearted indifference' towards the vulnerable, most visible in Hong Kong's treatment of mainlanders.[14] The Immigration Department was accused of 'discrimination' and of 'lax attitudes and prejudices' for its officers having assumed that a boy whose clothing seemed 'too cheap for a Hong Kong youth' must hail from the mainland.[15] The police likewise were criticised for their 'disdainful attitude towards mainlanders'. Cyd Ho Sau-lan, a LEGCO member, said, 'This also shows the officers judge people from their looks. The boy did not wear famous brands but was in very casual dress, therefore he was treated this way.'[16] A public opinion survey at the end of September 2000 reported that 66 per cent of the public placed the blame for Man-hon's disappearance entirely on the Immigration Department, whilst 64 per cent

11 Hong Kong Legislative Council, Panel on Security, Information Report CB(2)86/00-01(01), Agenda Item III, 'Report on the incident of Master Yu Man-hon', 24 October, 2000.

12 Hong Kong Legislative Council, Panel on Security, Information Report.

13 *SCMP*, 12 September 2000.

14 *SCMP*, 25 January 2003.

15 *SCMP*, 17 December 2000.

16 *SCMP*, 24 September 2000.

thought that the Immigration Department discriminated against handicapped people, as well as people from mainland China.[17] A BBC interview with the Yu family linked Man-hon's fate to wider criticisms of Hong Kong immigration officials' treatment of those they suspected of being illegal immigrants ('IIs').[18] Pejorative stereotypes of 'IIs' were widespread in Hong Kong, and mainlanders were seen as rough 'country bumpkins', ignorant and uncouth compared to their sophisticated Hong Kong compatriots. Man-hon's failure to dress 'Hong Kong-style' or recognise local show business celebrities marked him down as 'Other'. Mrs Yu said that vulnerable persons, such as Man-hon, being 'unproductive' members of society, were regarded with indifference by the Hong Kong government.

BETWIXT AND BETWEEN

Man-hon disappeared in the seventh month in the Chinese lunar calendar – the time of the Hungry Ghost (*Yue Lan*) festival, when restless spirits are temporarily released from hell to wander the earth in search of sustenance.[19] Forming part of the repertoire of Hong Kong culture, stories of ghosts and lost souls mostly surface at those times of the year associated with the supernatural, liminal times in the Hong Kong calendar. Spirits of the dead not yet incorporated into the afterlife are said to be connected by a thin thread to the society to which they once belonged. Ghosts that surface to roam the earth are potentially harmful and must be appeased by ritual offerings. To stop them making trouble, incense is burned and meals placed outside the home for the spirits to consume.[20] The real and the imaginary become blurred as people go about their everyday lives acknowledging the presence in their midst of ghosts and lost souls. The 'hungry ghosts' are those who have no relatives or descendants to pay them the respect owed to ancestors. They must be propitiated with food and other offerings and kept amused by watching performances of Chinese

[17] *Singpoa Daily*, 25 September 2000. [18] BBC News, 31 August 2000.

[19] See generally D. Johnson (ed.), 'Ritual opera, operatic ritual: "Mu-lien rescues his mother" in Chinese popular culture', Papers from the International Workshop on Mu-lien Operas, Publications of the Chinese Popular Culture Project, (Berkeley: IEAS Publications and University of California, 1989).

[20] Johnson, 'Ritual operal, operatic ritual'.

opera.[21] Since ghosts are believed to be roaming the landscape of the living looking for amusement, opera troupes leave empty seats for 'these spectral spectators' so that they may find entertainment.[22] Paper boats and lanterns are set to sail on water to guide lost ghosts and spirits home; fake money (Hell bank notes), paper models of cars, computers, houses, TVs and mobile phones are all offered up to the dead spirits at roadside fires.[23]

The festival reaches its peak on the fifteenth day of the month (August in the Western calendar) fifteen days after which the ghosts must return to the underworld. During this period, children like Yu Man-hon are said to be vulnerable to being drowned or snatched away; they are warned to return home early and not to wander around at night.

In the days after his disappearance, Mrs Yu believed that Man-hon was still alive, roaming the streets of Shenzhen, that he 'may try to go out to look for food when there are fewer people in the streets'.[24] She believed that Man-hon 'knew the way home' but had become trapped in the no-man's land of the border. In Hong Kong, schoolchildren made cards of support for the Yu family; the press speculated about Man-hon trying to survive in lawless Shenzhen. Experts argued that 'seeking survival' was 'a basic instinct' and that Man-hon did not need to be intelligent to find food, stay warm and find shelter. He might fall down, drown, be assaulted or get ill by eating food which is dirty, 'but as long as he's in places with people he should be okay, as ... it's a Chinese tradition that people will offer help'.[25]

Eighteen days after Man-hon disappeared, a half-naked boy who looked like him was found wandering in the Buji district of Shenzhen at 2 A.M. in the morning.[26] A month later, a seven-year-old mentally handicapped boy was found at Yau Ma Tei MTR, almost three hours after escaping from the family's Shekkipmei flat whilst his mother was in the bath.[27] In late September 2000, a ten-year-old boy without

21 See S. Y. Chan, 'The offering to the white tiger in Cantonese opera', *Journal of the Hong Kong Branch of the Royal Asiatic Society*, 30, pp. 139–79, cited in S. Y. Martin, 'Of ghosts and gangsters: capitalist cultural production and the Hong Kong film industry', *Visual Anthropology Review*, 28, no. 1 (2012), pp. 32–49.

22 Martin, 'Of ghosts and gangsters', p. 36.

23 See J. S. Lee, *For gods, ghosts and ancestors: the Chinese tradition of paper offerings* (Seattle: University of Washington Press, 2007).

24 *SCMP*, 1 November 2000.

25 *SCMP*, 6 September 2000.

26 *SCMP*, 10 September 2000.

27 *SCMP*, 10 September 2000.

travel documents was found between the Lo Wu bridge and the SAR immigration counters; he was returned to Shenzhen only after the Social Welfare Department was called in to assist and the Shenzhen authorities were able to verify that he was a mainland resident. Another autistic boy was found in Lo Wu after running away from his mother in Shekkipmei.[28] A seventeen-year-old girl (on medication for depression) disappeared in November 2000. A seventy-two-year-old woman 'suspected of suffering from mental problems' was found in Beijing and returned to Hong Kong.[29] In November 2000, Chan Fong, an elderly Hong Kong woman suffering from dementia, was found by PSB officers wandering in Shanghai without any travel documents, the third time that month that an elderly Hong Kong person had been found wandering alone on the mainland.[30] Though they could not communicate with her in either Cantonese or Putonghua, officials managed to establish that she was a Hong Kong resident; she had officially passed through Lo Wu on 6 November. Having found her, officials were reluctant to let her go for fear that she would not be able to fend for herself, as Hong Kong officials refused to accept her back without first gaining the consent of her son, whom they could not trace.

Despite assurances of procedural changes following Man-hon's disappearance, then, such incidents continued. In February 2001, a twenty-two-year-old autistic man, Tsoi Wa-kau, was found in the departure hall on the Huanggang side of the border without any record of him having passed through Lo Wu. He had run away from a sheltered workshop near his home in Ma On Shan and boarded a bus to Dongguan. The next day mainland border guards, thinking that he might be Man-hon, approached him. Although he carried no identifying documents and could not communicate clearly, he understood the complex Chinese characters used in Hong Kong. When mainland authorities contacted their Hong Kong counterparts, the HKSAR police confirmed that they had received a report the previous day of a man answering his description. He was then returned to Hong Kong. In May 2001, a four-year-old girl, Lee Lok-lam, 'almost staged a repeat of the Yu Man-hon incident' when she ran away from her aunt in Hunghom KCRC station at 1 P.M. and was found half-an-hour later, wandering the platform at Lo Wu.[31] Another 'mentally retarded' teenage girl without any identification documents was found wandering

[28] *SCMP*, 20 September 2000.
[29] *SCMP*, 20 September 2000.
[30] *SCMP*, 18 November 2000.
[31] *SCMP*, 6 May 2001.

around the departure hall at Lo Wu with a rucksack on her back; no one had reported her missing.

On Mother's Day 2001, the Hong Kong media reminded the public that Mrs Yu was still waiting for news of her son, and she talked of the toll taken on her as she trekked through Guangzhou searching in vain for him. Mrs Yu travelled across the border each day at 7.30 A.M. to Shenzhen, hoping to hear news; each evening, she returned home.[32] She spent each day:

> wait[ing] by herself in a hotel room in Shenzhen. Her husband . . . works as a caretaker on a Kwun Tong estate and takes care of Yu-cho [Man-hon's brother] so he can make only occasional trips across the border. Her brother, Li Yuefang, spends every day searching for his nephew; he rings his sister with progress reports and she tells him about the latest apparent sightings, phoned in by the public. Some are crank calls, some might be genuine, but brother and sister have to sift through them all because someone, someday, might call with the information that will lead to Man-hon.[33]

The Man-hon disappearance forced an overhaul of surveillance at the border crossing. Mrs Yu lent her voice to the call for a cross-border unit to establish what had happened to Man-hon and to help others whose relatives had disappeared on the mainland. The Shenzhen-Hong Kong Land Boundary Police Co-operation Scheme unit, established in January 2003, strengthened cross-border liaisons and 'facilitated joint efforts on both sides in combating crimes at boundary areas'.[34] However, complaints that the mainland police extorted money from those they detained undermined endeavours to persuade Hong Kong people to report their victimisation to mainland authorities. The Hong Kong police established a command control centre as a focal point for all government departments checking on missing persons; training was improved and information more readily disseminated. The Immigration Department announced that it would be spending HK$134.8 million to improve border checkpoints, installing 114 security cameras. A LEGCO panel called for 'enhanced sensitivity' on the part of public officials dealing with persons with disabilities (mental or physical) and/or communication difficulties, so as to deal with them 'in a fair, just and

32 *SCMP*, 4 January 2001. 33 *SCMP*, 4 January 2001.

34 LEGCO Security Panel, 'Personal Safety problems encountered by Hong Kong residents in the Mainland', 6 July 2004, LC Paper No CB (2)2980/03–04(02).

sensitive manner'.[35] However, the experience of such persons did not improve. In January 2002, Lee Shung, a partially senile, 'bewildered seventy-one-year-old mainland tourist' was mistaken for an illegal immigrant and sent back over the border.[36] The man and his wife were mainland residents, two-way travel permit holders who had come to Hong Kong to visit their daughter on the Tai Hing Estate in Tuen Mun. Mr Lee was found wandering in Tin Shui Wai without travel documents or an identity card. The police mistook him for a Chinese illegal immigrant, held him in a detention centre and then repatriated him to the mainland, where he was briefly detained in Shenzhen before being sent back to his home town. After his wife reported him missing, he was returned to Hong Kong. Whilst 'he did not suffer the fate of Man-hon', Hong Kong reporters wanted to know why officials had sent Lee across the border without verifying his identity.[37] Such persons:

> face not only the depredations of criminals in our society, but are also potential victims of the forces of law and order . . . There is a dark side to Hong Kong, one that is not always visible except to the poor, the handicapped, the mentally impaired, the aged, the ill and the otherwise underprivileged – the most vulnerable members of our society. It is an uncaring attitude, a lack of sympathy for those less fortunate, which seems to characterise some of the people in power.[38]

In April 2002, another 'mentally retarded' man was detained awaiting repatriation to China. Cheung Hoi-sang, one of a number of mainland children born of Hong Kong residents, sought right of abode in Hong Kong after 1997. The Immigration Department detained him whilst considering his application because it feared he would otherwise abscond. This resulted in a demonstration of about a hundred protesters who 'stormed the Waterfront police station in Central to try to secure his release, and staged a sit-in outside Victoria prison in Central, where Mr. Cheung was later transferred to . . . His mother, Wong Yuet-yuen, who has visited her son in jail, said "He's terrified. His face is very pale. My heart broke when I saw him". [His lawyer] Mr. Chan said . . . "he cannot be expected to fend for himself in China. He has never travelled alone in his life."'[39]

[35] LEGCO Security Panel, 'Personal Safety problems encountered by Hong Kong residents'.
[36] *SCMP*, 5 October 2002.
[37] *SCMP*, 25 January 2003.
[38] *SCMP*, 25 January 2003.
[39] *SCMP*, 16 April 2002.

The second anniversary of Man-hon's disappearance in 2002 was marked by press reports that Ngan Yau-lan, an eighty-two-year-old woman with senile dementia, had disappeared after boarding a train in Kowloon Tong. Her children reported her missing that evening and searched for her in Shenzhen. She had slipped through the Lo Wu checkpoint without travel documents and was later found by staff at a bus terminus in Xiasha, more than five miles from Lu Wu on the mainland side. According to her family:

> When we went to Shenzhen, a [m]ainland immigration officer told us there was nothing he could do and blamed Hong Kong for letting her cross. On the Hong Kong side, an officer told us they had too many people crossing the border and losing a few was inevitable . . . It was so lucky some nice people found her and called us. If they hadn't, we could have lost her and she might never have come back.[40]

Man-hon's treatment by immigration officials was thus one in a series of incidents that testified to the abuse of vulnerable people by an unaccountable and powerful arm of government.

THE 'OTHER' SIDE OF THE BORDER

The Hong Kong press raised the uncomfortable question of whether Man-hon could survive in the Motherland. Children *did* survive on the streets of Shenzhen, but Mrs Yu said that many mainlanders had told her that 'mentally disabled people are often collected and dumped in remote areas'.[41] Over the months searching in Fujian, Jiangxi, Guangxi and Hunan, she herself had seen nearly 2,000 mentally disabled children wandering the streets.[42] She collected a box of photographs of such children:

> There was an unkempt boy squatting in bushes in the middle of a highway, and another perched on a drain pipe in the middle of God knows where. There was a Polaroid from a PSB station of an adolescent, grinning vacantly, propped against a stained wall by an officer. There was, unforgettably, a photograph of a naked boy, like a wolf-child, with a couple of nonchalant hawkers loitering in the background . . . None was Man-hon but, to his mother, they could have been; the message they send us is that if these little wrecks can bob along amid the tide of

[40] SCMP, 25 September 2002. [41] *SCMP*, 3 December 2000.
[42] *SCMP*, 8 March 2002.

> Guangdong humanity, perhaps he can too . . . At Shawan we saw this: a poor lad, sitting on the ground inside the PSB compound, occasionally picking his teeth, his face blackly spotted with filth and some skin disease, unable to speak. When PSB officers asked him if he was Yu Man-hon, he had nodded; but if they had asked him if he was Marilyn Monroe he would surely have agreed in the same, uncomprehending way. Charles Dickens could have written about that lost child: he looked like a nineteenth-century waif who had washed up in a concrete yard, in a concrete town, clutching several pieces of coconut and surrounded by a small crowd who stared at him as if he were a wild beast. He wasn't Man-hon, of course, but he must, once, have been someone's son: an unknown tragedy amid all the other desolate tales that have become part of this bigger story.[43]

The Yus also received hundreds of hoax calls and ransom demands from people who claimed to have kidnapped their son.[44] One demanded 50,000 yuan and asked Mrs Yu if she had ever heard of organ transplants and whether it had ever occurred to her that this fate might befall her son.[45] Another wrote that he did not want to harm Man-hon, that it was her enemies who were doing this to her, and if she wanted her son to come home she must send 500, 000 yuan.[46] Another said that if Mrs Yu wished to see her son alive again, she must send him one million yuan. After a fresh round of 'sightings' in 2002, Mrs Yu asked, 'I have faced such hoaxes many times over the past year. How long do I have to endure such torture? Such behaviour for cheating money was just so heartless – and it is just for a few thousand dollars'.[47] One caller claimed that Man-hon had been caught by Shenzhen police officers under a footbridge at Dongmen two days after his disappearance, detained at a police station for two days, starved, interrogated and beaten before he died in police custody and his body cremated.[48] A newspaper reported that Man-hon had, 'hung around the railway station for a few days, where someone saw him being beaten with a broom while he begged at a noodle shop. Then the reliable sightings ended, and the crank calls – cruel, greedy, unforgivable, prompted by . . . a reward of HK$1 million – began'.[49]

Such stories fed into Hongkongers' suspicions that the mainland was populated by indifferent officials, greedy hoaxers and predatory

43 *SCMP*, 16 April 2002.
44 *SCMP*, 14 May 2001.
45 *SCMP*, 4 March 2001.
46 *SCMP*, 4 March 2001.
47 *SCMP*, 17 May 2002.
48 *SCMP*, 5 March 2001.
49 *SCMP*, 17 December 2000.

criminals. In Shenzhen, street beggars were said to threaten visiting Hongkongers:

> Beggars in Shenzhen can be found in many places, such as places near the Lo Wu train station, outside big discos and nightclubs or near the border. Almost all Hong Kong people who have been to Shenzhen have experienced the nuisance caused by the beggars . . . some people pretend to be beggars and wander on the street for the purpose of collecting intelligence for the crime syndicates. Once they have chosen a 'target', they would snatch or rob their property . . . All these activities severely endanger the life and property of the Hong Kong people.[50]

In September 2000, three weeks after Man-hon disappeared, the Hong Kong press had carried a series of articles on this phenomenon, highlighting 'the extent of the problem on Hong Kong's doorstep', and estimating that there were at least 200,000 street children (*liu lang er tong*) in China, half of whom were orphans. Others were runaways and/or the indigent children of migrant workers who flocked to Shenzhen in search of work.[51] The children were said to gather at points of transit, such as the railway station and the border checkpoints, begging or scavenging for food left by tourists, accosting strangers crossing the footbridge from Hong Kong to China, asking for money and sometimes acting in an aggressive fashion.[52] Mainland criminal syndicates used vulnerable children such as Man-hon, with physical or mental incapacities, as part of a begging ring:

> These criminals also kidnap children from different places in [m]ainland China, then beat them up so as to prevent them from resisting. The children are organised into begging syndicates. In each begging syndicate, there are 20–30 children . . . [S]ome child beggars are brought to Guangdong to beg by their parents because the amount of money that child beggar can get in Guangdong in one year is the equivalent of 10 year's income for the family in their hometown. These beggars . . . are still required to pay 'protection fees' in order to beg in a 'territory' controlled by the crime syndicate concerned. The begging syndicates . . . each have their own territory . . . [T]he police never deal with the problem seriously . . . [they] just tell the beggars to go away . . . they do not sincerely try to help Hong Kong people.[53]

[50] *The Sun*, 10 October 2000. [51] L. Yeung, *SCMP*, 17 September 2000.
[52] Yeung, *SCMP*, 17 September 2000. [53] *Xin Bao*, 3 September 2000.

Street children rounded up by the PSB typically ended up in detention centres, awaiting repatriation to their home town. These centres were 'little more than holding pens for all those whose presence on the streets on the city is deemed unseemly or inconvenient.'[54] Those released without being sent home typically ended up back on the streets, making a living by selling flowers, opening taxi doors, begging or scavenging from litter bins. Some slept on the streets, 'a dangerous existence in a city where fear of being the victim of violent crime causes many residents to think twice before venturing out at night'.[55] Few in Hong Kong, reading such accounts, had much doubt about the fate of children like Yu Man-hon.

The roll call of the lost and missing grew. Seven years after Man-hon's disappearance, another autistic child, Tai Chi-kwan, aged seven, was spotted by three Hong Kong visitors as she wandered around a shopping centre in Shenzhen (Glory Plaza) more than twenty hours after she disappeared from Hong Kong.[56] The press reminded the public of Yu Man-hon, who had 'slipped across the border undetected . . . [and had] never been found since.'[57]

THE SOCIOPOLITICAL CONTEXT

The Yus were grassroots Hongkongers. Their difficulty in looking after Man-hon was typical of many poor families caring for the disabled or elderly. In a city dominated by a discourse of 'bootstrap capitalists' and laissez-faire, self-reliance is valorised and state support remains minimal. Mrs Yu herself suffered from muscular dystrophy after contracting polio when she was three. Caring for Man-hon tested her endurance – diagnosed as autistic when he was two years old, he was unable to speak, sometimes overactive, strong and sometimes violent; he also enjoyed running away, seeing it as a game of 'chase'.[58] She did her best in her circumstances. It was, she said, 'like a war every time I take him out. I have to repeatedly tell him not to run away and to stick close to me. But sometimes he won't listen and we end up having a tug-of-war in the street. I used to be on my knees on a busy road begging my son not to run away as I could not catch him up'.[59] She tried to discipline Man-hon with rules and punishments: 'When he ran away, I would

54 *SCMP*, 17 September 2000. 55 *SCMP*, 17 September 2000.
56 *Hong Kong Standard*, 30 May 2007. 57 *Hong Kong Standard*, 31 May 2007.
58 *SCMP*, 31 August 2000. 59 *SCMP*, 31 August 2000.

scold him loudly and when he didn't go to the toilet properly, I would make him clean up . . . Sometimes I wanted to beat him, but I simply couldn't. When I got angry and spoke loudly, he would come close to me and kiss me'.[60] To keep Man-hon safe, she routinely locked the doors to their twentieth-floor flat, but 'Man-hon was always trying to escape'. A key hangs on a long ribbon near the kitchen. When Man-hon and his mother came home from school every day, she locked the front door immediately and hung the key round her neck. She made sure the windows were fastened. She had a nightmare that Man-hon would run away and she would never find him:

> he went missing for several days in 1998. He came home from school as usual with his mother, and as she put down her bag and reached for the key he slipped out and ran. That night, he was found hiding in a private housing estate in Ma On Shan; the residents thought he was an illegal immigrant and he was taken to the . . . hospital, but it was a week before the police got round to telling his mother where he was . . . At the beginning of the summer Man-hon bolted in Lok Fu MTR station. The police found him, hours later, sitting in MacDonald's in Diamond Hill. When he ran away from Yau Ma Tei station on . . . August 24th . . . the first clue Yu had that he might be on the [m]ainland came when a friend told her she'd glimpsed him on the Chinese side of the border the following day.[61]

Facing public criticism over the handling of Man-hon's disappearance, in October 2000 the administration took the unprecedented step of publishing two internal reports by the police and the Immigration Department. The LEGCO Security Panel argued that publication of the two reports was in the interests of transparency and public accountability, both notably lacking in the post-1997 regime. Less committed to welfare colonialism than the British had been, it demonstrated 'a keen appreciation for the models of patrician leadership exercised in Hong Kong during the sixties', appointing senior figures to positions of power, shrinking the franchise and adopting a highly-centralised, top-down executive-led approach to governance. The gap between rich and poor had also widened; unemployment had risen. The Tung regime was seen as adopting policies of direct benefit to Hong Kong's elite rather than the grassroots. Demonstrations grew. The 1 July 2003 march created 'the worst governance crisis to date . . . [and] a widening

[60] *SCMP*, 31 August 2000. [61] *SCMP*, 17 December 2000.

[of] the political gap between Hong Kong's government and citizenry'.[62] Opinion polls showed that Tung enjoyed lower popularity than the last British Governor. His administration was even 'more colonial', elitist, more closed, more remote and less democratic than the British,[63] even more 'skewed in favour of the 'business' sectors'.[64]

At the time Yu Man-hon went missing, an air of deep pessimism and anxiety about Hong Kong's future prevailed. The promise of Hong Kong people ruling Hong Kong sounded hollow; a series of administrative fiascos deepened the public's lack of confidence in the government. Apart from the Avian flu and SARS crises, poor handling of the Asian Financial Crisis and the humiliation surrounding the new airport's opening, the government provoked a deep constitutional crisis by inviting the NPCSC to intervene in a decision by the CFA. It was at this moment that Yu Man-hon disappeared. At the time, rumours were rife of Hong Kong people being robbed and/or drugged in the toilets at the Lo Wu border crossing and their kidneys being removed for sale on the mainland. In 2003, a story appeared of the four-year-old son of a Hong Kong hawker being kidnapped at Lo Wu, taken to Shenzhen and held for ransom.[65] The boy:

> went to the toilets of the third floor of the Wanjia Supermarket. His uncle waited outside but did not see him come out ... 'We waited and searched everywhere in the supermarket until past midnight, but did not find him,' Ms Ma [his mother] said ... The family says the Shenzhen police and the supermarket were slow to help. The supermarket allegedly declined to let family members see the [CCTV] tape until last night, while the local police did not take any action until [the next day] ... The boy is a Hong Kong permanent resident although he stays with his mother and goes to school in Shenzhen. His father, a fruit seller in Hong Kong, rushed back from Hong Kong and offered 10,000 yuan ... to anybody who helps find his son. The family distributed hundreds of pamphlets bearing the boy's photograph to passers-by

[62] A. B. L. Cheung and P. C. Wong, 'Who advised the Hong Kong government?: the politics of absorption before and after 1997', *Asian Survey*, 44, no. 6 (November-December 2004), pp. 874–94.

[63] See S. Vickers, 'More colonial again?: the post-1997 culture of Hong Kong's governing elite', *Journal of Public Administration* (2000). See also L. F. Goodstadt, 'China and the selection of Hong Kong's post-colonial elite', *China Quarterly*, 163 (September 2000), pp. 721–41.

[64] Cheung and Wong, 'Who advised', p. 882.

[65] *Hong Kong Economic Times*, 31 May 2002.

> in Shenzhen . . . The case has revived memories of missing Hong Kong autistic boy Yu Man-hon.[66]

SEEKING HELP FROM 'UNCLE TUNG'

The post-1997 Tung administration was characterised by, 'a reinforced paternalism . . . Uncle Tung's patronising style and his top-down, executive-led government echoed an older colonial era, but it suited the new sovereign very nicely'.[67] It was a government extolling Confucian values – when Man-hon disappeared, a 'Confucian values' campaign was underway, emphasising the conservative aspects of Chinese culture and actively promoting Putonghua, the language of the 'Motherland'. This Confucian paternalism meant that 'Uncle Tung' himself came to be seen as the ultimate locus of power. In the manner of subjects petitioning their imperial Emperor, it was to Tung himself that Mrs Yu now turned for justice. The Yus argued that the government's failure to provide support quickly had harmed their chances of finding Man-hon. As one reporter put it, 'All that these parents needed was a little help from people who are supposed to be leaders and organisers'.[68] Others demanded that someone be held accountable:

> It would be reasonable to expect that after such an incident a concerted effort would have been made to bring those responsible to account and to take clear, precise and transparent measures to ensure that such a travesty would never happen again . . . [P]erhaps the Government could tell us who shall be held accountable over the Yu Man-hon tragedy and what specific measures the Hong Kong Government . . . has taken to ensure such an incident will never happen again.[69]

Another writer commented that, 'I am sure that if this boy had come from a family belonging to the "elite" of Hong Kong society, the [g]overnment would not be absolving itself of responsibility in this matter'.[70] The Yus were left largely to their own devices, printing and distributing their own missing person's posters, traveling to and from Shenzhen every day, conducting the search and footing the bill. They juggled their jobs with searching the streets of Shenzhen, Zhuhai and Dongguan. In 2001, Man hon's father was even considering early

[66] *Hong Kong Economic Times*, 31 May 2002. [67] Vickers, 'More colonial again', 6.
[68] *SCMP*, 10 December 2000. [69] *SCMP*, 30 August 2001.
[70] *SCMP*, 6 September 2001.

retirement and cashing in his pension to fund the costs of finding his son.[71]

A month after Man-hon's disappearance, Mrs Yu wrote to Mr Tung seeking urgent help: 'My poor boy has been lost and left on his own for a month now. We have terrible visions of bad things happening to him every night in the past month ... Please make use of all channels of communication with mainland authorities to come up [with] any possible way to get him back'.[72] Apart from a brief fifteen-minute meeting, Tung did not speak a word to the Yu family until another petition was handed to him in 2001. In between, Mrs Yu unsuccessfully requested several meetings. In April 2001, she asked to meet Tung and Regina Ip Lau Suk-yee, Secretary for Security. Mrs Ip was said to be too busy; Mrs Yu was advised to go home. Mrs Yu then staged a protest sit-in outside government headquarters, whilst Mr Yu returned home to look after their other son, leaving his wife to camp outside the government offices all night before he rejoined her in the morning.[73] Then they both submitted a petition to Chief Executive Tung Chee-hwa:

> after waiting for three hours from 7 A.M. outside the Central Government Offices. Mr Tung talked briefly to the parents and promised to arrange for someone to meet them after taking the petition letter at about 10 am. But the couple had to wait until about noon before Mr. Tung's special assistant, Chan Kin-ping, met them for about 30 minutes ... Yu Wai-ling said she was disappointed with the attitude of the Government. 'The government is very insincere. They're playing around with us. Mr. Tung said he would arrange for someone to meet but later I was asked to leave, and told that Mr. Chan was out ... When I insisted on meeting Mr. Tung they asked me to wait for Mr. Chan, who was in a meeting. When I met him, he just kept recalling what the Government had done to help find Man-hon. But what's the use of talking about this?'[74]

Tung finally held a ten-minute meeting with Mrs Yu and assigned two aides to liaise with mainland authorities in the search for Man-hon. On the anniversary of Man-hon's disappearance in 2001, Mrs Yu wrote a second letter to Tung asking, 'Do you still remember? A year ago today, the Hong Kong Government handcuffed my son with a pair of handcuffs used for criminals and forced him to leave his birthplace – Hong

[71] *Apple Daily*, 21 August 2001. [72] *SCMP*, 22 September 2000.
[73] *SCMP*, 19 April 2001. [74] *SCMP*, 25 August 2001.

Kong . . . The fate of the boy was changed on that day . . . the child has suffered for a year. His parents have also suffered the pain for a year'.[75] Mrs Yu tried to present another petition to Tung in May 2002 but, after a three-hour wait, he failed to appear.[76]

Five years after Man-hon's disappearance, in September 2005, Mrs Yu reiterated that the family had 'very much been on our own all these years' and that the government had done little to help them: 'they keep saying they sympathise with us but in reality they do very little to help us'.[77] Border officials even mocked Mrs Yu when she tried to use the counters for disabled people at Lo Wu in order to cross the border faster on her daily trips to Shenzhen to look for Man-hon.[78] Interviewed in 2007, Mrs Yu said that, 'Just like any other mother' she would 'not give up the search for my child until and unless I see his body'.[79] She visited the mainland 'the minute any possible information on Man-hon is received'.[80] She also continued to write to the CE in the hope that he would press the mainland government to help with the search.[81]

Ho Hei-wah, chair of the Human Rights Commission, called the Man-hon case 'the most serious mistake I have ever heard of . . . The Immigration Department has not treated the boy as a human being. Any person with minimal conscience would not have abandoned a child in Shenzhen, especially if he cannot express himself'.[82] Highlighting the systematic failings of the Tung administration, he argued that, 'It is not just about having Tung Chee-hwa make a call to the Shenzhen mayor. The officials have to work out concrete plans to search for the boy'.[83]

TURNING TO THE LAW

The rule of law served the Yus poorly. The ombudsman's report into the Immigration Department's handling of the case identified systematic errors and recommended disciplinary action. However, in July 2001, the Civil Service Bureau's internal disciplinary inquiry cleared all those involved of negligence and unprofessional conduct. A public outcry followed. James To Kun-sun, acting chairman of the LEGCO

[75] *SCMP*, 24 August 2001. [76] *SCMP*, 22 May 2002.
[77] *SCMP*, 1 August 2005. [78] *SCMP*, 3 December 2000.
[79] *SCMP*, 3 December 2000. [80] *SCMP*, 3 December 2000.
[81] *SCMP*, 3 December 2000. [82] *SCMP*, 30 August 2000.
[83] *SCMP*, 2 September 2000.

Security Panel, expressed shock at the discrepancy between the two sets of findings and pressed the administration to give a public account.[84] Responding to the acquittal of the Immigration Officers, Man-hon's parents said that they did not wish to see them lose their jobs as they too had their own families: 'we just want justice to be seen to be done'. The real responsibility, the Yus felt, lay with the Hong Kong government:

> They said there were many missing children on the [m]ainland. I know many children go missing on the [m]ainland. But it's not us who took Man-hon there. He has gone missing because of a series of mistakes by the SAR and [m]ainland authorities. Had they kept Man-hon at a reception centre instead of releasing him in Shenzhen on his own, he could have been found by now.[85]

Government officials did eventually acknowledge their failures. However, they did so out of court and without admitting liability. The Commissioner for Immigration apologised to Man-hon's parents, admitting that his department had been wrong.[86] A senior immigration officer visited the Shenzhen hotel (Yu Wai-ling's base during her search) to apologise to her. According to the press, he told her that 'Even if we have to say sorry 1,000 or one million times, we'll do it'.[87] However, Mrs. Yu herself said that she still had not received a direct apology from Tung, and she was disappointed with the attitude of officials. Officials insisted that an apology had been made, on a number of occasions, by high-ranking HKSAR officials.

In December 2001, following legal advice, the Yus submitted a High Court writ seeking justice from the police and Immigration Department and/or compensation from the HKSAR.[88] Security Bureau officials contested the family's claim,[89] but in 2003, the parents received an offer of HK$1 million compensation, which they rejected. In 2006, it was reported that they had eventually accepted a HK$2 million out of court offer.[90] However, the Yus still felt let down by the legal system, stating that the HKSAR government had done less than it could – or *should* – have done. Mrs Yu accused the government of 'coldness and apathy . . . the high ranking officials [treating] this disabled child like

[84] *SCMP*, 18 July 2001. [85] *SCMP*, 28 April 2001.
[86] *Ming Pao Daily*, 24 September 2000. [87] *Ming Pao Daily*, 24 September 2000.
[88] *Singpoa Daily*, 31 December 2000. [89] *SCMP*, 4 January 2001.
[90] *Singpoa Daily*, 1 January 2006.

dead grass ... something worthless, ground down into bureaucratic dust and blown away'.[91]

TURNING TO THE MOTHERLAND

Neither the universalistic rights of the law nor the particularistic paternalism of 'Uncle Tung' had delivered the justice sought by the Yus. They turned to the Motherland, where initially, officials proved more helpful. During a meeting with Shenzhen public security officials and two NPC delegates in March 2001, Mrs Yu was told that 'The officials ... had children of their own and would do their best to help find her son'.[92] In January 2001, as the family marked Man-hon's sixteenth birthday, the Shenzhen PSB pledged that it had not given up the search for Man-hon: 'Tens of thousands of officers' from Guangdong Public Security searched for Man-hon.[93] When, in November 2000, twenty-three Civil Aid rescuers volunteered to conduct a search in the hills of Shenzhen, they were welcomed by mainland authorities as long as they remembered 'to abide by mainland laws'.[94] According to the Shenzhen PSB, this kind of response 'had never happened before ... To my understanding, it's the first time that such a large-scale operation has been conducted by the Public Security Bureau to find a missing boy'.[95] Over 7,000 Shenzhen Public Security Bureau staff combed the cities as well as remote rural areas.[96] Radio and television stations in Shenzhen and Guangdong – as well as China National Radio – appealed for the public's help in finding Man-hon. The Acting Assistant Director of HKSAR Immigration, Tang Man-kit, and Mrs Yu appeared together on Shenzhen television. Posters showing a black-and-white photograph of Man-hon were displayed on mainland streets, buses, trains and border control points as well as in Man-hon's favourite eating place, MacDonalds. Shenzhen community organisations were mobilised. Chinese language paging companies disseminated information about Man-hon; Chinese websites carried the boy's details under the banner 'Missing in China'. The KCRC displayed posters about Man-hon at its rail stations; Shenzhen Transport Bureau did likewise. By October 2000, the Shenzhen Public Security Bureau was receiving on average one hundred calls a day about Man-hon. Hospitals and

91 *SCMP*, 4 March 2001. 92 *SCMP*, 7 April 2001. 93 *SCMP*, 8 January 2001.
94 *SCMP*, 23 November 2000. 95 *SCMP*, 5 September 2000.
96 LEGCO Security Panel Report, Appendix B.

'centres for the mentally handicapped' were checked; China National Radio extended its broadcasts about Man-hon to Fujian, Guangxi and areas south of the Jiangxi River.

But the mainland search also ran into obstacles. In October 2000, Man-hon's father, with a group of thirteen relatives and reporters, was detained for four hours by the authorities at a railway station in Jianxi province, en route to Shenzhen; the reporters were ordered to surrender their film.[97] Around the Lunar New Year 2001, Man-hon's uncle was 'almost attacked by a group of people with knives' when he went to check an abandoned housing complex in his search for Man-hon.[98] When Mrs Yu flew to Beijing to seek the help of then Premier Zhu Rongji and Hong Kong delegates to the NPC, the Hong Kong Deputies told her it was 'inappropriate' for her to petition Beijing directly, that the premier could not handle every petition and that whilst officials in Guangdong were already trying their best to search for her son, the chances of finding him were slim. Mrs Yu was 'threatened by the Beijing Liaison Office and Shenzhen security officials that the search for her son might be suspended if she took the case to Beijing'.[99] In Hong Kong, Beijing's response was interpreted as showing that the mainland's liaison office was 'unwilling to help Hong Kong people to communicate with the central Government'.[100]

Having failed in her attempts to reach the Chinese leadership, Mrs Yu sent a petition to the United Nations (UN) and to the then British Prime Minister, Tony Blair, urging them both to pass on her request for help to Beijing.[101] In 2002, she met with the Deputy Director of the Guangdong Public Security Bureau, Zheng Shaodong, in the lobby of a hotel in Dongguan. According to the Hong Kong press, Yu Wai-ling 'knelt sobbing' in front of the deputy director, begging him to 'find me an answer, whether he's alive or dead'. After helping Mrs Yu to a seat, Mr Zheng 'reassured her that Guangdong officials would continue to look for Man-hon. If he's here, we will find him'.[102] However, when questioned about the matter, Guangdong Party Secretary Li Changchun said he 'had no idea who Yu Man-hon was'.[103]

Having found both the Motherland and 'Uncle Tung' less than helpful, the Yus fell back on their own resources and on those of the

[97] *SCMP*, 9 October 2000.
[98] *SCMP*, 4 March 2001.
[99] *SCMP*, 15 March 2001.
[100] *SCMP*, 15 March 2001.
[101] *SCMP*, 24 August 2001.
[102] *SCMP*, 23 May 2002.
[103] *SCMP*, 23 May 2002.

media. On 28 August 2007, the seventh anniversary of Man-hon's disappearance, Mrs Yu, aided by friends, made a YouTube video appealing to ordinary citizens of China and Hong Kong for help.[104] Two years later, in November 2009, she was interviewed on an RTHK programme devoted to her son's disappearance.[105] She remained angry with the government, reiterating that it had not really helped her look for Man-hon. It had not done anything more, she felt, because she was only an ordinary citizen and the life of the underprivileged was cheap; if her son had been the son of Tung Chee hwa, he would have been found. As it was, he was devoid of any value, an autistic, mentally retarded child who could not work and thus made no contribution to society – the government did not esteem such people; it despised them and 'always looked down on disabled kids'. She wanted to know the truth about what had happened; until she did, she could not hold a requiem service for him, could not 'bring his soul back to Hong Kong'.

THE LIMINAL SPACE

When Man-hon disappeared, the border with the mainland was already established in Hong Kong folklore as a place of danger. In 1992, a KCRC advertisement for its through-train from Hong Kong to Guangzhou was removed from television channels after provoking a territory-wide flurry of rumours. Filmed in a wood on the mainland, the advert showed children playing at being a train:

> It was supposed to be a cutesy clip of innocent fun, but it disturbed more than a few souls after it aired. For most of the ad, six children are clearly seen playing the game, but from the 25th second to the 27th second, a seventh child suddenly appears – and the director swears there were only six children on location. A young girl joins the end of the train, her hair loose, and, even more disturbingly, the chubby boy she is holding appears to have blood smeared across his lips. According to legend, the boy died soon after filming ... *feng shui* masters, exorcists, psychics, priests and even psychologists [gave] their own interpretation of the phenomena ... According to various 'expert opinions' the woods had acquired negative energy following the death of a young girl ... [It was] perhaps the most terrifying TV commercial in the history of Hong Kong

[104] Mrsyeunguk 28.08.07 Youtube.com/watch?v=pHsDm2H5Ojc. The original YouTube video has disappeared.
[105] 'Wei Yu Hon mother whispers'. www.youtube.com/watch?v=mxLGesVeppw.

> ... The ad ran for a month in 1993, before being re-shot with no ghostly seventh child. But the campaign was soon pulled.[106]

The territory, Evans argues, became enthralled by the ghost story: 'In trains, buses, schools, offices and homes people swapped information, investigated and discussed the "ghosts" which allegedly had appeared in [the] ... TV commercial'.[107] Rumours varied in their accounts of how many children had died during the making of the commercial in mainland China. One child – the ghost – was said to have caused the death or disappearance of the others. In some versions, four children had died or disappeared; in another version, the third child had a trace of blood at his/her mouth; in another, the children's feet were not touching the ground but hovering over the ground, like ghosts.[108] Evans links the rumours with anxieties about China's angry reaction to the new governor's policy address in October 1992. The period was one of intense political conflict. The rumour flourished, Evans argues, in the context of revelations about secret talks between the British and Chinese over Hong Kong. In the absence of openness, he argues, 'rumours will ... attempt to fill the gaps in our knowledge either in a direct or displaced way'.[109] The children in the advert and the rumours mediated anxieties about the future of Hong Kong that could not easily be expressed through other channels.[110] The appearance of ghost stories at such a time and in such a place was a sign of unfinished business.[111]

The original KCRC video was withdrawn by the company from circulation.[112] A revised version, showing a 'train' of smiling Santa Clauses, was issued in 1993 to counteract the negative publicity it had generated. Unfortunately for the KCRC, the 'Through-Train', itself a leading motif of the Hong Kong retrocession, was derailed. Beijing had promised that those elected to LEGCO before 1997 would continue in

106 A. Cheung, 'Ghost Town', *Hong Kong Magazine*, 11 August 2005. http://hk-magazine.com/city-living/article/ghost-town.

107 G. Evans and M. S. Tam, 'Ghosts and the new governor: the anthropology of a Hong Kong rumour' in Evans and Tam (eds.), *Hong Kong: The Anthropology of a Chinese Metropolis* (Richmond: Curzon, 1997), pp. 267–98.

108 Evans and Tam, 'Ghosts and the new governor'.

109 Evans and Tam, 'Ghosts and the new governor'.

110 Evans and Tam, 'Ghosts and the new governor'.

111 J. T. Zeitlin, *The Phantom Heroine: Ghosts and Gender in Seventeenth Century Chinese Literature* (Honolulu: University of Hawaii Press, 2007).

112 'Hong Kong Train Ad', uploaded by chuamike on YouTube, https://www.youtube.com/watch%3Fv=6100jCPZVA0.

power throughout the transition. This promise evaporated with Patten's 1992 proposals to extend the franchise.

Trains, missing children and the ghosts became imbued with multiple meanings within Hong Kong popular culture. Jess Lowe's 2005 collection of stories, *The Train to Lo Wu*, for example, used the metaphor to explore the themes of dislocation and discontinuity. In 2006, the Hong Kong MTR banned another poster advertising a Japanese horror film from its trains to the Chinese border, because they depicted a ghost child and the movie itself ('*Ghost Train*') dealt with people who were haunted after picking up lost items on the train.[113] As Abbas has noted, the supernatural ghost figure is one of the most popular genres used to represent the complexities of Hong Kong's cultural space.[114] As an entrenched customary symbolic form, Cohen argues, the ghost can be used in radically changed circumstances.[115] Sometimes such symbols can massage away the disruptions of social change and the tensions between the ideal and the actual, the familiar and the unfamiliar, the feared and the resented. Ghost films have a long history in the territory, one of the most famous – *Rouge* – specifically dealing with a dead woman (Fleur) who returns to Earth as a ghost after fifty years to search for her missing lover – Abbas describes her as 'a revenant who has just stepped out of freeze-frame "unchanged for fifty years" . . . and obvious ironic reference to the Sino-British Joint Declaration and the future of Hong Kong, which specifies that it will remain the same for fifty years after 1997'.[116]

The Man-hon incident thus fed into a repository of Hong Kong folklore of lost souls caught between worlds. Children are marginal in that they are not yet adults. In Hong Kong culture, Evans says, they are an 'extremely potent cultural symbol . . . [which] like most powerful symbols . . . articulate simultaneously several discourses. Children as a potent polyvalent symbol are the reason why the KCRC's "charming, innocent" commercial could become such an effective vehicle for Hong Kong society's anxieties'.[117] For Abbas, the ghost represents a 'space of otherness', symbolising fear of the unknown, the world of the dead (*yin*, as opposed to that of the living, *yang*).[118] In an attempt to bring Man-

[113] 'Hong Kong Train Ad'.
[114] Abbas, *Hong Kong: Culture and the Politics of Disappearance*, p. 42.
[115] Cohen, *The Symbolic Construction of Community*, p. 91.
[116] Abbas, *Hong Kong: Culture and the Politics of Disappearance*, pp. 40–1.
[117] Evans, 'Ghosts and the new governor', p. 285.
[118] J. Bosco, 'Young people's ghost stories in Hong Kong,' *Journal of Popular Culture*, 40, no. 5 (2007), pp. 785–807.

hon back from such a place, the Yus consulted a *fung-shui* expert 'who recommended a golden-coloured quilt and pillowcase' be placed on Man-hon's bed, as well as 'a tank filled with bright, endlessly pulsating plastic fish ... There is a *lai-see* packet under the pillow. Nothing is to be moved until Man-hon returns. A huge poster of the Hong Kong cityscape, pictured from the Peak, hangs above the empty bed'.[119] As the Lunar New Year approached, Mrs Yu observed the tradition of buying new clothes for Man-hon as a gift'.[120] On his birthday she did not make him a cake because 'I don't know when he will be back'.[121] She also prayed for her son at Wong Tai Sin temple, 'where she drew a lot that carried an oracle suggesting her son would be found in a few months. A fortune-teller told her the oracle spoke of the blooming of Plum Blossom in Guangdong, suggesting the boy was healthy, would get help and return home by spring'.[122] At least ten psychics claimed knowledge of Man-hon's whereabouts, some demanding thousands – hundreds of thousands, millions – of yuan. Yu and her brother went to the expense of hiring a car 'so that psychics might be driven, uselessly, around Guangdong; such people, having insisted on payment in advance ... they evaporated when Man-hon did not materialise'.[123]

Man-hon has never materialised. In 2005, a United Nations working group on forced and involuntary disappearances specifically asked Hong Kong's Society for Community Organisations to submit a report on the Man-hon case.[124] In January 2007, a UN report on disappearances in China urged the Chinese government to 'elucidate the fate of whereabouts of persons who have allegedly disappeared, including children and mentally challenged individuals'.[125]

Man-hon's story is a reminder to Hongkongers of the Motherland's looming disorderliness that threatens to smother Hong Kong. The border with the mainland is seen as an 'Other-worldly' place of abductions, killings and disappearances. Hong Kong's own transition to Chinese sovereignty occurred at a liminal point, midnight on 30 June during the hours of darkness. Hongkongers became instant 'marginals' whose complete reintegration is not destined to take place until 2047.

[119] *SCMP*, 17 December 2000. [120] *SCMP*, 28 January 2001.
[121] *SCMP*, 4 January 2001. [122] *SCMP*, 14 September 2000.
[123] *SCMP*, 8 March 2002. [124] *SCMP*, 1 August 2005.
[125] United Nations General Assembly Human Rights Council Implementation of General Assembly Resolution 60/251 on 15 March 2006, Report of Working group on Enforced or Involuntary Disappearances A/HRC/4/41.

Until that time, they live in a continuous state of uncertainty. The question they have is whether, like Man-hon, they will fail to reappear. No one knows for sure whether he is dead or alive. He can neither be brought back nor buried. He can only be remembered. Paradoxically, his absence keeps him present in Hong Kong memory. As one local journalist wrote at the time, when Man-hon, 'sprang out of the train carriage at Yau Ma Tei and began his journey into the headlines, [he] thought he was free [but] ahead of him there were handcuffs and unkindness and awful fear'.[126] By stepping over the threshold between Hong Kong and China at such a time, he slipped from the orderly and safe world of Hong Kong into a world reversed. In April 2014 the Hong Kong press reported that Mrs Yu 'still dreams of her lost son almost 14 years after he vanished'. She was 'still angry with the government too'.[127]

[126] *SCMP*, 17 December 2000.

[127] W. Lo, 'Hong Kong mother still looking for autistic son Yu Man-hon last seen 14 years ago', *SCMP*, 1 April 2014.

Child vanishes — [illegible]
see Gorker as dangerous space —
— uncertain
HK elite complacent
authorities no use

6

Patrolling the walls of law

Early on in its reign, the HKSAR government acquired an image as pro-big business and pro-Beijing. Government bodies were accused of riding roughshod over the law and tycoons were seen as the principal beneficiaries of government policies, not everyone was equal before the law. At the other end of the social spectrum, the poor were getting poorer, and the government was accused of treating the 'livelihood issues' of ordinary Hongkongers with indifference. Growing public discontent with this state of affairs fuelled numerous street protests after 1997. Students demonstrated against Secretary for Security Regina Ip; even the elderly 'learned to take to the street'.[1] There were over 2,000 public meetings and processions each year, earning Hong Kong the nickname 'city of protests'. Journalists, human rights activists, lawyers and pro-democracy politicians were all, Ma Ngok says, allied in defence of civil liberties, press freedom and the rule of law.[2] The courts themselves remained an important channel for discontent – judicial review was increasingly used to call government to account.[3]

The explosion of demonstrations by social activists translated into legal controversies on questions about the exercise of police powers, the

[1] A. Lee, 'Subversion law stirs student activism', *SCMP*, 30 October 2002.
[2] Ma Ngok, *Political Development in Hong Kong: State, Political Society and Civil Society* (Hong Kong: Hong Kong University Press, 2007), p. 207.
[3] Ngok, *Political Development in Hong Kong*.

restriction of civil liberties and the powers of the CFA.[4] Along with the Societies Ordinance, the pre-1997 administration had liberalised the Public Order Ordinance to reduce government control over protests and societies. After 1997, these reformist measures were reversed. In 1998, the Provisional LEGCO also exempted state organisations from HKSAR law, contradicting the Basic Law's provision that all Chinese government organisations in the HKSAR 'shall abide by the laws of the region'. This was criticised by the Hong Kong Bar Association as raising fundamental constitutional issues.[5] The then Secretary for Justice, Elsie Leung, justified the measure as a mere transfer of the power of state immunity, previously enjoyed by the Crown, to the new state authorities. However, there was considerable uncertainty as to the definition of a state organ since the PRC took a wider view of this than the British administration.

Yash Ghai observed that this privilege was based on the mistaken assumption that Hong Kong is a colony of China, whereas 'the new Hong Kong is supposed to have considerable autonomy from the Chinese government'.[6] Nevertheless, when the occasion arose, a 'state organ', the *Xinhua* news agency, was never prosecuted for breaching the law, in this instance the Personal Data (Privacy) Ordinance. This was despite the complainant (Emily Lau) producing clear evidence that it had done so. *Xinhua* was required by the ordinance to respond to Lau's request for information within forty days. It failed to do so. No action was taken against it. State organs, however, were not the only parties to be exempted from the rule of law.

THE SALLY AW CASE

The belief that no one is above the law is central to the rule of law. Before 1997, there were fears that it would be eroded by the intrusion of mainland-style patronage, cronyism and corruption. In January 1999, these fears appeared to be borne out in the Sally Aw case. Two executives of the *Hong Kong Standard* were imprisoned for their part in a fraud involving the falsification of newspaper circulation figures. Following an ICAC raid on the newspaper's premises, three people

4 See *HKSAR* v. *Ng Kung Siu*, (1999) 2 HKCFAR 442; *Yeung May Wan and Others* v. *HKSAR*, (2005) 8 HKCFAR 137; *Chan Hau Man Christina* v. *Commissioner of Police* (2009) 4HKLRD 797.

5 Vines, *China's New Colony*, pp. 237–8.

6 Vines, *China's New Colony*.

were initially charged, including the proprietor and chairwoman of the *Sing Tao* Publishing Group, Sally Aw. She was a member of the Chinese People's Consultative Conference and a friend of the Tung family.[7] Although she was originally charged, she was not prosecuted. A subsequent report as to what Aw said during her questioning by the ICAC indicated that she knew what was happening at the newspaper but blamed her co-conspirators for the fraud.[8] However, Aw was never prosecuted and walked free. Elsie Leung defended the decision not to prosecute on the grounds that it was not in the public interest. At the time, the *Sing Tao* group was facing financial difficulties and was negotiating restructuring with banks. If Sally Aw had been prosecuted, Leung said it would have been a serious obstacle for restructuring. If the group should collapse, its newspapers would be compelled to cease operations. Apart from losing employment, the failure of a well-established important media group at that time could 'send a very bad message to the international community'.[9] This statement was widely understood to imply that a rich employer would not be prosecuted for certain crimes, whereas a poor employee would.

A LEGCO 'No confidence' vote in Leung was subsequently tabled by Margaret Ng. During the debate, Anson Chan, for the government, argued, 'I can assure members that we have acted out of principle, not expediency; that we have acted not to undermine the rule of law but to observe it; that we have acted not to challenge the independence of the judiciary but out of respect for it. We know precisely what is the rule of law'.[10] This did not explain, however, why Sally Aw 'is free at her home ... while the manager to whom she gave the green light is in jail'.[11] Ng's motion stood a good chance of success until government officials – 'knowing the impact a defeat would have' – put pressure on the businessmen who 'pulled the strings' of the functional constituencies represented by the Liberal Party.[12] The Liberal Party abstained, allowing the vote of 'no confidence' to be narrowly defeated by 29 votes to 21. Fenby remarked that 'the Chief Executive hails the result as a vote of confidence in the integrity of the legal system. One pro-China legislator says that Ng, not Leung, threatens the rule of law ... [T]here is also an intriguing suggestion in a remark by a legislator to a reporter

[7] Gittings, 'Changing expectations'.
[8] Fenby, *Dealing with the Dragon*, pp. 72–3.
[9] Fenby, *Dealing with the Dragon*, pp. 84–5.
[10] Fenby, *Dealing with the Dragon*, pp. 106–7.
[11] Fenby, *Dealing with the Dragon*.
[12] Fenby, *Dealing with the Dragon*.

some time later. "Only once", he says, "was I lobbied by Chinese officials: not to vote for the motion of no confidence on Else Leung"'.[13]

RULE-BREAKING

Disregard for the principle of equality before the law made post-1997 Hongkongers vigilant for further signs of official impropriety and declining standards in public life. These included behaviour which, whilst not illegal, was perceived to infringe communal norms, such as the equal application of rules, regulations and laws. Any sign of *guanxi*, lack of probity or prudence in public life, was regarded as a sign of mainlandisation. In 2003, for example, the former Financial Secretary, Antony Leung, was forced to resign after it was discovered that he had purchased a Lexus car shortly before he himself had raised the tax on luxury cars in the annual budget. The press also drew attention to the fact that Tung Chee-hwa's wife had requested the 'A1' seat on a flight, simply because of her husband's position. This kind of behaviour marked a shift away from the merit-based society extolled pre-1997, to one in which favours were done for those with connections to the rich and powerful. The fact that it caused a scandal, however, indicated that more generally society adhered to the principles of rule-following and equity.

As the decade wore on, the infractions became more common. Donald Tsang, who succeeded Tung as CE in 2005, was severely criticised for his excessive use of public funds on hotels, cars and overseas trips. Known as a 'son of Hong Kong' for his 'rags to riches' background, Tsang's popularity sank following revelations of his lavish expenditures. Tsang was also alleged to have accepted favours from tycoon friends, such as flights in their private jets, trips on their yachts and the lease of a luxury Shenzhen penthouse at a knock-down rent. Tsang's successor, Leung Chun-ying, was also found wanting. Leung was already unpopular: thousands had protested at his 'small circle' election. He was seen as 'Beijing's man', but his integrity was questioned when he was found to have constructed several illegal structures at his house on the Peak. Leung initially denied all knowledge of the structures and allegedly lied about them before hastily arranging their removal. The allegations led to public demands for his

[13] Fenby, *Dealing with the Dragon*.

resignation because Leung himself had attacked the integrity of his rival in the race for CE, Henry Tang, for constructing an illegal basement at his house in Kowloon Tong. This lost Tang the election and struck many as hypocritical. Pan-democrats launched a legal challenge to Leung's election, accusing him of making false statements during the campaign.

The saga dragged on. In late 2012, there were calls for a vote of 'no confidence' in the CE. Leung's administration had a particularly poor track record of probity. Mak Chai-kwong, whom Leung had appointed as secretary for development, was accused of having abused his rental allowance by cross-leasing his apartment, a practice every civil servant knows is forbidden. Arrested by the ICAC, he was forced to resign. In July 2012, this scandal was superseded by the highest-level corruption cases in Hong Kong's history, with charges levelled against the former chief secretary in the Tsang administration, Rafael Hui.[14] It was followed by allegations that the former head of the ICAC, Timothy Tong, had brought the organisation into disrepute by his 'unduly close' relationship with mainland officials. A LEGCO report into his stewardship of the ICAC concluded that '[t]he ways he handled such matters are not commensurate with the values of probity and integrity advocated by the ICAC and fall short of public expectations of the commissioner of the ICAC, and have damaged the image of the ICAC, thus tarnishing its reputation'.[15] Leung's closeness to mainland political influence had long been an issue. He intended to appoint Rimsky Yuen as his justice secretary when Yuen still held a position on the Guangdong's Provincial People's Political Consultative Conference, raising questions about his impartiality. Yuen replaced Wong Yan-leung, the Tsang government's most popular minister, hailed as having upheld the independence of the Legal Department and the rule of law. Yuen's close association with the mainland, on the other hand, fuelled speculation about a conflict of interests.

[14] The cases involved Sun Hung-Kai Properties co-chairmen, Thomas Kwok Ping-kwong and Raymond Kwok Ping-luen, former Chief Secretary Rafael Hui Si-yan and two others.

[15] Select Committee to Inquire into Matters Relating to Mr Timothy Tong's Duty Visits, Entertainment, and Bestowing and Receipt of Gifts during his Tenure as Commissioner of the Independent Commission against Corruption, Hong Kong. Legislative Council of the HKSAR, 9 July 2014.

The scandals that beset successive post-1997 administrations indicated that the 'fair', 'open' and 'clean' society described by Patten was withering from within. Leung's government was weak, an administration whose lack of credibility called into question its ability to rule.[16] As in the days of the Tung regime, top government officials were 'mocked and ridiculed'.[17] Officials were nicknamed 'eunuchs', a reference to sycophants in Imperial China.[18] Public concern grew about increased interference from Beijing in internal matters.[19] An opinion poll on the eve of the fifteenth anniversary of the handover revealed that people's mistrust of the mainland government stood at 37 per cent, the highest since 1997.[20] Falling standards in public life, as well as inefficiency and imprudence in government, fuelled the sense that 'mainland ways' had indeed penetrated the walls of law to infect Hong Kong's way of life. This sentiment was fuelled by a series of 'law wars' in the years following 1997.

THE PUBLIC ORDER ORDINANCE

The Provisional LEGCO reversed amendments to the Public Order Ordinance made by the Patten administration to remove police powers to curtail gatherings. It restored these powers, giving the authorities greater legal controls over public gatherings.[21] Marches of more than thirty people or demonstrations of more than fifty people required a seven-day advance notification to the commissioner of police, as well as a notice of no objection from the police.[22] The police were empowered to ban demonstrations on the basis of national security, public safety and public order. These amendments subjected citizens to detailed restrictions and surveillance, requiring official registration of organising bodies.[23] Heavy criminal penalties were attached to

[16] T. Chong, C. Lee and T. Cheung, 'Credibility crisis engulfs Leung', *SCMP*, 13 July 2012.
[17] A. Lo, 'A political system heading for collapse', *SCMP*, 28 September 2012.
[18] Wee Kek Koon, 'Reflections; unnatural leaders', *SCMP*, 7 August 2011.
[19] T. Cheung, 'Democratic future for HK "in doubt"', *SCMP*, 25 June 2012.
[20] A. Cheng, 'Action needed to quell rising Hong Kong-mainland tension', *SCMP*, 23 June 2012.
[21] Cheng, 'Action needed to quell'.
[22] A. S. Ku, 'Negotiating the space of civil autonomy in Hong Kong: power, discourses and dramaturgical representations', *The China Quarterly*, 179 (September 2004), pp. 647–64.
[23] Ku, 'Negotiating the space of civil autonomy'.

non-compliance – a demonstration could, for example, be criminalised for failure to give enough notice, which was subject to a penalty of up to five years imprisonment.

Ku argues that, post-1997, the police increasingly drew on a 'law and order' discourse to justify a more forceful approach to demonstrations.[24] Complaints arose of hard-line police tactics. In 1998, for example, defendants convicted of obstruction and assaulting the police during a demonstration claimed they had been treated with excessive violence by the police.[25] Similar charges were levelled during the 2005 World Trade Organisation meeting in Hong Kong. Civil society activists were publicly demonised in an attempt to gain public backing for a crack-down on demonstrations during the WTO meeting. Security drills and anti-riot preparations were stepped up, building on an already formidable internal security capability. For the business elite, rule of law meant law and order, a line of thinking that is shared by Beijing. For this reason, though the courts may occasionally act as a restraint on state power, the Public Order Ordinance remains firmly wedded to an ideology of control.

Ku documents civil activists' struggles over the Public Order Ordinance in 2000 and argues that these were key moments in the working out of post-1997 state-individual relations.[26] An anti-Public Order Ordinance campaign of the time eventually died down, but controversy continued to dog public order policing. Subsequently, she argues, the public became less susceptible to the authorities' argument that hard-line tactics were in fact necessary for the preservation of law and order. As a consequence, the government has had to vie with activists for public credibility and legitimacy.

The case of *Leung Kwok-hung and Others* brought the issue of how far the police could restrict the constitutional right to demonstrate before the CFA.[27] The accused were convicted of holding an unauthorised public procession in February 2002 at Chater Gardens. They had deliberately failed to comply with the requirement under the Public Order Ordinance to give notification of the assembly to the commissioner of police because, they argued, the right to

[24] Ku, 'Negotiating the space of civil autonomy'.
[25] 'Demonstrators convicted for obstructing police', *Hong Kong Voice of Democracy*, 19 May 1998.
[26] Ku, 'Negotiating the space of civil autonomy', p. 652.
[27] *Leung Kwok-hung and Others* v. *HKSAR* (2005) 8 HKCFAR 229, CFA.

peaceful assembly was provided by Article 27 of the Basic Law and Article 17 of the Bill of Rights. The commissioner of police, therefore, should not have the power to prohibit a march or impose restrictions on it. They attacked the manner in which the police power was exercised and the fact that the commissioner could restrict protests if he reasonably considered it 'necessary in the interests of national security or public safety, public order (*ordre public*) or for the protection of the rights and freedoms of others'.[28] The government argued that the right to freedom of assembly was not an absolute right and could be restricted. However, the CFA held that permissible restrictions must be provided by law, be necessary and be proportionate.

The majority of the judges in the CFA agreed that 'the discretion to restrict the right to peaceful assembly for the purpose of "*ordre public*"' failed to satisfy the constitutional requirement for a restriction to be prescribed by law '"because [it] "plainly does not give an adequate indication of the scope of that discretion"'.[29] Justice Bokhary argued that 'where a scheme contains powers to impose conditions in respect of a public meeting or procession, the scheme should specify the sort of conditions that can be imposed rather than leaving them at large. The wider the concepts in the service of which conditions may be imposed, the more clearly and carefully must the scheme circumscribe the conditions that may be imposed'.[30]

As a consequence of the case, '*ordre public*' was severed and references to it excised from the texts of the Public Order Ordinance and the Societies Ordinance. This represented a partial victory for the defendants, their actions in deliberately flouting the law having forced the courts and the public at large to re-consider Hong Kong's public order legislation. In doing so, they wrought from the CFA a statement that freedom of speech and freedom of assembly were fundamental rights which, along with tolerance, the ability to voice criticisms and seek redress, were of cardinal importance to the stability and progress of society.

28 P. Y. Lo, *The Judicial Construction of Hong Kong's Basic Law: Courts, Politics and Society after 1997* (Hong Kong: Hong Kong University Press, 2014), pp.120–2.

29 *Leung Kwok-hung and Others* v. *HKSAR*. See Lo, *Judicial Construction of Hong Kong's Basic Law*, pp. 122–4.

30 *Leung Kwok-hung and Others* v. *HKSAR*.

The notification system remained in place, however, and protesters still require prior written notification to the commissioner of police one week before any intended procession.[31] It must include details of the organisers, the meeting's purpose and subject matter, the date, precise route, time of commencement, duration, location and number of people expected. In practice, this is a system which requires the permission of the commissioner – only if he/she does not object is the assembly lawful. In 2012, protesters again complained that the ordinance restricted their rights, and in 2013, the CFA overturned public order convictions against two other social activists. In 2014, the courts were again required to consider the difference between someone participating in an unauthorised assembly and organising it. The battle between civil society and the state thus remains unresolved and ongoing.

To this litany of legal issues from the start of the handover there was added the fact that 'built into the very fabric of the new SAR legal system is its subservience to the judicial and law-making process on the Chinese mainland'.[32] Despite promises that the legal system would remain unaltered, the new regime would proceed to undermine the rule of law, 'the one legacy of British colonial rule which practically everyone agrees was a major contribution to the success of Hong Kong'.[33] It did this most visibly in 1999, when the Court of Final Appeal decided against the government in a test case regarding the right of abode in the HKSAR, the first interpretation of the Basic Law by the NPCSC.[34]

[31] The provision applies to assemblies of fifty or more persons, or thirty or more if there is to be a public procession on a highway or thoroughfare.

[32] Vines, *China's New Colony*, p. 239.

[33] Vines, *China's New Colony*, p. vii.

[34] Hong Kong Transition Project, 'Parties, Policies and Political reform in Hong Kong', report for the National Democratic Institute for International Affairs, May 2006.

7

The law wars: wayward children and the right of abode

Writing in 2014, a Hong Kong lawyer remarked that the CFA's 1999 ruling in the *Ng Ka-ling* case was still reverberating in Hong Kong and Beijing.[1] *Ng Ka-ling* v. *Director of Immigration*[2] provoked 'the worst constitutional crisis' in the early years of the HKSAR.[3] The state's reaction and the NPCSC's subsequent intervention exemplified what Jacob calls the 'crisis by mistake' scenario.[4] It was a case involving children, doubly-liminal for their being not-quite-adult and not-quite Hongkongers. It was their desire for a resolution of their status that provided the CFA with the opportunity to deliver 'the most extensive exposition … on the high degree of autonomy of the HKSAR'; it also provided an opportunity for the central authorities to put the CFA in its place.[5] The court survived, but this – and subsequent interventions by the NPCSC – damaged the belief that the rule of law was safe from destabilisation by Beijing. The case also signalled the emergence of a

[1] C. Buddle, '15 years on, landmark court ruling on right of abode still reverberates', *SCMP*, 29 January 2014.

[2] See *Ng Ka Ling and The Director of Immigration* (FACV No. 14 of 1998); [1999] 1 HKLRD 315; *Ng Ka Ling* v. *Director of Immigration* (No. 2) [1999] 1 HKLRD 577; *Tsui Kuen Nang and The Director of Immigration* (FACV No. 15 of 1998); *The Director of Immigration and Cheung Lai Wah* (FACV No. 16, 1998) (Jan. 29, 1999); *Chan Kam Nga* v. *Director of Immigration* [1999] 1HKLRD 304. See also *Lau Kong Yung* v. *Director of Immigration* 3 HKLRD 778.

[3] D. Gittings, 'Changing expectations'.

[4] Hong Kong Transition Project, 'Parties, policies and political reform'.

[5] Lo, *Judicial Construction of Hong Kong's Basic Law*, pp. 28–9.

new bloc in the Hong Kong legal system: mainland legal experts, often academics in Beijing, with a direct channel to the central authorities. Their opinions on the constitutional position of the HKSAR were to become increasingly influential in the coming years, ranged against Hong Kong's lawyers, judges and academics of the common law world.

At issue in the case was the right of abode for 2,000 children born on the mainland to parents who were Hong Kong residents. The government wished to deport them back to the mainland. According to the Basic Law, however, Hong Kong residents of Chinese descent qualified for right of abode provided that at the time of birth at least one parent was a Chinese citizen with right of abode status in Hong Kong.[6] The legal challenge arose following new ordinances passed by the Provisional LEGCO in 1997 restricting existing procedures for proving eligibility. The government claimed that, should the children be granted right of abode, another 1.6 million similarly placed people on the mainland would demand the right of abode in the HKSAR, putting its infrastructure and resources under intolerable pressure. A great deal of controversy surrounded the validity of these figures.[7]

The CFA eventually ruled in favour of the children seeking right of abode, at which point the government effectively refused to accept the verdict and invited the NPCSC to intervene to provide an interpretation of the Basic Law. In doing so, it was accused of 'opening the front gate to invite Beijing's direct judicial interference in order to salve the SAR's executive arm from certain defeat on purely legal grounds in vital matters of great consequence'.[8]

In pre-1997 negotiations, it was understood that the question of who possessed the right of abode in Hong Kong was likely to prove problematic. In 1996, the Hong Kong government had estimated that between 60,000 and 100,000 children would be eligible to come to Hong Kong after 1997; to this, Guangdong authorities added 'hundreds of thousands' of spouses entitled to family reunion under the Basic Law.[9] Guangdong officials estimated that there were about 130,000 children in that province alone who had the right to migrate to Hong Kong, being the offspring of Hong Kong permanent residents.[10] In

[6] Carroll, 'Ten years later', pp. 14–15. [7] Carroll, 'Ten years later'.

[8] M. K. Chan, 'The Hong Kong SAR in flux' in M. K. Chan and A. Y. So, *Crisis and Transformation in China's Hong Kong* (New York: M.E. Sharpe, 2002), p. 7.

[9] C. K. Lau, 'Warm welcome for wealth of new arrivals', *SCMP*, 7 September 1996.

[10] Lau, 'Warm welcome'.

1994 and 1995, the Hong Kong authorities themselves increased the quota of migrants allowed into Hong Kong from the mainland to 54,700 per year, in an attempt to avoid a sudden influx by 'right of abode' claimants after 1997. However, rumours abounded on the mainland that an amnesty would follow for those who had entered Hong Kong illegally.

Government propaganda presented this as a tide of mainlanders waiting to rush the border at midnight on 30 June, overrunning the HKSAR. Official projections issued in September 1996 estimated that the territory's population would grow from 6.3 million to 7.3 million in 2006.[11] Less than a year later, in July 1997, the government forecast a rise of 30 per cent in the next twenty years, from just under 7 million to 8.21 million.[12] These figures encouraged the fear that 'if there were no rules on immigration the territory's well-being would be jeopardized ... "There are thousands like them"'.[13] At least 90,000 mainland-born children of Hong Kong parents were said to be waiting to migrate to Hong Kong.[14] According to one report, just a month before Hong Kong's return to China, 'a surge of illegal Chinese immigrants [was] storming the territory's ramparts'.[15] In total, the projected 'tide of mainlanders' would increase the population by almost 60 per cent within ten years. Another report talked of the 'Huddled Masses' of Chinese illegal immigrants 'escaping from China to Hong Kong' at the rate of 450 per day, 'putting a strain on Hong Kong's social system'.[16] Hong Kong was depicted as under siege. Though in fact crime had fallen, 'rising crime' was blamed on the influx of illegal immigrants from China; children as young as ten were allegedly entering Hong Kong 'numerous times' to commit crime.[17] Allowing migrants freer access would, it seemed, plunge the territory into disorder. There would be competition for housing, hospitals, schools and jobs. In 1999, when the issue came to a head, unemployment already stood at a thirty-five-year high and Hong Kong was in the midst of the Asian Financial Crisis; workers complained that their wages were already being undercut by

[11] Hong Kong Government Territorial Strategy Review, 1996, cited in Lau, 'Warm welcome'.

[12] Lau, 'Warm welcome'.

[13] Editorial, *Hong Kong Standard*, cited in Edward Gargan, 'Illegal Chinese immigrants swamp Hong Kong', *New York Times*, 23 May 1997.

[14] Editorial, *Hong Kong Standard*. [15] Editorial, *Hong Kong Standard*.

[16] 'Huddled Masses: Hong Kong', *The Economist*, 31 August 1996.

[17] 'Cross-border child criminals', *SCMP*, 14 September 1996.

mainlanders prepared to work in poorer conditions for less pay. Ruthless Chinese illegal immigrants were said to be robbing locals in country parks along the border, whilst others committed armed robbery right in the heart of the city. Alarmed by these forecasts and events, the government embarked on a 'zero tolerance' policy towards those attempting to enter the territory illegally. Approximately 1,400 illegal child migrants were returned to China,[18] and as 30 June 1997 approached, 'anti II' operations became constant:

> Hong Kong – In the still midnight air, only the coils of razor wire pointing in the harsh yellow floodlights hinted at the divide between the vast poverty of China and the compact neon glitter of Hong Kong ... Along the fence, in green camouflage fatigues and with a pistol strapped to his waist, the Hong Kong immigration inspector whispered into his radio to his ambush team ahead in the darkness ... The inspector ... explained 'Our job is to catch IIs' ... Far from the border, in the shadow of the gleaming towers of Hong Kong's business district, Ching Hau-ngoh tries to puzzle out how to outwit ... his forces ... Her chances are diminishing. Arrayed against her are Hong Kong's armed police and, in China, more armed police recently added to the border fence. At the land border are the fences topped with razor wire and in the harbour, high-speed patrol boats.[19]

The Ng Ka-ling case took place against this tense background. Article 24 of the Basic Law stated that people of Chinese nationality born outside Hong Kong, as well as those born in Hong Kong or who had resided there for seven years continuously before or after the establishment of the SAR, were entitled to permanent residency in Hong Kong. It had not excluded children born out of wedlock or children born before their parents became permanent residents. In 1996, however, the NPC had decided that children born out of wedlock and those born before their parents obtained permanent residency had no right of abode in the SAR. Though this was a decision made before the handover, mainland lawyers later insisted that it had the status of an 'annex' to the Basic Law which would apply in Hong Kong after 1997. The mainland authorities then revised the rules on the categories of persons allowed to emigrate to Hong Kong.[20] In 1999, however, the CFA declared that the children in the case before it were indeed

[18] 'Cross-border child criminals'. [19] Gargan, *Illegal Chinese Immigrants*.
[20] *Migration News*, 'China's Hong Kong border', June 1997.

entitled to right of abode in Hong Kong, whether they were the illegitimate or legitimate offspring of Hong Kong residents, and whether or not they were born before their parents had obtained the right of abode in Hong Kong. The government claimed that the judgment would 'open the floodgates' to mainland migrants, overwhelming Hong Kong's infrastructure. It continued to broadcast alarmist statistics, arguing that the ruling was enough to 'make any normal person agree that the judges were out of their minds to let those people in'.[21] Its 'Doomsday scenario' was backed by pro-Beijing groups, including mainland legal academics, some of whom had helped to draft the Basic Law. Four of these claimed that the CFA was putting itself above the NPCSC.

Surveys conducted in 1999 and 2000 showed that Hongkongers' anxiety about 'over population' stood at very high levels.[22] As Chow observes, 'it is the denial of secure protection to ... [those] who are reduced to "transients" and "migrants" that enables the pride and respectability of those who possess the right documents of permanent citizenship'.[23] Regarded as backward and inferior by the mainland, in this instance Hongkongers asserted themselves by denying the right of abode to others seen as more backward and powerless than themselves. The government's challenge to the CFA's judgment thus found much support amongst ordinary Hongkongers. The counter-arguments, articulated by liberal lawyers, legal academics and human rights groups, were portrayed as inimical to ordinary people's interests. The children's lawyers countered that, whatever the social situation, the Basic Law gave the children the right of abode.

In the same year that it opposed granting the right of abode to the mainland children, and despite all its warnings about population growth, the government introduced a scheme encouraging mainland professionals to migrate to Hong Kong. Between 2001 and 2003, further programmes were put in place to improve 'the quality of the population'.[24] A speech by Tung Chee-hwa to LEGCO suggested in fact that it was not the number of migrants that was a problem but their

[21] Fenby, *Dealing with the Dragon*, p. 159.

[22] Hong Kong Baptist University, The Hong Kong Transition Project, research report, 'Winter of despair: confidence and legitimacy in crisis in the HKSAR', December 2001. http://hktp.hkbu.edu.hk/Despair/Winter _of_Despair.pdf.

[23] Chow, 'Between colonizers', pp. 151–70.

[24] Chow, 'Between colonizers'.

'quality'.[25] The professionals were welcome as contributors to the economy. By contrast, a group of 350 'overstayers' camped outside the Government's Central Office were lambasted as 'repulsive'.[26] A Chinese University opinion poll revealed that between 60 and 80 per cent of locals regarded mainlanders as 'uneducated, unhygienic welfare scroungers out to take jobs from locals'.[27] Fenby recalls an occasion when, after a lunch with a government official that included a lecture on how Hong Kong people should not feel so superior towards their fellow Chinese, 'my host glanced at a group of men in boxy suits getting out of the lift and murmured: "Mainlanders. You can tell from the way they dress"'.[28]

With a slightly different twist, the discourse of 'pollution' was to reemerge in 2012 when the government, instead of preventing mainlanders from entering Hong Kong, positively favoured their entry in large numbers. In 1999, in opposing the CFA, the government presented the judges as enemies of the people and itself as their protector. In 2012, it was hoisted by its own petard.

In 1999, the public was ambivalent about the rule of law for whilst law promised protection of their rights, in this case it granted rights to people who threatened its way of life. The discourse of pollution and degradation encouraged a swell of xenophobia, supporting a government otherwise lacking in popular legitimacy. At the same time, however, the CFA's judgment was widely heralded as a 'victory for the rule of law', something the public cherished. The CFA's judgment was described as 'almost a perfect demonstration of the rule of law'[29] and 'the best shot in the arm for the rule of law since the handover'.[30] But, since the verdict made Chinese leaders 'see red',[31] the government challenged it.

The judges on the CFA had argued that the CFA had the power 'to invalidate actions of the National People's Congress ... and its

[25] H. C. Leung, 'Politics of incorporation and exclusion' in Ku and Pun, *Remaking citizenship*', pp. 97–114.

[26] Fenby, *Dealing with the Dragon*, pp. 92–3.

[27] Fenby, *Dealing with the Dragon*.

[28] Fenby, *Dealing with the Dragon*.

[29] Y. Ghai, 'Abode verdict a resounding victory for the rule of law', *SCMP*, 31 January 1999.

[30] 'Two systems', *SCMP*, 8 February 1999.

[31] R. Jacob, 'Hong Kong's threatened rule of law', *The Financial Times*, 24 February 1999.

Standing Committee . . . if they breached the Hong Kong Basic Law'.[32] The courts of Hong Kong, it argued, had the right to determine whether an act of the NPC or NPCSC was inconsistent with the Basic Law, and if it was, the courts had the right to declare it invalid. Based on Article 2, interpretation of the Basic Law on issues involving Hong Kong's autonomy was within the province of the CFA. Article 2 of the Basic Law authorised the SAR to exercise a high degree of autonomy and to enjoy independent judicial power, including the power of final adjudication. Critics responded that the Basic Law had not granted sovereignty to the HKSAR and that the CFA had exceeded its authority in attempting to delimit the constitutional supremacy of the NPC in Hong Kong.[33] Senior PRC officials and pro-Beijing lawyers denounced the ruling. A Basic Law Committee member, Dr Wu Wai-yung, criticised the judges for failing to take the 'public interest' into account in their judgment, remarks that prompted leading lawyers and Democrat Martin Lee to accuse him of advocating that courts should decide cases not according to the law but according to 'political consequences'.[34] Mainland legal experts claimed that the CFA's decision amounted 'to an attempt to turn Hong Kong into an independent political entity, that it was "in direct opposition to the interests of Hong Kong residents and has hindered efforts to maintain stability and prosperity"'.[35] They insisted that the ultimate power to interpret the Basic Law on this matter resided with the NPCSC.

In mid-February 1999, Yash Ghai, leading Constitutional Law expert and Professor at the University of Hong Kong warned that it was 'imperative to avoid a major showdown over the Court's decision'.[36] He argued that the courts were obliged not to enforce any laws that contravened the rights of Hong Kong residents. Furthermore, that the courts were obliged by the Basic Law to decide questions on the compatibility of legislation, whether local or mainland, with the Basic Law. This being the case, he asserted, they were merely carrying out their duties. None of the critics, he argued, had attempted to follow the

[32] Jacob, 'Hong Kong's threatened rule of law'.

[33] H. C. K. Liu, 'Sovereignty inviolable in context of "one country, two systems"', *Hong Kong Standard*, 10 February 1999.

[34] A. Li, '"Step down" call to Beijing adviser', *SCMP*, 4 February 1999.

[35] Fenby, *Dealing with the Dragon*, p. 86.

[36] Y. Ghai, 'When doing the right thing is amending the Basic Law', *SCMP*, 10 February 1999.

CFA's rationale, nor did they show any understanding of the common law of Hong Kong. The error lay not with the CFA but with the Basic Law Drafting Committee, which provided for the entry of mainlanders. The remedy, therefore, was to amend the Basic Law.

Increasingly venomous attacks by pro-Beijing bodies further polarised opinion.[37] China informed the Secretary for Justice that parts of the ruling needed to be 'revisited' and 'rectified'.[38] The CFA's decision was an 'intolerable attack on the authority of the highest sources of constitutional power in China'.[39] The government then invited the NPCSC to intervene, presenting this as necessary for the continued stability of Hong Kong.

After the original CFA ruling there had been long queues at immigration offices on both sides of the border, as applicants inquired about their entitlement to right of abode. A poll conducted in January 1999 showed that almost 87 per cent of respondents regarded the influx of mainlanders seeking right of abode as 'bad for Hong Kong', 53 per cent worried about the effect on the job market and almost 67 per cent stated that the Basic Law should be amended to prevent their claims.[40] However, there was ambivalence about asking for the NPCSC's intervention. *Ming Pao*, in an editorial, urged Beijing to let the HKSAR itself resolve the right of abode issue, warning that if it did interfere, the international community would see this as undermining the HKSAR's legal system. The public, it argued, 'definitely did not want to see Beijing overturn the verdict'.[41] An *SCMP* editorial argued that, if the rule of law meant anything, it meant that the law was above politics, a principle the government was undermining by appealing to a political body when the decision of the highest court went against it.[42] This clearly placed the supreme court in Hong Kong in a subservient position to the NPC, and when the NPCSC demanded a 'clarification' of the CFA's ruling, *Ming Pao's* view was that:

> two years after the handover, the major challenge to Hong Kong's system has come not in the political arena, as many had expected, but

[37] Ghai, 'When doing the right thing'. [38] Ghai, 'When doing the right thing'.
[39] Gittings, 'Changing expectations'.
[40] Survey conducted by the Democratic Alliance for the Betterment of Hong Kong, January 1999.
[41] 'Serious debates on the jurisdiction of the Court of Final Appeal', *Ming Pao*, 8, 9, and 10 February 1999.
[42] 'Serious debates on the jurisdiction'.

> in the legal field. In a sense, this makes what has happened all the more serious ... what had appeared to be a bedrock of Hong Kong's way of life ... has become subject to an essentially political process. The NPC ruling was a stark statement of where power lies ... Within Hong Kong itself, there is a very real danger that application of the rule of law is becoming a partisan issue. Being for or against the interpretation route will be seen as a gauge of being for or against the government ... The Secretary for Justice branded those who make a link between interpretation and the rule of law as scaremongers who were destroying their own fortress ... [She] has made it plain that the one country comes first followed by the two systems.[43]

Faced with criticisms, the government promised that requests to the NPCSC for interpretations would be rare.[44] In the vanguard of the protests against seeking an interpretation were the barristers and liberal legal academe.[45] Johannes Chan argued that it would put the independence of the judiciary in jeopardy, and the Bar Association regarded it as a 'potentially dangerous precedent'. Other Hong Kong legal experts regarded it as 'extraordinary' and likely to open up a 'political Pandora's box which would shake international confidence in the HKSAR'.[46] The Bar organised a silent march in an unprecedented show of unity, their silence a symbolic representation of the silencing both of the law and of the Hong Kong judiciary. Against them were mainland-trained lawyers, NPC Deputies and official advisers, as well as local pro-Beijing academics, all of whom supported the NPCSC's intervention. Maria Tam, a Basic Law Committee member, argued that inviting the NPCSC to interpret the Basic Law 'had nothing to do with judicial independence' and that it would only help Hong Kong by preventing the extra burden of mainland children.[47] *Xinhua* published a lengthy article in which it quoted the opinion of four mainland legal experts (all former Basic Law drafters and members of the Basic Law Committee) that the court's decision had violated the Basic Law. Their remarks were broadcast nationwide.[48] During the protests marking

[43] 'Serious debates on the jurisdiction'.

[44] S. Lo, 'The mainlandization and recolonization of Hong Kong', in Cheng, *The Hong Kong Special Administrative Region in its First Decade*, pp. 208–9.

[45] See *Ming Pao*, 10 February 1999; RTHK, 'Letter to Hong Kong', 28 February 1999.

[46] C. Buddle, A. Li, A. Parwani, 'Judges asked to clarify right of abode decision', *SCMP*, 25 February 1999.

[47] K. Y. No, 'NPC "no threat to judicial status"', *SCMP*, 25 February 1999.

[48] 'Mainland criticism fuels bitter abode row', *Hong Kong Standard*, 8 February 1999.

1 July anniversary of the handover, however, it was the liberal lawyers whose message found public support. Groups of demonstrators wore black armbands symbolising 'the demise of the rule of law' and carried placards accusing the government of 'ruining the rule of law'.[49] A cartoon of the time depicted Tung Chee-hwa jumping on the prostrate corpse of the rule of law.

There being no precedent for a 'clarification' by the CFA, the legal procedure was unclear. Eventually, counsel for the HKSAR Government stood before the bench of CFA judges asking them to clarify the meaning of certain statements in its earlier judgment: 'the learned barrister ... said that the court had a duty to clarify its judgment because it had become highly controversial, whilst conceding that it was a correct judgment'.[50] In 'revisiting' its earlier decision, the CFA did not formally depart from the substance of its earlier position. However, it issued a 'supplementary judgment' that contained enough deferential language about the supremacy of the NPCSC for Beijing 'to view it as an apology'.[51] Chief Justice Andrew Li declared that the CFA's judgment did not question the authority of the NPCSC to make an interpretation under Article 158 of the Basic Law and that 'the court accepts that it cannot question the authority of the NPCSC to do any act which is in accordance with the provisions of the Basic Law and the procedures therein'.[52] Yash Ghai described the process as a 'farce':

> Highly improbable, irrelevant and sometimes misleading submissions by the [g]overnment, completely lacking in legal principle, were admitted by the court without any real probing ... Instead of sending in the red guards ... our own Department of Justice ... despatched the gentle and fair-minded Mr Ma to assist in the judicial humiliation ... The Hungarian Marxist philosopher George Lukacs once said that to destroy liberalism, it must be forced into violations of its own legality. This would destroy the myths which sustained liberalism's major institution of oppression. Is there a lesson for us here?[53]

Gittings argued that a 'chastened court' was in no position to resist, accepting that it was bound by the NPCSC's unlimited power to

[49] Carroll, 'Ten years later', pp. 18–19.
[50] Y. Ghai, 'The theatre of the law', *SCMP*, 1 March 1999.
[51] Gittings, 'Changing expectations'.
[52] Zheng Caixiong and Joseph Li, 'Court reaffirms NPC's authority', *China Daily*, 27 February 1999.
[53] Caixiong and Li, 'Court reaffirms'.

interpret the Basic Law. Its rapid retreat 'was ... memorably described by Professor Jerome Cohen ... as the court veering from being "unnecessarily provocative" to the opposite extreme of having "unnecessarily prostrated itself before Beijing" within less than a year'.[54]

Would-be migrants, left in limbo as this politico-legal see-saw swung back and forth, tried to follow each step in the complex legal argument, delivered in a language they did not understand. As the Ng Ka-ling case was still in train, another seventeen right of abode migrants won their challenge in the Court of Appeal against removal orders issued against them by the government. In October 1999, nevertheless, the government urged the CFA to overturn a Court of Appeal's ruling. The Ng Ka-ling case was seen as the 'last hope' for the migrants. In a touching demonstration of their belief in law, over 200 people gathered outside the CFA to listen to the October hearing:

> some held banners ... most listened intently to the arguments broadcast via a television link, even though they could not understand the English used. They have pledged to come every day until the hearing ends. Mrs Lui, 45, from Guangzhou said the court was her last hope: 'I started applying for a one-way permit to Hong Kong when I was five. Now 40 years have passed but I still do not have one. My elderly mother is very sick now. I want to stay to take care of her'. Eung Kit-kwai, whose husband has stayed in Hong Kong for less than seven years, said she had been fighting for the right of abode for her elder son from the mainland: 'If he really cannot stay here, I will take him back to the [m]ainland. I want him to receive formal education instead of being an illegal immigrant ... Now Hong Kong is under Chinese rule, I don't have much confidence. But of course we still want to try our luck. We will keep waiting'.[55]

On 1 and 9 February 1999 – shortly after the final right of abode ruling by the CFA – Immigration Department officials arrested sixteen overstayers, repatriating them immediately. At the time, Fenby argued that the fact that they were permitted to stay during the legal process was 'a testament to the strength of the rule of law' – as long as their case was

[54] Gittings, 'Changing expectations', citing J. A. Cohen, 'Hong Kong's Basic Law: an American perspective', International Symposium to Commemorate the 10th Anniversary of the Promulgation of the HKSAR Basic Law, 1 April 2000; *Lau Kong Yung v. Director of Immigration* [1999] 3 HKLRD 778.

[55] Ambrose Leung Tsung-Yan and Ella Lee, 'Hearing is last hope for migrants', *SCMP*, 26 October 1999.

going through the courts, they would not be deported'.[56] The fact was that the government would have removed them sooner had it not been for the ongoing legal proceedings. In July 1999, it introduced further changes to its immigration controls.[57]

The final defeat of the migrants' case demonstrated Beijing's determination to retain control over Hong Kong affairs. Ku argues that the outcome also revealed the play of two competing discourses of the rule of law, one which stressed the idea of civil rights and one which emphasised authoritarian law and order.[58] The HKSAR government, she argues, became more inclined towards the 'law and order' discourse after the handover, calling for a quick and drastic resolution to what was actually a tricky political question in order to maintain social stability:

> Within the broad framework of rule of law, the government's strategy ... was first of all to reduce the whole problem to a matter of legal means and speed – constitutional amendment through the local legislature (slow) versus re-interpretation by the NPCSC (quick). The former conformed to the rule of law tradition whereas the latter was based on the legal tradition in China. Finally, the government succeeded in overturning part of the ruling of the Court of Final Appeal in Hong Kong. It justified the move on the grounds of legality, speed, and effective population control. Apparently, the government's turn to national law was overlaid with a concern about 'law and order' that privileged political and administrative expediency. Within civil society, the government's action was fiercely challenged as signifying a breach of the rule of law.[59]

In August 2000, a small number of desperate right of abode protestors in Immigration Tower, Wanchai, set fire to flammable liquid, which some said they had intended to pour over themselves in a suicide bid. In the resulting conflagration, two immigration officers died and several of the protesters were badly injured. The entire episode was a vivid demonstration of the failure of law to live up to its ideological promise. They were caught in a politico-legal contest, trapped for a lengthy period of time in 'extended legal liminality'.[60] Many already lived a

[56] Tsung-Yan and Lee, 'Hearing is last hope for migrants'.

[57] C. Buddle, 'Migrant changes "threat to self-rule"', *SCMP*, 27 October 1999.

[58] Ku, 'Negotiating law', pp. 157–74. [59] Ku, 'Negotiating law'.

[60] C. Menjivar, 'Legal liminality: Salvadorean and Guatemalan immigrants' lives in the United States', *American Journal of Sociology*, 111, no. 4 (January 2006), pp. 999–1037.

half-life in clandestine circumstances 'at once no longer classified and not yet classified'.[61]

Pun and Wu argue that the right of abode cases revealed 'the constitutive process of defining who is and who is not the Hong Kong citizen *proper*'.[62] According to Fernandez, membership of the social world 'signifies inclusion into a public culture of beliefs and values, symbols and ideas', communicated in social encounters between insiders and outsiders.[63] A person's legal membership of a society, on the other hand, is communicated by nationality, passports, freedoms, rights, law, courts and other institutional means.[64] In Hong Kong, the category of 'citizen' does not exist in the Basic Law, its residents being either permanent or non-permanent.[65] The rights and freedoms which citizens elsewhere enjoy are in Hong Kong granted to 'residents', and the central concept used in the Basic Law to indicate community membership is 'the right of abode'.[66] As the right of abode claimants discovered, the full menu of rights associated with the liberal view of the rule of law did not adhere to persons falling between cracks in the politico-legal contest.

The instability generated by the right of abode cases owed much to the government's efforts to scare the population into supporting 'stability', the nation state and Beijing's 'right to rule'. In these, it was successful, but in the longer term the outcome was much more ambiguous. A survey conducted in July 1999 showed the public's perception of the fairness of the judicial system had fallen to an all-time low.[67] In its first report on the HKSAR, the United Nations Human Rights Committee expressed serious concern about the implications of the NPCSC's intervention. Coming within eighteen months of the handover, it unsettled commercial interests, for whom the independence of

61 Menjivar, 'Legal liminality'.

62 N. Pun and K. M. Wu, 'Lived citizenship and lower class Chinese migrant women', in Ku and Pun (eds.), *Remaking Citizenship*, p. 139.

63 C. Fernandez, 'The stranger within', in Petersson and Clark, 'Identity Dynamics', p. 165.

64 See T. H. Marshall, *Citizenship and Social Class and Other Essays* (Cambridge: Cambridge University Press, 1950).

65 Y. Ghai, 'Citizenship and politics in the HKSR: the constitutional framework', *Citizenship Studies*, 5, no. 2 (2001), pp. 143–64.

66 D. K. L. Ho, 'Citizenship as a form of governance', in Ku and Pun, *Remaking Citizenship*, pp. 19–36.

67 University of Hong Kong, HK POP survey, 7/1997–10/2001 http://hkupop.hku.hk/english/popexpress/judiciary.

the Hong Kong judiciary underpinned business confidence in the territory. The attack on the CFA opened up the possibility that China might in future overrule court decisions of which it disapproved, including decisions which went against mainland business interests. The Washington-based Heritage Foundation declared that the legal system had now been rendered unpredictable, and that the law was up for grabs. The local American Chamber of Commerce reiterated that the rule of law and an independent judiciary were of paramount importance to Hong Kong's status as a centre for international commerce and finance.

Commenting on the controversy, Fenby recalls a remark by Chris Patten about China's desire to have a mechanism for a 'post-remedial verdict' on the CFA: 'The Governor characterised this as "if we don't like the result we've got to find some way to overturn it"'. China had achieved this without Beijing having to issue a directive – the HKSAR government had done it all by itself.[68] A senior British official from the Department of Justice suggested that the administration could in fact now ask for an interpretation from the NPC 'whenever it wished – before, during or after a court hearing'.[69] Fenby observes that the government was exultant over the defeat of the CFA – he recalls an NPC Deputy from Hong Kong inviting his friends to tea 'to celebrate, as Hong Kong is about to rid itself of a disaster'.[70] According to one report, the 'surgery' was seen by Beijing as a necessary evil: 'If there is a lot of pain, so be it. At least there will be no more attempts at independence'.[71] A cartoon of the time depicted the phrase 'Court of Final Appeal' with the word 'Final' crossed out and replaced by 'Semi'. In September 2011, WikiLeaks published a diplomatic cable in which the US Consulate in Hong Kong reported that Mr. Justice Bokhary had informed him that the CFA judges had seriously considered resigning at this time, but they did not do so in case they were replaced by less competent jurists.[72] A poll at the time indicated that the right of abode controversy had seriously weakened public confidence in cross-border political relations and that confidence in the 'one country, two systems'

[68] Fenby, *Dealing with the Dragon*, p. 179. [69] Fenby, *Dealing with the Dragon*.
[70] Fenby, *Dealing with the Dragon*, pp. 193–5.
[71] 'NPC will have "final say" on Basic Law', *Hong Kong Standard*, 10 February 1999.
[72] G. Cheung and C. Ip, 'All City's top judges "considered quitting"', *SCMP*, 8 September 2011.

formula had plunged.[73] Hong Kong citizens' approval rating of Chinese rule dropped drastically from 60 per cent in 1998 to 42 per cent after the CFA incident.[74] By the second anniversary of the handover, 43 per cent of those polled said that the rule of law had deteriorated.[75]

In June 2012, a University of Hong Kong law professor stated that the rule of law had deteriorated and was in continuous decline.[76] In 2013, Beijing officials expressed the view that the separation of powers was not sacrosanct and that there ought to be more cooperation between the executive, legislature and judiciary. In 2014, for the fifth year running, senior legal figures gave speeches at the opening of the legal year reiterating the importance of the separation of powers and an independent judiciary.[77] The government had pursued one hegemonic objective – upholding 'one country' – but in the process had damaged another – the legitimacy that flows to rulers from the rule of law.

[73] Hong Kong Policy Research Institute Poll, 8 February 1999. 60 per cent of respondents said that criticism by mainland experts of the CFA's ruling had affected their confidence.

[74] 'Citizens' approval rating for Chinese rule drastically drops', *Apple Daily*, 2 March 1999.

[75] Fenby, *Dealing with the Dragon*, 198.

[76] S. Lau, 'Rule of law declined under Tsang, says scholar', *SCMP*, 25 June 2012.

[77] Editorial, *SCMP*, 19 January 2014.

8

The law wars: the flag cases

The issue of the extent of freedom of expression post-1997 came before the courts shortly after the handover in 1998 when two political activists were prosecuted for defacing the Chinese national flag.[1]

In 1997, the colonial flag was replaced by the flag of the PRC; Hong Kong also acquired a new regional flag. The construction, design and display of the new flags were regulated by protocols set out in the National Flag and Regional Flag Ordinances; the national symbol and regional symbol were similarly protected by law.[2] The new regional flag was to be flown at official and cultural venues throughout Hong Kong on PRC National Day (1 October), New Year's Day and HKSAR Establishment Day (1 July). At other times, it was to be flown daily from the chief executive's official residence, the airport and all border crossings; it was also to fly at the Court of Final Appeal, the High Court and LEGCO when these were sitting. It was to be raised at 8 A.M. and lowered at 6 P.M. It was to fly alongside the PRC national flag, but the national flag had to be flown in a more prominent position than the regional flag. The regional flag was also smaller in size. The national flag had to be raised before the regional flag and lowered after the regional flag.[3]

[1] *HKSAR* v. *Ng Kung Siu And Another* [1999] HKCFA 10; [1999] 3 HKLRD 907; (1999) 2 HKCFAR 442; [2000] 1 HKC 117; FACC4/1999 (15 December 1999).

[2] National Flag and National Emblem Ordinance, 116 of 1997; Regional Flag and Regional Emblem Ordinance, 117 of 1997.

[3] Stipulations for the Display and Use of the National Flag and the National Emblem and the Regional Flag and Regional Emblem, Protocol Division HKSAR

Flags which were damaged, defiled, faded and substandard were not to be displayed. Desecration and/or inappropriate use of the national and regional flags were prohibited. Publicly and wilfully burning the flags, mutilating them, scrawling on them, defiling them or trampling them were criminal offences.

DESIGN

The (re)union of Hong Kong and the mainland was clothed in a rhetoric of return to the Motherland, as if some mysterious maternal bond invisibly united the two. The design of the regional flag was supposed to express this mystery. Locals had been invited to help choose their new flag, but this idea was abandoned after one proposal depicted a hammer and sickle on one side and a dollar sign on the other. The design that was eventually accepted was replete with cultural, regional and political symbolism:

> The colour itself is significant; red is a festive colour for the Chinese people, used to convey a sense of celebration and nationalism. Moreover, the red colour is identical to that used in the PRC national flag, chosen to signify the link re-established between postcolonial Hong Kong and China. The juxtaposition of red and white on the flag symbolises the *one country two systems* political principles applied to the region. The stylised rendering of the Bauhinia blakena flower . . . is meant to serve as a harmonising symbol for this dichotomy.[4]

On the choice of the bauhinia, one of the judges, Tao Ho, is said to have 'wandered into his garden . . . looking for inspiration. He picked up a Bauhinia blakeana flower. He observed the symmetry of the five petals, and how their winding pattern conveyed to him a dynamic feeling. This led him to incorporate the flower into the flag to represent Hong Kong'.[5] According to the chairman of the drafting committee of the Basic Law, the regional flag's design 'implies that Hong Kong is an inalienable part of China and prospers in the embrace of the

Government Secretariat. See also The National Flag and National Emblem Ordinance Statutory Instrument A401 and the Regional Flag and Regional Emblem Ordinance Statutory Instrument A602.

[4] The Regional Flag and Regional Emblem Ordinance Cap 2602 Schedule 1, the Specifications for the Regional Flag of the Hong Kong Special Administrative Region of the People's Republic of China

[5] http://www.thefullwiki.org/Flag_of_Hong_Kong.

motherland. The five stars on the flower symbolize the fact that all Hong Kong compatriots love their motherland, while the red and white colours embody the principle of one country, two systems'.[6] The regional emblem had a red circular edge, an outer ring marked with English words and Chinese characters reading 'Hong Kong Special Administrative Region' and an inner ring with a swaying bauhinia with five star-shaped stamens, each dotted with a red five-pointed star.

Unlike the British, China has strict laws for its flags. Article 1 of the PRC's National Flag law is meant to defend the dignity of the national flag, enhance citizens' consciousness of the State and promote the spirit of patriotism. Article 3 states that 'All citizens and organizations shall respect and care for the National Flag'. Anyone who desecrates the national flag by publicly and wilfully burning, mutilating, scrawling on, defiling or trampling upon it is liable to imprisonment for not more than three years, criminal detention, public surveillance or deprivation of political rights.[7] In the HKSAR, similar criminal sanctions apply.[8] The National Flag Ordinance provides that a person who desecrates in any of these ways is liable on conviction to a fine and to imprisonment for three years.[9] Similarly, anyone who desecrates the regional flag or regional emblem is liable to a fine and imprisonment for three years, or on summary conviction, to a fine and imprisonment for one year.[10]

In January 1998, Ng Kung-siu and Lee Kin-yun were part of a peaceful demonstration organised by the Hong Kong Alliance in Support of the Patriotic Democratic Movement in China. The demonstration began in Victoria Park and processed through Central towards the Government Offices. The two defendants were seen carrying a defaced national flag and the regional flag; Lee was also seen carrying an undamaged Taiwanese flag. At the end of the march, they tied these flags to some railings outside Government Headquarters. During the procession, they had chanted 'build up a democratic China'. The second defendant was reported to have stated that the damaging and defiling of the national and regional flags were a way to express the

6 Ji Pengfei, 4 April 1990 at the Third Session of the Seventh National People's Congress.

7 Article 299 of the Criminal Law of the People's Republic of China.

8 Annex III of the Basic Law.

9 See National Flag and National Emblem Ordinance, no. 116 of 1997, which implements PRC law on the national flag and national emblem.

10 Regional Flag Ordinance, sec. 7.

dissatisfaction and resistance to the ruler who was not elected by the people. Both were charged with publicly desecrating and wilfully defiling both the national and regional flags. The national flag had the centre cut out and black ink daubed over the large yellow five-pointed star; the star itself was punctured. Similar damage appeared on the reverse side. The Chinese character 'shame' was written in black ink on the four small stars, and on the reverse side a black cross was daubed on the lowest of the four small stars. One section was torn off the regional flag. A black cross was drawn across that design, and three of the remaining four red stars had black crosses daubed over them. The Chinese character 'shame' was written on the flag in black ink. Similar damage appeared on the reverse side.[11]

At the Magistrates Court, the defence argued they had no case to answer. Because freedom of expression was a recognised right under the Basic Law and the ICCPR, it could not be restricted by the Flag Ordinances. Government lawyers countered that in this instance restricting freedom of expression was justified for the protection of public order. Harking back to the riots of 1956, prompted by the removal of a Taiwanese flag from a housing estate in Kowloon, the magistrate argued that a responsible government could not afford to overlook that social disorder might be provoked by the public desecration of the flags. He held that freedom of expression could be restricted on public order *(ordre public)* grounds and convicted both defendants. On appeal, the appellants argued that just because 'a symbol such as a flag may be respected or venerated by many people does not justify criminalizing those who disapprove of that symbol and/or wish to change it ... the essence of free expression is the right to express unpopular ideas through any medium'.[12] They also pointed out that none of the leading common law jurisdictions criminalized the defacing of the national flag. The Court of Appeal rejected the public order argument that the Flag Ordinances were necessary for the normal operation of the HKSAR. It overturned the convictions, agreeing that the defendants' actions amounted to freedom of expression, a right protected under Article 19 of the ICCPR and Article 27 of the Basic Law.

[11] Regional Flag Ordinance, sec. 7.

[12] *HKSAR* v. *Ng Kung-Siu and Lee Kin-Yun*, Court of Appeal Judgment 23 March 1999, Magistracy Appeal No. 563 of 1998, HCMA 563/98.

Coming at a time when local and international observers were watching for signs that retrocession had adversely affected the independence of the Hong Kong courts, this ruling was interpreted as a sign that rule of law was alive and well. But the government took the case to the CFA. On 15 December 1999, Chief Justice Andrew Li delivered the court's judgment. He acknowledged that the case hinged on the right to freedom of expression, which was a fundamental freedom in a democratic society and lay at the heart of Hong Kong's way of life. Flag desecration was a 'form of non-verbal speech or expression', a 'symbolic expression'[13] – the protesters were using desecration of the flag to protest against the mainland government. Li agreed that the courts must give a generous interpretation to the constitutional guarantee of freedom of expression, stating that 'This freedom includes the freedom to express ideas which the majority may find disagreeable or offensive and the freedom to criticize governmental institutions and the conduct of public officials . . . The Basic Law contains constitutional guarantees for the freedoms that are of the essence of Hong Kong's civil society'.[14] However, this freedom of expression was not an absolute and could, under certain circumstances, be subject to restriction. In this instance, some degree of restriction was justified, since protecting the dignity of the national and regional flags was a legitimate matter of community interest; restriction was also justified 'for the protection of national security or of public order *(ordre public)*. According to the CFA, '*ordre public*' considerations included safety, public health, aesthetic and moral considerations and economic order as well as peace and good order. At this particular point in Hong Kong's history, it argued, the protection of the flags should also be included:

> The resumption of the exercise of sovereignty is recited in the Preamble of the Basic Law, as 'fulfilling the long-cherished common aspiration of the Chinese people for the recovery of Hong Kong'. In these circumstances, the legitimate societal interests in protecting the national flag and the legitimate community interests in the protection of the regional flag are interests which are within the concept of public order *(ordre public)* the national flag is the unique symbol of the one country, the People's Republic of China, and the regional flag is the unique symbol of the Hong Kong Special Administrative Region as an inalienable part of

[13] Hong Kong Court of Final Appeal, Final Appeal No. 4 of 1999 (Criminal) *HKSAR* v. *Ng Kung-siu and Lee Kin Yun*.

[14] *HKSAR* v. *Ng Kung-siu and Lee Kin Yun*.

> the People's Republic of China under the principle of 'one country, two systems'. These legitimate interests form part of the general welfare and the interests of the collectivity as a whole ... Hong Kong is at the early stage of the new order following resumption of the exercise of sovereignty by the People's Republic of China. The implementation of the principle of 'one country, two systems' is a matter of fundamental importance, as is the reinforcement of national unity and territorial integrity. Protection of the national flag and the regional flag from desecration, having regard to their unique symbolism, will play an important part in the attainment of these goals. In these circumstances, there are strong grounds for concluding that the criminalisation of flag desecration is a justifiable restriction on the guaranteed right to the freedom of expression.[15]

This was a reunification judgment. Its rhetoric extolled individual freedoms, but its substance protected the state. Protecting the flags was necessary to the post-1997 order. The court thus sought to socially and politically suture Hong Kong to the nation, in the process constructing an 'imagined community'. The national flag was:

> the symbol of a nation ... a unique symbol ... the symbol of the State and the sovereignty of the State. It represents the People's Republic of China, with her dignity, unity and territorial integrity ... The regional flag is the unique symbol of [Hong Kong] ... as an inalienable part of the People's Republic of China under the principle of 'one country, two systems' ... The intrinsic importance of the national flag and the regional flag ... as such unique symbols is demonstrated by the fact that at the historic moment on the stroke of midnight on 1 July 1997, the handover ceremony in Hong Kong to mark the People's Republic of China's resumption of the exercise of sovereignty over Hong Kong began by the raising of the national flag and the regional flag. And the speech, which the President of the People's Republic of China then delivered, began with the words: 'The national flag of the People's Republic of China and the regional flag of the Hong Kong Special Administrative Region of the People's Republic of China have now solemnly risen over this land'.[16]

Though it is questionable how widely the community itself shared its view, the court held that Hongkongers had a legitimate interest in protecting the flags. Restrictions on the right to freedom of expression

[15] *HKSAR* v. *Ng Kung-siu and Lee Kin Yun*.
[16] *HKSAR* v. *Ng Kung-siu and Lee Kin Yun*.

were justified because Hong Kong was trying to 'integrate itself into the Chinese motherland'.[17] Protecting the flags played an important part in the attainment of these goals. Therefore, there were 'strong grounds for concluding that the criminalisation of flag desecration is a justifiable restriction on the guaranteed right to the freedom of expression'.[18]

At the time, one observer remarked on the strangeness of seeing 'the scholarly, reasonable Chief Justice' quoting at length from the sayings of Jiang Zemin and reminding the population that flags symbolised the fact that 'all Hong Konger compatriots love their motherland'.[19] Despite the fact that the CFA ruled against the protesters, Lo argues that case was a landmark for the legal system, since 'the executive authorities accepted in this case the ... proposition that the ICCPR was incorporated into the Basic Law by its Article 39' and by the BOR.[20] This was to prove important for future cases and established that, even after 1997, Hong Kong continued to 'use the methodology of international and comparative jurisprudence to determine whether a restriction or limitation to an internationally or constitutionally guaranteed fundamental right is justified, necessary or reasonable'.[21] What was good news for the legal system was, however, bad news for the accused, whose convictions were reinstated.

The case went to the heart of the single most serious issue worrying Hongkongers – freedom of expression. On the eve of the handover, Margaret Ng, LEGCO member and barrister, had presciently argued that:

> to the general public, deprived of a democratic government and therefore the power to influence government decisions, the freedom to disagree, to criticise, to express strong discontent about policies, what the government does or fails to do, is regarded as sacrosanct, as the most fundamental right. The curtailment of that is intolerable. This high regard for freedom of expression in all its manifestations ... is respected by the [colonial] administration and is one of the main features of Hong Kong's way of life and political culture'.[22]

[17] M. Landler, 'Top court in Hong Kong upholds ban on defacing Chinese flag', *The New York Times*, 16 December 1999.

[18] Landler, 'Top court in Hong Kong'.

[19] Fenby, *Dealing with the Dragon*.

[20] P. Y. Lo, *The Judicial Construction of Hong Kong's Basic Law: Courts, Politics and Society after 1997* (Hong Kong: Hong Kong University Press, 2014), 80–1.

[21] Lo, *The Judicial Construcction*.

[22] M. Ng, 'Taking stock: the political culture in Hong Kong as of June 1997', unpublished paper.

For Ng, freedom of expression was an identifying feature of Hong Kong identity. There was, she argued, 'a deep reliance on the rule of law as the foundation of fair play, restraint on arbitrary power and a safeguard against corruption . . . The link between the rule of law and democracy is beginning to be appreciated . . . democracy as the means by which people may safeguard their rights and freedoms, particularly the freedom of expression, has become deeply ingrained among the masses'.[23]

Post-handover, however, the flag cases raised the uncomfortable possibility that the courts might not always reliably uphold freedom of expression. The flag cases, coming so soon after the CFA was forced to 're-visit' the right of abode decision, suggested that law was a double-edged sword in the fight to protect freedoms. This partly explains why other, non-legal steps recommended themselves to a civil society worried about freedom of expression. There were numerous sites of contest. The government was accused of interfering with the editorial independence of RTHK. In discussion programmes, a reference had been made to independence for Tibet and the 'two states' theory expounded by Taiwan's president, Lee Teng-hui. Pro-Beijing figures put pressure on the government to move the head of RTHK, Cheung Man-yee, to another post in Japan.[24] The dismissal of a *South China Post* editor was also alleged to have been politically motivated. A survey conducted in 2001 indicated that the public felt that freedom of the press and freedom of speech were under threat.[25] Tung Chee-hwa was forced to reaffirm the government's commitment to freedom of speech,[26] but since his unpopular administration could always rely for support on pro-communist groups, it was possible to persist with measures designed to instantiate the new national identity and uphold PRC sovereignty, many of which had a chilling effect on freedom of speech.

23 Ng, 'Taking stock'.
24 C. Yeung, 'Tung challenges RTHK sceptics', *SCMP*, 26 October 1999.
25 Hong Kong Transition Project report, 2001, p. 28.
26 Hong Kong Transition Project report, 2001, p. 32.

9

The law wars: Article 23

The term 'social movements' captures the emergence of a relatively recent Hong Kong phenomenon.[1] As Cohen reminds us, social movements can operate as a kind of 'ideological hat-stand – a single piece of furniture which, nevertheless, can accommodate a large number and wide variety of hats'.[2] This precisely captures what happened when the government issued its proposal to introduce mainland-type anti-subversion laws under Article 23. The ensuing fight brought together otherwise disparate social groups in a common cause, defence of freedom and the rule of law. Pro-democracy groups and lawyers were joined by journalists; academics; workers; human rights activists; actors; artists; homosexual groups; civil servants; university and school students; negative-equity homeowners; social welfare recipients; medical, legal and other professionals; women's groups; political parties; Christian churches; and individuals.[3] What this showed, Ku argues, is that 'the ruling hegemony of the government was undermined to the extent that it could no longer contain widespread discontent in society at large'.[4] For Sing, the sheer number of participants, the diversity of the social

[1] See L. Butenhoff, *Social Movements and Political Reform in Hong Kong* (Westport: Praeger, 1999).

[2] Cohen, *Symbolic Construction of Community*, p.108.

[3] A. S .M. Ku, 'Civil society's dual impetus: mobilisations, representations and contestations over the July 1 march in 2003', in M. Sing (ed.), *Politics and Government in Hong Kong: Crisis under Chinese Sovereignty* (London: Routledge, 2009), p. 42.

[4] Ku, 'Civil society's dual impetus' in Sing, *Politics and Government*.

groups involved 'and the robust demands they voiced, powerfully underscored the pervasive public frustration with governmental performance'.[5] Their collective demand for more democracy and better governance was 'reminiscent of the explosion of civil society amid democratic transitions in various parts of the world'.[6]

Writing in 1990, David Clark identified Article 23 of the Basic Law as problematic. It attempted to restrict free political activity, contradicting Article 27, which stated that Hongkongers would enjoy freedom of speech, of the press and of publication.[7] It prohibited acts of treason, secession, sedition and subversion, the last an offence not known to the common law. In 1998, the Hong Kong Voice of Democracy also flagged concerns about Article 23 noting Lau Siu-kai's remarks that it had been inserted into the Basic Law after Tiananmen to curb all activities that threatened Beijing.[8] The government released its proposal for public consultation on 24 September 2002 after being reminded by Beijing of its obligation under the Basic Law to enact laws to prohibit 'any act of treason, secession, sedition, subversion against the Central People's Government, or theft of state secrets, to prohibit foreign political organizations or bodies from conducting political activities in the Region and to prohibit political organizations or bodies of the Region from establishing ties with foreign organizations or bodies'. Beijing's reminder reflected a long-standing fear that Hong Kong could become a base for subversion. Throughout the handover negotiations, Beijing had insisted on the inclusion of the anti-subversion law, partly as a reaction to Hongkongers' support for the Tiananmen demonstrators in June 1989. The prospect of an anti-subversion law had been 'a sword of Damocles hanging over social activists ever since'.[9]

That the SAR administration decided to enact Article 23 when it did showed a signal lack of understanding of the public mood. Government legitimacy was already poor. Opinion polls in December 2002 already indicated that 54 per cent of Hongkongers were opposed

5 M. Sing, 'Introduction', in Sing, *Politics and Government*, p. 1.
6 Sing, 'Introduction', in Sing, *Politics and Government*.
7 D. Clarke, 'Sedition and Article 23', in *Hong Kong's Basic Law: Problems and Prospects* (Hong Kong: University of Hong Kong Faculty of Law, 1990), pp. 31–2.
8 'What's Wrong with Article 23 of the Basic Law', *Hong Kong Voice of Democracy*, 25 July 1998.
9 Ma, Ngok, *Political Development*, pp. 210–12.

to the legislation.[10] Most of the offences were in any case already covered by existing legislation, such as the Public Order Ordinance and the Societies Ordinance. In 1997, the little-known Emergency Regulations Ordinance was also re-enacted, giving the CE unrestrained internal security powers. Taken together with other police powers, these laws signalled what Ku terms the post-1997 government's turn to an ideology of law and order,[11] stressing control over rights, political discretion over legal consistency and state power over procedural justice.

Significant reservations were expressed by those opposed to the proposals (the Article 23 Concern Group) as to what exactly constituted 'subversion', sedition, 'state secrets' and secession. There was widespread awareness of how such laws operated in China – in 1994, a former reporter with *Ming Pao Daily News*, Xi Yang, had been arrested in Beijing for theft of state secrets, for which he received a sentence of twelve years imprisonment. Xi had published information on China's gold reserves which, it was alleged, he had obtained by encouraging a Bank of China employee to steal 'state financial secrets'. The offence for which he was convicted, however, was refusal to disclose his sources. Likening the charges to those available under Article 23, Hong Kong lawyer and LECGO member Margaret Ng asked: 'Is it any comfort that in [the] future, Hong Kong reporters in Xi Yang's shoes may be likely to be sentenced to fewer years than he?'[12] She saw the way in which the Article 23 proposals were handled as a crucial test of the 'one country, two systems' formula.[13] There was, she said, hardly anything 'more crucial to the preservation of Hong Kong's separate systems and way of life than the rights and freedoms people enjoyed, 'in particular, a free press, the free flow of information, freedom of speech and of association and free and open debate of political, religious or cultural views, no matter how distasteful they may be to government . . . It is universally appreciated that this should remain unchanged after

[10] Ma, Ngok, *Political Development*, pp. 210–12. See *Ming Pao Daily News*, 14 December 2002.

[11] Ku, 'Civil Society's dual impetus', p. 44.

[12] M. Ng, 'Government sharpens its knives against the media', *SCMP*, 23 October 2002.

[13] M. Ng, 'Draconian measures threaten Hong Kong freedoms', *SCMP*, 14 October 2002.

reunification, and that the situation in the rest of China should not spread to the SAR'.[14]

The *China Daily*, the mouthpiece of the Communist Party, had already condemned LEGCO member Emily Lau Wai-hing for shaking hands with former Taiwanese president Lee Teng-hui during a trip to Taiwan – was shaking hands now to be considered 'subversive'? Lau also allegedly stated that Taiwan's independence should be a matter for the Taiwanese. This was interpreted as encouraging a movement for independence, leading the *China Daily* to call for national security legislation to deal with such 'separatists'. Secretary for Justice Elsie Leung and the Secretary for Security Regina Ip insisted that Hongkongers 'must follow mainland China's policy on Taiwan' and that 'secessionist' activities would indeed be an offence under Article 23.[15] As Gittings notes, the government also slipped a provision into the draft legislation allowing it to ban the Falun Gong or any group it deemed undesirable on national security grounds.[16] If successful, this would have 'risked importing the mainland's harsh definitions of national security – and suppression of peaceful protests – into Hong Kong'.[17] Qualms were also expressed about the suggestion that special tribunals, rather than the courts, would try 'national security' cases. On the mainland, state security police dealt with national security, sedition and subversion in a highly secretive fashion. In Hong Kong, it was argued, these should be dealt with openly, by the courts, 'because people in Hong Kong are now trusting our judges more than any other institution'.[18]

Ku argues that the government's determination to proceed turned the consultation into a 'fake consultation' and Leung and Ip into emblems of authoritarianism and arrogance.[19] By cocooning himself in a circle of like-minded individuals, Tung Chee-hwa 'isolated himself from the society he was supposed to lead and became more stubborn because alternative viewpoints did not reach him ... In a time when society demands democracy, ... accountability, openness and transparency, it is indeed unwise to shut oneself off from the real world'.[20]

[14] Ng, 'Draconian measures'.
[15] E. Leung, 'Two Systems will remain', *SCMP*, 18 October 2002.
[16] Gittings, 'Changing expectations'. [17] Gittings, 'Changing expectations'.
[18] Chairman of the Hong Kong Bar Association, Alan Leong Kah-kit, cited by C. Buddle, 'Lawyers attack security law tribunal plan', *SCMP*, 27 October 2002.
[19] Ku, *Civil Society*, p. 46.
[20] E. Chan and J. C. W. Chan, 'Social Cohesion and governance problems in the Tung Chee-hwa era', in Sing, *Politics and Government*, pp. 102–3.

There was a widespread sense that, unless the community spoke out, it would be silenced forever.[21] The government's consistent refusal to listen to the public on any issue fuelled a mass protest against Article 23 on 1 July 2003.

As Cohen says, communities respond assertively when their members:

> feel themselves to be under so severe a threat from some extrinsic source, ... they feel the message of this vocal assemblage, though general, to be informed directly by their own experiences and mentalities ... and ... their members find their identities as individuals through their occupancy of the community's social space: if outsiders trespass in that space, then its occupants own sense of self is felt to be debased and defaced. This sense is always tenuous when the physical and structural boundaries which previously divided the community from the rest of the world are increasingly blurred. It can therefore easily be depicted as under threat: it is a ready means of mobilising collectivity. Thus one often finds in such communities the prospect of change being regarded ominously, as if change inevitably means loss.[22]

Article 23 provided a lightning rod around which hitherto quite disparate social groups could rally in a symbolic defence of the rule of law. Surveys showed that liberty had by this time become 'a much treasured societal value', identified with the rule of law, democracy and the right to demonstrate.[23] The pro-Beijing camp called upon all Chinese to support the law in the name of patriotism.[24] Expressing reservations about Article 23 was, they said, 'unpatriotic', an allegation contested by Martin Lee, who urged 'brave nationals' to fight it. Doubters were accused by Vice Premier Qian Qichen of having the 'devil' in their hearts. Calling for 'independence' opened up protestors to the charge of 'splittism',[25] something more usually associated with campaigners for Tibetan, Uighur or Taiwanese independence. One commentator warned the administration that the 'one country, two systems' formula was being watched from Taiwan by those sceptical of China's plans for 'Great China' unification.[26]

[21] Cohen, *Symbolic Construction of Community*, p. 109.
[22] Cohen, *Symbolic Construction of Community*.
[23] Chan and Chan, 'Social cohesion and governance problems', pp. 102–3.
[24] A. Li, '"Brave nationals" urged to fight Article 23', *SCMP*, 4 November 2002.
[25] Yeung Sum, 'We don't want independence', *SCMP*, February 19 2004.
[26] Li, 'Brave nationals'.

The attempt to marginalise Article 23 opponents as a deviant few failed. In all, 500,000 people took to the streets to demonstrate against Article 23 on 1 July 2003. This was, Ma Ngok says, 'the largest indigenous social movement in Hong Kong's history'.[27] Cheung and Lee described protesters, '[b]randishing anti-Tung placards and chanting slogans against the government, protesters, dressed mostly in black, braved scorching heat to vent their anger. They carried effigies of Mr Tung and the Secretary for Security, Regina Ip Lau Suk-yee as they walked from Causeway Bay to Central'.[28]

In what some call the 'Hong Kong style' of protest, behaviour during the march was 'impeccable'; marchers 'behaved admirably', showing 'great self-control'.[29] Protestors were calm and patient, showing that 'we know how to behave and to claim our rights peacefully . . . Though we shouted "Down with Tung Chee-hwa" in united voices . . . the people who marched there were not gangsters or rebels. They were ordinary well-behaved citizens demanding their voices be heard'.[30] Others said that they 'saw constant waving from bus drivers and passengers in taxis crawling along the flyover, which was returned with hearty cheers from a perspiring and good-natured crowd. We stood for five hours . . . The police in any other place would have had an impossible task . . . we Hong Kong people are so reasonable, intelligent and . . . good humoured. [Mr Tung should] give us universal suffrage immediately'.[31] Another said that, 'before joining the march, I wondered: would enough people turn up to make the government listen? When I found myself stuck in a vast sea of people for hours on end, it was at once extremely uncomfortable, but mostly inspiring. Who said that the people of Hong Kong are not ready for democracy? . . . I, an ordinary citizen, knew this would be the mother of all marches . . . Families came along with their small kids . . . the self-appointed cheering squads . . . encouraged us not to lose our enthusiasm. "Watch your step. Keep going. Watch the old folks. Help them down the steps. You're not alone. There are hundreds and thousands of us. Your voices will be heard. You will be counted. Be patient"'.[32]

The march became a landmark in Hong Kong's political history. It changed people's lives. Hong Kong's core values, uppermost of which

[27] Ma, Ngok, *Political Development*, 210.
[28] J. Cheung and K. Lee, '500,000 take to the streets', *SCMP*, 2 July 2003.
[29] 'Voices from the crowd', *SCMP*, 4 July 2003. [30] 'Voices from the crowd'.
[31] 'Voices from the crowd'. [32] 'Voices from the crowd'.

was the rule of law, had already been undermined by mainland intervention in the legal system; it was now threatened by Article 23. International reaction was, however, carefully calibrated not to upset China. The US stated that, 'It is in the US and international interests that a predictable, transparent, and fair system of law allow citizens in Hong Kong to continue to exercise their fundamental freedoms and civil liberties as protected by international human rights instruments'.[33] Britain warned that the legislation threatened to compromise the 'one country, two systems' model. However, neither country translated their disapproval into action, and it was left to the Hong Kong people to do what Patten had exhorted them to do, to stand up and fight for themselves.

Mainland leaders were shocked by the scale of the demonstration. Anthony Neoh, a member of the Basic Law Committee, sought a compromise by arguing for wider participation in the consultation process to facilitate a better understanding of the legislation,[34] a contrast with Ip's position that there was no need to consult the likes of 'taxi drivers, restaurant waiters and McDonalds' staff'. On 6 July 2003, Liberal Party Chairman and EXCO member James Tien Pei-chun resigned over the issue. He was followed on 16 July by Regina Ip.[35] Tien's departure came after visiting Beijing officials. His action effectively forced the bill to be abandoned, at least for the time being. This did not rescue the Tung administration, and calls for his resignation accelerated. Along with Ip, he became a figure of fun, openly lampooned in comic books. Coming so soon after his invitation to the NPCSC in the right of abode cases, the Article 23 episode illustrated how, when faced with mainland pressure, his administration was too weak – or unwilling – to defend Hong Kong.[36] Polls conducted after the 1 July march revealed that public mistrust of both the Tung regime and Beijing had increased.[37] A November 2003 poll revealed that only 51 per cent of respondents were satisfied with life in the HKSAR.[38] Ip sought to assuage the public's fears by telling them: 'You're scared?

[33] A. Li and C. Snyder, 'US eyeing possible dangers of Article 23', *SCMP*, 25 October 2002.
[34] A. Neoh, 'Voices of Hong Kong', *SCMP*, 10 July 2003.
[35] Neoh, 'Voices of Hong Kong'. [36] Ngok, *Political Development*, 223.
[37] J. Cheung, 'Trust in Beijing falls after Basic Law interpretation', *SCMP*, 7 July 2004.
[38] DeGolyer, M. E., 'Hong Kong people's economic attitudes 1997–2007', in Cheng, *The Hong Kong Special Administrative Region*, p. 363.

What are you afraid of? We have the rule of law'.[39] Chief Secretary Anson Chan also argued that freedom under the rule of law remained the defining marker of Hong Kong's identity:

> We remain committed to maintaining the pillars of our society that sets us apart from other parts of the country, and other countries in the region. The rule of law upheld by an independent judiciary; a level playing field for business; the free flow of information, capital and goods; and a clean administration ... It's about having the freedom to read what you like whether it be a newspaper, a magazine, or on the internet; it's about speaking your mind, whether it makes sense or not; it's about having the freedom to come and go as you please; it's about settling your differences in court with a tried and trusted legal system; it's about going to mosque on a Friday, the synagogue on Saturday, or the church on Sunday without fear of attack or reprisal.[40]

Chan praised Beijing for its 'hands off' approach to Hong Kong issues since 1997 and the transition process for having kept Hong Kong a free, open and vibrant place. Any laws relating to national security would, she promised, be debated by 'our own legislature' and interpreted 'by our own courts'. However, when she retired from the Hong Kong Civil Service, she admitted that Article 23 had been the 'most important', 'sensitive' and 'challenging' measure facing Hong Kong since 1997.

'Article 23 undoubtedly provoked the biggest political crisis since the handover. Beijing blamed four types of "troublemakers" – politicians, media professionals, academics and foreigners'.[41] Mainland politicians used the phrase *'fanzhong luangang'* to describe the demonstration, words that accuse Hong Kong's own dissidents of 'rebelling or causing turmoil'.[42] Beijing responded to the crisis by appointing Zheng Qinghong, a member of the Standing Committee of the Political Bureau, to oversee Hong Kong affairs and by setting up a coordination Committee comprising eighteen members, including officials from the State Council's Hong Kong and Macao Affairs Office, the Liaison

39 C. Yeung, 'Article 23 to test Hong Kong's autonomy', *SCMP*, 14 October 2002.

40 A. Chan, 'One country, two systems', Heritage Foundation Lecture, Heritage Foundation Policy Research & Analysis, 2 October 2003.

41 Y. Zheng and S. K. Tok, 'Democratisation in Hong Kong: a crisis brewing for Beijing?', in Zheng and Yew, *Hong Kong under Chinese Rule*, p. 191; S. Lo, 'The mainlandization and recolonization of Hong Kong', in Cheng, *The Hong Kong Special Administrative Region*, pp. 181–2.

42 Ng, *Paradigm City*, p. 38.

Office in Hong Kong, the Liaison Office in Macao, the Ministry of Public Security, the Ministry of National Security, the Party Central Committee's United Front Department and the PLA. These measures were intended to tighten Beijing's 'behind-the-scenes' grip On Hong Kong affairs, take a hard-line policy towards the 'unpatriotic' democrats and prevent them from winning half the seats in the September 2004 LEGCO elections.[43]

Beijing's hard line was supplemented by the 'velvet glove' of various propaganda initiatives, such as visits to the HKSAR by the PRC's Olympic athletes and the Chinese astronaut Yang Liwei. 2003 also saw the inauguration of CEPA and an agreement to relax the rules of mainland visitors to the HKSAR. These measures were designed to 'win the hearts and minds' of Hong Kong people and increase patriotic sentiments. But although they improved the territory's immediate economic prospects, they also made it more economically dependent on the mainland and stored up future resentment against mainlandisation.[44] Moreover, capitalist promises, Ng says, 'no longer seemed sufficient to restrain the political desire of the people'.[45] On 1 July 2004, another half million people took part in a protest against the Tung administration, fuelled by reports that three popular radio phone-in hosts had resigned due to intimidation.[46] These confirmed Hongkongers feared that 'mainland' ways were seeping into Hong Kong, eroding core values such as freedom of speech. Clamping down on the pro-democracy movement in Hong Kong, Lo argues, was also one means of firing a shot across the bows of Taiwanese independence. In late 2003, pressure was also brought to bear on Tung to decelerate the pace of democratisation in Hong Kong. His subsequent report paved the way for the NPCSC's interpretation of the Basic Law in April 2004, which held that the 2007 election of the CE and the 2008 LEGCO elections would not be by universal suffrage.

43 Lo, 'Mainlandization and recolonization', in Cheng, *The Hong Kong Special Administrative Region*, p. 205.
44 Lo, 'Mainlandization and recolonization', in Cheng, p. 198.
45 Ng, *Paradigm City*, p. 39.
46 Lo, 'Mainlandization and recolonization', in Cheng, *The Hong Kong Special Administrative Region*, pp. 181–2, 205. The talk show hosts were Albert Cheng, Wong-Yuk-man and Allen Lee.

The attempt to introduce Article 23 was a step too far in what Lo calls Tung's unpopular mainlandization policies.[47] These, he argues, attempted to Sinicise the territory, bringing its political and legal processes more in line with those of the mainland and restricting people's civil liberties. In particular, this mainlandisation policy sought to make Hong Kong more reliant on the NPCSC's interpretation of the Basic Law. In April 2014, however, the issue resurfaced. Peking University law professor and Basic Law Committee member Rao Geping remarked that some mainland academics wanted to see the mainland's national security law enacted in Hong Kong until the HKSAR enacted Article 23. Another Basic Law Committee member, Wang Zhenmin, called for Article 23 to be implemented after six demonstrators from the Hong Kong Independence movement broke into the PLA's base in Hong Kong carrying the British colonial flag.[48] In an interview with the mainland newspaper, *Global Times*, Geping accused the group of opposing the Basic Law, challenging national sovereignty and damaging national security. However, the Basic Law stipulates that – with certain named exceptions – national laws shall not be applied in Hong Kong. Pro-Beijing legal academics then suggested changing the Basic Law.[49] The pro-Beijing president of LEGCO Jasper Tsang Yok-sing expressed his shock at the suggestion, arguing that he did not think it represented the view of the central authorities. Whilst it was thought unlikely that the HKSAR government would risk reviving Article 23, the idea was planted that the Occupy Central civil disobedience movement could provide Beijing with an opening to impose national security legislation on the HKSAR.

47 Lo, 'Mainlandization and recolonization', in Cheng, *The Hong Kong Special Administrative Region*, pp. 185–6.

48 'Radical Hong Kong protesters trespass onto PLA headquarters', *Chinasmack*, 29 December 2013. www.chinasmack.com/2013/stories.

49 J. Lam and G. Cheung, 'Hong Kong "should adopt national security law until own version is ready"', SCMP, 7 April 2014.

10

The law wars: law as politics, politics as law

After the first occasion, the government reassured Hongkongers that NPCSC intervention would be exceptional. Yet between 2004 and 2005, two further NPCSC interpretations occurred. The first began in 2004 and was intended, after the 1 July march, to stymy the pace of democratisation by vetoing universal suffrage for the 2007 CE and 2008 LEGCO elections. The second, in April 2005, concerned the period of office of the CE and arose following Tung's resignation from office in March 2005. Under the Basic Law, a new CE had to be elected within six months. The question arose as to whether the new CE should serve out the remainder of Tung's term of office (two years) or a full five-year term.

THE NPCSC'S INTERPRETATION ON THE PACE OF DEMOCRATIC DEVELOPMENT

The second NPCSC intervention of the Basic Law since 1997 began with steps by Beijing to slow the pace of democratisation in 2004. After the July 2003 march, the pro-democracy camp demanded that the election of the LEGCO and the chief executive after 2007 should proceed on a more democratic basis, preferably universal suffrage. However, the extent of dissatisfaction evidenced by the 1 July 2003 protest had also convinced Beijing that it needed to clamp down on democratic 'troublemakers'. In December 2003, four prominent Communist Party legal experts published an essay refuting the idea that the electoral agenda could be determined by the Hong Kong electorate, claiming it was an erroneous interpretation of the Basic Law'.[1] The four legal scholars quickly became the butt of local satire, dubbed 'the Four Divine Monks' after characters from popular knight-errant novels, 'representing inflexible orthodoxy'.[2] As the debate became more heated, and liberal legal experts challenged this view, the mainland experts became 'more hostile and aggressive in their demeanour and rhetoric', reasserting Beijing's right to interfere in Hong Kong's legislative reform and declaring that it 'would definitely interfere/control to the end'.[3]

According to Article 68 of the Basic Law, 'the method for forming the Legislative Council shall be specified in the light of the actual situation in the Hong Kong Special Administrative Region and in accordance with the principle of gradual and orderly progress. The ultimate aim is the election of all members of the Legislative Council by universal suffrage'. Problematically, it is left up to the NPCSC to decide what the 'actual situation' is at any given time, and its view is coloured by national interests. It is, therefore, unsurprising that the views of the NPCSC and Hong Kong people seldom coincide. The procedure for informing the NPCSC of the 'actual situation' involves the CE filing a report to the NPCSC. It then decides if Hong Kong is ready for democracy. If it decides that Hong Kong is not ready, it can spell out what the future pace of development should be. In 2004, the CE provided such a report, recommending that direct elections should not be introduced in 2007 and 2008, which was when everyone else was expecting them to take place.[4]

Surveys conducted between 2003 and 2009 indicated that Hongkongers were ready for democracy – 47 to 53 per cent of respondents supported the direct election of the CE, and 17 to 30 per cent supported direct election of the CE by universal suffrage;[5] most understood this to be promised by 2007 for the CE elections and thereafter for the LEGCO elections. However, pro-Beijing forces had different ideas about the timetable for universal suffrage set out in the Basic Law. At issue was the interpretation of Article 7 of Annex I and Article 3 of

[1] Ng, *Paradigm City*, p. 39. [2] Ng, *Paradigm City*. [3] Ng, *Paradigm City*.

[4] See B. Y. T. Tai, 'An unexpected chapter two of Hong Kong's constitution: new players and new strategies', in Sing, *Politics and Government*, p. 231.

[5] S. H. Lo, *Competing Chinese Political Visions: Hong Kong v. Beijing on Democracy* (Santa Barbara: Praeger, 2010), p. 10.

Annex II.[6] The NPCSC held that no modification to the election process could be introduced by the CE or LEGCO without NPCSC approval and that direct elections for LEGCO and the post of CE would violate the Basic Law. The pan-democrats proposed a referendum to test public opinion on what method should be used to elect both the CE and LEGCO. This too was criticised by pro-Beijing groups as unsanctioned by the Basic Law. Nonetheless, Lo says, Martin Lee revealed that during the drafting of the Basic Law in 1989, it had been mooted that all Hong Kong citizens could vote for the methods of election.[7]

At this point in time, the public's dissatisfaction with the government's handling of relations with Beijing was at its highest level since 1997.[8] Survey data showed that public dissatisfaction peaked in June and July 2004, just after this NPCSC ruling.[9] The reining in of pro-democracy aspirations was Beijing's response to the 1 July 2003 rally. The Bishop of Hong Kong, Joseph Zen Ze-kiun, called the NPCSC's intervention 'our own June 4th', shattering Hongkongers hopes for full democracy: 'The June 4 we experienced did not shed any blood, there were neither tanks nor machine guns. But in their fierce shape, the so-called "guardians of the Basic Law" came to lecture us about patriotism, and certain [Beijing officials] claimed some people wanted to achieve independence [for Hong Kong] ... Before we had chance to discuss the issues surrounding universal suffrage in 2007–2008, the committee had already made a decision for us'.[10]

In October 2005, the HKSAR administration floated its own reform proposals for the 2007 and 2008 elections. These were endorsed by the

6 Article 7 of Annex 1 states that: 'If there is a need to amend the method of electing the chief executive for the terms subsequent to the year 2007, such amendments must be made with the endorsement of a two-thirds majority of all the members of the LEGCO and the consent of the chief executive, and they shall be reported to the NPCSC for the record'. Article 3 in Annex II states that: 'In regard to the method of forming the legislature ... [i]f there is a need to amend the provisions, such amendments must be made with the endorsement of a two-thirds majority of all the members of LEGCO and the consent of the chief executive, and they shall be reported to the NPCSC for the record'.

7 Lo, *Competing Chinese Politics*, p. 63.

8 Carroll, 'Ten years later', p. 15.

9 M. E. DeGolyer, 'Electoral structures and public opinion in the 2004 Hong Kong legislative council elections', in Sing, *Politics and Government in Hong Kong*, pp. 206–7.

10 P. Hui, 'Basic Law interpretation was our own June 4, says bishop', *SCMP*, 5 June 2004.

PRC President, Hu Jintao.[11] They increased the number entitled to vote in what remained a 'small circle' election of the CE and stipulated that half of the LEGCO seats could in the future come from geographical constituencies. Since, Lo argues, Annex I and Annex II of the Basic Law stipulated that any change to the electoral process had to obtain the support of two-thirds of LEGCO members, in 2005 this meant that the government proposals required at least forty votes.[12] Controversially, in 2014, the NPCSC announced an even more restrictive system (see Chapter 1).

THE NPCSC'S INTERPRETATION REGARDING THE CE'S TERM OF OFFICE

The third NPCSC intervention followed close on the heels of this attempt to slow democratisation by legal means. It was seen by the Article 45 Concern Group as yet a further attempt to undermine the judicial autonomy of the HKSAR.[13] Between July 2004 and March 2005, it became evident that Tung's legitimacy had fallen to the point of no return. In March 2005, he resigned, three years into his five-year term. The issue which then arose was whether his successor and Acting CE, Donald Tsang, should serve out the remaining two years of the CE's term of office or serve a full five-year term. Article 46 of the Basic Law gave the CE's term of office as five years; Articles 52 and 53, though dealing with the election of a replacement in the event of the CE's resignation, did not specify what term the replacement should serve. Because a new CE had to be elected within six months, the government announced that the election would take place in July 2005. The NPCSC was asked to intervene to decide the matter. Lo observes that prior to this, there had been 'a carefully orchestrated consultation' with the Hong Kong elites, including the visits of researchers, public security personnel and military officers.[14] Incentives were also given to some democrats to support the intervention, whilst a special committee was established to conduct local lobbying efforts.[15]

11 Lo, *Competing Chinese Political Visions*, p. 66.
12 Lo, *Competing Chinese Political Visions*.
13 Lo, "Mainlandization and Recolonization," in Cheng, *The Hong Kong Special Administrative Region*, p. 209.
14 Lo, *Competing Chinese Political Visions*, pp. 206–7.
15 Lo, *Competing Chinese Political Visions*.

Initially, the government had preferred a five year term. It reversed its position following a visit to Beijing by Secretary for Justice Elsie Leung and the advice of mainland legal scholars who had participated in drafting the Basic Law. However, since Article 46 of the Basic Law clearly stated that the CE should serve a five-year term, the question arose as to whether the government's suggestion was compatible with the Basic Law. As Tai notes, the text of the Basic Law can be manipulated by the NPCSC to achieve whatever objective it seeks.[16] In this instance, the government introduced a bill to LEGCO to amend the Basic Law to specify that in such an event, the replacement CE should serve out whatever was the remaining term of office. Two applications for judicial review arose on the matter and were still before the courts when, in April, the Acting CE, Donald Tsang, announced that the government was requesting an NPCSC interpretation. Because the NPCSC was able to decide this matter before it could complete its journey through the legal system, this was a pre-emptive strike against the due process of law-making and the independent judicial power of the courts, another 'quick fix' to a political problem. It was also seen by some as an indication of the government's fears that it would lose the judicial review.

This request for yet another NPSC interpretation prompted a silent march of about 900 lawyers led by the Article 45 Concern Group, many of whom had previously led the Article 23 Concern Group (four of this group were elected to LEGCO in 2004, an indication of how far law and politics overlapped). They argued that the NPCSC's intervention raised questions about how statutes, including Hong Kong's 'mini-constitution', should be interpreted – according to common law or civil law traditions. As things stood, the NPCSC's interpretation allowed the government to:

> fall in line with Beijing's wishes and overc[o]me the obstacle of giving an initial two-year term to Mr Tung's successor ... by explicitly disregarding the common-law principles of interpretation used by the courts in favour of interpreting parts of the Basic Law, according to the more flexible principles that apply under the mainland legal system ... [It] did so at the price of raising questions about which legal system the Hong Kong government was committed to protecting and what fundamental rights might end up being restricted if the provisions on

[16] Tai, 'An unexpected chapter two' in Sing, *Politics and Government*, p. 234.

> civil liberties in the Basic Law were now also interpreted according to the [m]ainland's more flexible rules.[17]

Members of the Article 45 Group, along with pro-democracy lawmakers and academics, were invited to attend a meeting with mainland officials and the 'four guardians of the Basic Law' in Shenzhen to discuss whether the issue could be settled by the Hong Kong courts. Democracy Party members, being barred from entering the mainland, were unable to attend. The outcome of this meeting was a statement by the deputy-secretary of the NPCSC to the effect that the NPCSC had unfettered powers of interpretation, that it would interpret the Basic Law on the matter and that it would decide if a two-year term of office was correct.

Lo argues that this contest revealed the existence of two different constitutional cultures in the HKSAR – the Bar and its supporters, who regarded the CFA as the ultimate authority on interpretation of the Basic Law, and the government and Beijing's legal experts, who regarded NPCSC interpretation as authoritative.[18] He suggests that, whilst the government saw the interpretations as a legal move, Hong Kong's lawyers regarded them as essentially political and a violation of the territory's common-law system. However, if the legal community is to act as a bulwark against the administration's encroachment on civil liberties, it must be politically engaged. Though several leading members of the Bar Association are elected members of LEGCO and well-known for their advocacy of democratic reform, the profession only has a relatively short history in political activism. In the 1960s, for example, just five – a combination of academic lawyers and members of the Bar – campaigned against the government's use of detention without trial. This changed in the 1990s, with the rise of greater human rights litigation following the introduction of the Bill of Rights. However, it is noticeable that throughout this history, the solicitor's branch of the profession has proved either quiescent in the face of attacks on the rule of law or opposed to the Bar's position.

This division was repeated in 2014, when the Bar criticised and the Law Society supported Beijing's White Paper. The divide is partly

[17] Gittings, 'Changing expectations'. The CFA laid out the common-law principles of interpretation in the cases of *Ng Ka Ling* v. *Director of Immigration* [1999] 1HKLRD 577 and *Chong Fung Yuen* [2001] 2 HKLRD 533.

[18] Lo, 'Mainlandization and Recolonization', in Cheng, *The Hong Kong Special Administrative Region*, p. 210.

explained by the difference in the structural position of the two branches of the profession, for whilst the Bar operates principally in the Hong Kong courts, the solicitors' branch is involved in cross-border legal work with mainland commercial and legal firms. It is, thus, difficult to speak of a Hong Kong legal community united around rule of law as a core value.

CIVIL SOCIETY'S REACTION TO THE NPCSC INTERPRETATION ON DEMOCRATIC REFORM

In December 2005, following the NPCSC's rejection of universal suffrage for the 2007 CE and 2008 LEGCO elections, the pan-democrats mobilised hundreds of thousands to demonstrate in support of direct elections.[19] The PRC responded with indifference. It reiterated that democratic development must proceed in accordance with the Basic Law. The government had by this point launched its own reform package. When LEGCO voted on this, the government failed to achieve the forty votes it needed to succeed.

Lo identifies this as the point at which the HKSAR administration began to view the pan-democrats as 'the opposition'; former Basic Law members called for the enactment of Article 23 before any chance of direct elections.[20] This threat of enacting Article 23 to deal with 'unpatriotic' elements would recur in 2013 and 2014 during Occupy Central's campaign for universal suffrage for the 2017 CE election.

Despite numerous attempts to make the issue disappear, the question of the pace of democracy persisted. In 2007, Tsang sought the NPCSC's view on the method for selecting the CE and LEGCO elections in 2012. The NPCSC ruled out universal suffrage but allowed it for 2017 CE election and LEGCO elections thereafter. However, it demanded that candidates be selected by a Nomination Committee. This opened up the possibility of electing the CE by universal suffrage in 2017 and for the LEGCO in 2020, but closed down the prospect of pro-democracy candidates being allowed to stand. The membership of the Nomination Committee would remain within Beijing's fiat and only 'patriotic' candidates would be eligible to stand for election as CE. In effect, the pro-Beijing elite would be able to retain control and no pan-democrat would be eligible for election. This attenuated version of

19 Lo, *Competing Chinese Political Visions*, pp. 71–5.
20 Lo, *Competing Chinese Political Visions*, p. 79.

universal suffrage signalled Beijing's fears that universal suffrage would result in the election of a candidate opposed to the policies of the political centre. This reflects what Zheng and Tok describe as the two different centres of loyalty carved out by the Basic Law: the office of the CE – endowed by and answerable to Beijing and lacking a popular mandate – and LEGCO, which enjoys greater popular legitimacy and is more answerable to the general population.[21] The contest between the two is increasingly played out not in the law courts but on the streets.

[21] Y. Zheng, and S. K. Tok, 'Ending the Governance Crisis?' in Zheng and Yew, *Hong Kong under Chinese Rule*, p. 97.

Beijing blocks democ reform –
cites local troublemakers –

11

The law wars: law and civil society

The decision to resort to street protests reflects the fundamental incapacity of the HKSAR's legal and political institutions to cope with rising discontent. The dominance of pro-establishment forces in LEGCO means that it has not been able to serve as an effective channel for the resolution of the conflicting views of the community.[1] Not all political issues are, however, justifiable.

Judicial review is a process that explicitly thrusts courts into a political role.[2] Rule of law, Chan argues, is probably best exemplified by judicial review. It is 'a process by which the exercise of public power is brought under scrutiny by an independent and impartial judiciary'.[3] The former chief justice, Andrew Li, argues that judicial review has 'redefined the legal landscape' of the HKSAR and significantly influenced the conduct of government business and public debate on many issues.[4] Since 1997 social activists have increasingly employed legal means to challenge the government's and developers' plans. To do this, they have turned to judicial review. Applications for judicial review have increased since 1997, Chan notes, partly reflecting the public's rising expectations of good governance, frustration with the political

[1] J. Chan, 'Administrative Law', in Young and Ghai, *Hong Kong's Court of Final Appeal*, pp. 417–46.

[2] Halliday, Karpik and Feeley, *Fighting for political freedom*, p. 6.

[3] Chan, 'Administrative law'.

[4] Chan, 'Administrative law', referring to a speech given by the chief justice at the opening of the Legal Year, 8 January 2007.

system, the willingness of the legal profession to take such cases sometimes on a *pro bono* basis and increased avenues of challenge through the provisions of the Bill of Rights and the Basic Law. Applications have enjoyed a high success rate, leading some to argue that there are 'too many' and the CFA to raise the threshold 'perhaps to discourage the legalisation of political issues'.[5] However, Chan concludes overall that the CFA has delivered some major judgments that have had far-reaching implications and, perhaps more importantly, have facilitated access to justice and 'enhanced procedural due process'.[6]

Lo describes this as the 'gathering politicisation of the judicial process' and argues that it was the resort to the courts by civil society groups that probably 'kick-started the judicial review phenomenon in the HKSAR'.[7] As evidence of this, Lo cites the use of judicial review in 2002 by housing activists and by the Society for the Protection of the Harbour in 2003. These were followed by another application for judicial review in 2004, when the government sought to proceed with the stock market launch of the Link Real Estate Investment Trust (LinkReit). The LinkReit trust portfolio included Hong Kong Housing Authority properties occupied by grassroots Hongkongers. The initial public offering was substantially delayed, however, when a sixty-seven-year-old tenant living on social security, Lo Siu Lan, challenged its legitimacy. She, along with many other public housing tenants, feared that the move would result in a loss of public amenities as well as rent increases for flats and shops, provoking price rises. The extent of public support for Lo took the government by surprise. Her application for judicial review was dismissed in December, but she was set to appeal. When the Housing Authority applied to abridge the time for her to appeal, the Appeal Committee of the CFA refused its application, further delaying the offering.[8] Though her legal challenge eventually failed, Lo had managed to hold up the billion dollar plans of developers, the government and investors. The old formula of 'big business, small government', Chu suggests, no longer exacted public support.[9] Instead, the government was criticised for privatising public assets, helping the rich and ignoring the poor.

[5] Chan, 'Administrative law', p. 422. [6] Chan, 'Administrative law'.

[7] Lo, *Judicial Construction of Hong Kong's Basic Law*, p. 147.

[8] See Lo, *Judicial Construction of Hong Kong's Basic Law*, pp. 111–12.

[9] Chu, *Lost in Transition*, p. 55.

It was alleged that political activists were behind Lo's legal action, prompting the CE to call the use of judicial review to challenge government initiatives 'ill-intentioned' and accusing those who encouraged litigants of pursuing 'unspeakable ends'.[10] In 2011, this charge was again levelled against those who supported a litigant, Chu Yee-wah, in her argument that the environmental assessment for the development of the Hong Kong-Zhuhai-Macau Bridge failed to comply with the regulations. Chu was a retiree dependent on social security payments; she lived in public housing in Tung Chung, and it was alleged that she had been encouraged to apply for judicial review by the Civic Party. Her success 'stunned the HKSAR government', propelling its appeal. The CE, addressing LEGCO, stated that:

> a certain political party and politicians make use of legal proceedings or other means, under the excuse of environmental protection or conservation, to block large-scale projects when works are about to start to achieve their own political interests but harming Hong Kong's interests, such as the timely opportunity of economic integration with mainland China, the competitiveness of Hong Kong and the creation of jobs.[11]

Over seventy other major development projects had to be put on hold pending the outcome of the case, which eventually ended with victory for the government. In the process, the Court of First Instance was attacked for 'prescribing environmental standards "as if there were judges ruling Hong Kong"'.[12] Pro-Beijing supporters accused the courts of interfering in politics and taking the place of the government. What the case also revealed, however, was that economic integration with the mainland was not a popular policy and that the legal challenge to this integration project was only the start of popular discontent with the entire mainlandisation project.

The use of law by civil society activists might have been regarded by the government as a good sign. People were, after all, abiding by the law rather than taking to the streets; legal cases could act as a warning that

[10] Lo, *Judicial Construction of Hong Kong's Basic Law*, p. 147.

[11] Hong Kong Legislative Council, 8 June 2011, question by the Hon Lam Tai-fai and reply by the Acting Secretary for the Environment, Dr Kitty Poon, LCQ6: Regarding the judicial review of Hong Kong-Zhuhai-Macao Bridge.

[12] Lo, *Judicial Construction of Hong Kong's Basic Law*.

unresolved issues needed to be addressed. However, the government saw judicial review as troublesome and its supporters as troublemakers.

In the absence of democracy, moreover, the courts were being asked to bear a burden they were ill-equipped to carry. A repeated refrain of successive chief justices has been that the courts cannot resolve the HKSAR's political problems. This is, perhaps, to lose sight of that people look to the courts for. One effect of court hearings is that matters are openly discussed and, sometimes, arguments from other places are aired, including arguments about democracy and human rights. This in itself adds to political discourse in Hong Kong. In addition, procedural fairness – even when litigants fail – helps satisfy the search for justice and the sense that one has at least been listened to.

There are few platforms available to Hongkongers for the airing of grievances and calling a remote government to account. Even if success in the courts is infrequent, the fact that it happens at all is key to the efficacy of rule of law ideology. As Lo argues, the courts have come to be regarded as 'the last redoubt', putting up legal barricades against the erosion of Hong Kong's 'core values'.[13] But public faith in the rule of law has been hollowed out. Cumulatively, the high-level corruption trials as well as accusations of maladministration and malfeasance have convinced the public that 'mainland ways' have indeed undermined the way of life they knew before 1997. Observers warn of a weakening of watchdogs as senior prosecutors leave the prosecutions department, judges step down or are forced to leave the bench and the various bodies appointed to oversee the government's conduct of its own business are depleted. Legal aid is administered not by an independent body but by a government department. Judicial review is on the decline – the number of applications peaked at 149 in 2005, but by 2011 had fallen by 20 per cent to 120. Government and business leaders stated that ways needed to be found to curb the delays caused by challenges to government decisions.[14] Nor is it easy to find lawyers prepared to take on the government – the vast majority of Hong Kong's law firms serve international commerce and are loath to criticise mainland policies. In addition, the poor have very little access to justice. Civil justice reforms promote mediation in place of litigation, removing

[13] Lo, *Judicial Construction of Hong Kong's Basic Law*, p. 11.
[14] 'A bulwark against the abuse of power', *SCMP*, 11 October 2012; *Ming Pao*, 18 June 2007.

many issues from the public eye. Law schools train students to serve the needs of global capital rather than those of ordinary citizens, though since 2012 there has been a rise in activism on the part of law students, whilst public interest law has become a positive choice for would-be lawyers.

The gradual closing down of these avenues of justice since 1997 means that Hongkongers have had to turn to other means to challenge the government, defend their freedoms and protect their rights. Cartier notes the role of artworks in this movement, and in particular the 'Back to the Basic' exhibit of July 2007. This invited artists to develop work based on their own understanding of the Basic Law and to 'reveal complex relationships between people and the Basic Law through symbolic meanings'. One artist, Leung Po-shan, performed 'Basic Law in Burning', in which he read a page or two from the Basic Law to an individual, removed the pages from the booklet, burned them, collected the ashes in a plastic bag and presented them to the participant:

> in this act, the audience receives that which Hong Kong is denied: the central government issued repeated statements that Hong Kong had no residual power under the Basic Law in the run-up to 1 July 2007 ... [Leung] spoke closely into the ear of the listener as if to ensure that Hong Kong people hear the reality of the absence of local interpretation of the Basic Law – after all, Hong Kong people had effectively no representation in its drafting.[15]

Cultural works increasingly question the place of law in Hong Kong society. Another performance piece illustrates this point. The TengSeWong/Voice-Writer series processes the text of the Basic Law, translating it from spoken Cantonese into Mandarin using computer voice-software. The resulting gibberish raised the questions, 'What is the meaning of the Basic Law? Is it even translatable or worth the effort? Could it be a duplicitous document? Does it have any meaning at all?'[16] Part of the reason these works are so effective is that they create public participation 'from mere passers-by' and are thus much more difficult to contain than protest marches. Since 1997, Cartier argues, they have become part of the landscape of Hong Kong, 'etched indelibly into spaces of experience and into many people's memories'.[17]

[15] Cartier, 'Power plays', pp. 36–7.
[16] Cartier, 'Power plays', p. 35.
[17] Cartier, 'Power plays', p. 40.

What she calls 'wordplay' in spoken and written Cantonese (punning, deployment of linguistic tropes and use of Chinese characters that are unique to the Cantonese language) demonstrate 'not only how words or characters and meanings are changed and even lost, but the symbolic miscues and even incommensurability between perspectives among Hong Kong people and elite state interests in Hong Kong and Beijing'.[18] Contesting interpretations of the law through culture has become an art of resistance.

The turn to law on the part of social activists was partly a legacy of the rhetoric of the last governor.[19] As Turner argues, Patten presented Hongkongers with a more politicised version of themselves, one in which they themselves could play an active role in determining their future.[20] This conception of Hong Kong resonated with popular culture's representation of Hongkongers themselves as active agents, capable of carving out their own future, defending their distinct culture and identity.[21] For Lau Siu-kai, the growing realisation by Hongkongers of their own agency and the 'vast difference in values' between Hong Kong and mainland people meant that the post-1997 identity potentially contained within it seeds of conflict with the mainland.[22] As Armentrout astutely notes, this analysis 'posits Cantonese culturalism as a threat to stability and suggests a race between those who are seen to be encouraging centrifugal forces that pull Hong Kong Chinese away from being a clone of the mainland and those who are determined to create a "harmonious society" . . . at whatever cost to Hong Kong's unique identity'.[23] If politically active Hongkongers succeeded in challenging their own government in the courts, they might begin to challenge mainland rule.[24]

[18] Cartier, 'Power Plays', p. 35.

[19] Sum, 'War of words'.

[20] M. Turner, '60s/90s, Dissolving the People', Hong Kong, Hong Kong Arts Centre Installation.

[21] Sum, 'War of words'.

[22] S. K. Lau, cited in F. Armentrout, '*Canto-culture:* Loving a Floating City', *Hong Kong Journal* 6 (2007).

[23] Armentrout, '*Canto-culture*'.

[24] E. Vickers, *In Search of an Identity: The Politics of History as a School Subject in Hong Kong 1960s–2002*, 2nd ed. (Hong Kong: Comparative Education Research Centre, 2005, p. 76, citing Lin Yuan, '*Gangren zhi gang, shei shi 'Gangren'?*' (Hong Kong People Ruling Hong Kong – Who are 'Hong Kong People'?) in J. Wu and Z. W. Zhang (eds.), *Yue du Xiang-gang pu ji wen hua 1970–2000* (Reading Hong Kong Popular Culture 1970–2000) (Hong Kong: Oxford University Press, 2002).

12

The law wars: interpreting the law

As the foregoing demonstrates, interpretation of the Basic Law has been at the heart of politico-legal disputes since 1997.[1] As Tai has written, in almost all the constitutional controversies in Hong Kong, 'disputes focused on the interpretation of certain provisions of the Basic Law'.[2] He argues that the 'correct' legal meaning cannot simply be read-off from the legal text itself since many different legal meanings can be derived from the rules of interpretation and using different rules can also lead one to the same interpretation.

Article 158 of the Basic Law specifies that the power of interpretation is split between the courts of Hong Kong and the NPCSC.

[1] See generally J. M. M. Chan and C. L. Lim (eds.), *Law of the Hong Kong Constitution* (Hong Kong: Sweet & Maxwell, 2011); A. H. Y. Chen, 'The theory, constitution and practice of autonomy: the case of Hong Kong' in J. Oliveira and P. Cardinal (eds.), *One Country, Two Systems, Three Legal Orders – Perspectives of Evolution* (Berlin: Springer-Verlag, 2009), pp 751–67; M. C. Davis, 'Interpreting constitutionalism and democratisation in Hong Kong', in H. Fu, L. Harris and S. Young (eds.), *Interpreting Hong Kong's Basic Law: The Struggle for Coherence* (New York: Palgrave Macmillan, 2007); Y. Ghai, 'Hong Kong's autonomy: dialects and institutions' in Y. Ghai and S. Woodman (eds.), *Practising Self-Government: A Comparative Study of Autonomous Regions* (Cambridge: Cambridge University Press, 2013), pp. 315–47; A. D. Jordan, 'Lost in translation: two legal cultures, the Common Law Judiciary and the Basic Law of the Hong Kong Special Administrative Region', *Cornell International Law Journal* 30, pp. 335–80; Young and Ghai, *Hong Kong's Court of Final Appeal*.

[2] Tai, 'An unexpected chapter two', in Sing, *Politics and Government*, pp. 221–3.

But, Ghai argues, Hong Kong's common law system often seems impenetrable to the Chinese authorities. The Chinese are:

> not tuned in to the niceties of Western procedures and are more at home with the more flexible standards of Chinese law. The two legal systems have very different traditions, styles of interpretation, and capacity for accommodation to political pressures. The presence of a strong legal system in Hong Kong and the absence of a fully democratic system, tend to convert contentious political, and sometimes social, matters into legal issues, but China prefers legal issues to be treated as political matters in which it has the upper hand.[3]

The doctrine of the separation of powers is foreign to China. Its courts and judiciaries are not independent from the legislature and executive. Mainland courts must follow party directives and 'cannot refuse to enforce a law because it might be considered to contravene the Constitution'.[4] Differences of approach are part of the problem of policing the new legal boundary, but differences of politics are thus equally influential.

As Ghai argues, the Achilles heel of autonomy is that the ultimate responsibility for the interpretation of the Basic Law lies with the NPCSC. The assumption underlying the Basic Law is, he says, 'that the responsibility for policing the boundaries between Hong Kong's institutions lies with the HKSAR's courts, but the policing of boundaries between them and the central authorities is with the NPCSC'.[5] The power of interpretation is, he says, 'intertwined deeply in the relationship between Beijing and Hong Kong; it is not simply about the meaning of laws, but about power relationships'.[6] What has become clear since 1997 is that, whilst the Hong Kong courts have power of final adjudication – and in some instances can also interpret certain provisions of the Basic Law – the NPCSC has the power of final interpretation, and it employs a different approach to this task of the common law. The difference between the two legal

[3] Ghai, 'Themes and arguments', in Young and Ghai, *Hong Kong's Court of Final Appeal*, pp. 2–3.

[4] Ghai, 'Themes and arguments', in Young and Ghai, *Hong Kong's Court of Final Appeal*.

[5] Ghai, 'Autonomy and the Court of Final Appeal', in Young and Ghai, *Hong Kong's Court of Final Appeal*, p. 58.

[6] Ghai, 'Autonomy and the Court of Final Appeal', in Young and Ghai, *Hong Kong's Court of Final Appeal*.

systems is nowhere better revealed, Ghai argues, than in their systems for interpreting the law.

In this regard, since 1997 all Hong Kong's courts (but especially the CFA) have been policing the line between the two systems. The CFA has had to make decisions on 'momentous matters in largely uncharted territory' relating to the Basic Law,[7] and in doing so, has butted against a very different idea of the relationship between the courts and the executive. As Tai notes, in *Ng Ka Ling* v. *Director of Immigration*, the CFA had already positioned itself 'as the guardian of Hong Kong's high degree of autonomy, the guardian of Hong Kong's rule of law, and the guardian of human rights in Hong Kong'.[8] But the NPCSC issued an interpretation of the Basic Law which, in effect, overruled the CFA's judgment.

In 2001, in another right of abode case,[9] the battle recommenced when the CFA held that the NPCSC's ruling did not apply to the particular provision of the Basic Law in the case before it.[10] It then reaffirmed that the courts of the HKSAR were bound to apply the common law approach to the interpretation of law, since the Basic Law itself provided for a separate legal system in the HKSAR based on common law. The common law approach was to construe the language used in the Basic Law to ascertain the legislative intent, avoiding a 'literal, technical, narrow or rigid approach', looking at the context and purpose to ascertain the meaning of the language used but not giving it a meaning which it could not bear. The CFA concluded that the language of the relevant section of the Basic Law, when considered in the light of its context and purpose, had a clear meaning, which was that Chinese citizens born in Hong Kong before or after 1 July 1997 had the status of permanent residents.

Though heavily criticised by mainland lawyers, the judgment, 'chalked up a much-needed victory for the court'.[11] The case, however, continued to irritate mainland lawyers, who looked for opportunities to nullify the CFA's approach, reiterating that there was a single, correct

[7] Ghai, 'Autonomy and the Court of Final Appeal', in Young and Ghai, *Hong Kong's Court of Final Appeal*.
[8] Ghai, 'Autonomy and the Court of Final Appeal', in Young and Ghai, *Hong Kong's Court of Final Appeal*.
[9] *Director of Immigration* v. *Chong Fung Yuen* (2001) 2 HKLRD 533.
[10] *Director of Immigration* v. *Chong Fung Yuen* (2001) 4 HKCFAR 211, CFA.
[11] *Director of Immigration* v. *Chong Fung Yuen* (2001) 4 HKCFAR 211, CFA.

interpretation, and that, under Article 158 (1) of the Basic Law, the power of interpretation was vested in the NPCSC. However, under Article 158 (2) of the Basic Law, the courts of the HKSAR are constitutionally authorized by the NPCSC to interpret *on their own* in the course of adjudicating cases provisions of the Basic Law that are within the limits of the autonomy of the HKSAR. The Hong Kong Bar Association argued that this means that there is no 'correct' meaning of the Basic Law which exists separately as an objective fact:

> under the common law system, statutes and constitutions mean what the Courts interpret them to mean, based on well-established and long-developed principles of statutory and constitutional interpretation, upon hearing adversarial arguments between the parties and considering the facts and evidence placed by the parties (including the Government) before the Court, in an open and transparent judicial setting. It is not the case ... that in deciding cases judges and the Courts in Hong Kong need to (or can) learn, understand, or take instructions, about any definitive 'correct' meaning of the Basic Law from anyone else, be they public officials or scholars, here or elsewhere.[12]

Commenting on the fact that Basic Law cases and 'ordinary' statutory interpretation cases were now being interpreted in different ways, in 2005 Buddle argued that a 'two-stream legal system has developed', which was 'not good either for the legal uncertainty or the rule of law'.[13] Elsie Leung herself perpetuated this legal uncertainty when, in 2012, she returned to the theme that the Basic Law should be interpreted not according to common law principles but according to Chinese principles. Leung was seen locally as a Beijing mouthpiece. Her statement came amidst the 2012 controversy about mainland mothers giving birth to babies in local hospitals. She urged the government to push for an NPCSC intervention to stop the practice, reviving memories of the CFA's 2001 decision. This was an opportunity for pro-Beijing groups to cast the judiciary once again in the role of villain harming Hong Kong and the NPCSC as its saviour. Lo argues that legislators, seeking a quick means to fix the problem, pushed for a way to nullify the CFA's decision in the 2001 *Chong Fung Yuen* case, which

[12] Hong Kong Bar Association, Response to the State Council White Paper, *The practice of 'one' country, two systems' in the Hong Kong Special Administrative Region*, 11 June 2014.

[13] C. Buddle, 'Bridging a legal gulf between HK, Beijing', *SCMP*, 17 April, 2005. See also Y. Ghai, 'Just what can Beijing teach us?' *SCMP*, 13 April 2005.

pro-Beijing groups wished to see 'rectified'.[14] That case, concerned with the interpretation of whom, under Article 24 (2) of the Basic Law was a permanent resident, had followed the common law approach to interpretation of the Basic Law.[15] Leung attacked the local judges' 'lack of understanding' of the mainland/HKSAR relationship, accusing them of making mistakes in their previous rulings and trying to supersede the central government's power.[16]

In March 2012, thirty of the thirty-six deputies to the NPC from Hong Kong signed a petition suggesting that the NPCSC should consider interpreting the Basic Law to provide a solution to the mainland mothers problem.[17] This step was seen as a 'blatant disregard of the rule of law' and an attempt to 'destroy our legal system and the spirit of the law'.[18] According to Lo, the officials responsible for Hong Kong affairs preferred that Hong Kong resolve the problem by 'legal means', but the fact that legislators were seriously considering such a step signals just how far NPCSC interventions had become part of Hong Kong's politico-legal life.

Leung's comments sparked an immediate controversy about judicial independence. The Bar Association issued a strong defence of the Hong Kong judiciary, arguing that Hong Kong's 'common law system had to be defended', and that it was, 'a cardinal principle of the common law that the interpretation of all enacted laws is a matter solely for the judges when deciding cases litigated before them . . . Any act which interferes, or which may be perceived as interfering, with the independence of the judiciary in Hong Kong must be viewed with great circumspection'.[19]

The Law Society argued that seeking yet another NPCSC interpretation would undermine the authority of the CFA and was 'likely to damage the rule of law'.[20] The Department of Justice was forced to issue a statement reassuring Hongkongers that judicial independence and the rule of law were 'core Hong Kong values', and reminding everyone that Article 85 of the Basic Law specified that Hong Kong courts 'shall

[14] Lo, *Judicial Construction of Hong Kong's Basic Law*, pp. 161–2.
[15] Lo, *Judicial Construction of Hong Kong's Basic Law*.
[16] J. Tam, 'Chief Secretary Carrie Lam defends Hong Kong's judicial independence', *SCMP*, 8 October 2012; A. Chiu, 'Law groups fight back after Elsie Leung attack', *SCMP*, 11 October 2012.
[17] Tam, 'Chief Secretary Carrie Lam defends'.
[18] 'Retirement of liberal judge', *SCMP*, 4 April 2012.
[19] 'Retirement of liberal judge'. [20] 'Retirement of liberal judge'.

exercise judicial power independently and free from any interference'. The Chief Secretary, Carrie Lam, also felt the need to reiterate that judicial independence was Hong Kong's 'core value'.[21]

Other events the very same year, however, raised doubts about this commitment, in particular the ousting of Mr Justice Bokhary, a judge in the CFA. Bokhary (described by Martin Lee as 'the Lord Denning of Hong Kong') had reached retirement age. However, instead of the government extending his appointment, he was forced to step down, only to be replaced by an even older judge, sparking claims that Beijing wished to rid itself of a judge known for his liberal decisions in leading cases on the right of assembly, the right of abode and freedom of expression.[22] In the *Congo* case,[23] for example, where the CFA was divided on whether to seek an interpretation from the NSPSC, he had argued that, 'It has always been known that the day would come when the Court has to give a decision on judicial independence. That day has come. Judicial independence is not to be found in what the courts merely say. It is to be found in what the courts actually do. In other words, it is to be found in what the courts decide'.[24] Bokhary had previously opposed Leung on the issue of seeking an interpretation over the issue of mainland mothers, and in April 2012 warned journalists against self-censorship. In the month before his departure, he criticised Leung's comments about the judiciary, arguing that they placed the rule of law under threat.[25] The local media speculated about the links between these incidents:

> Something stinks yet we are choosing not to smell it. We should demand answers but we are not even asking questions. Why? This business of Mr Justice Kemal Bokhary being ousted as a Court of Final Appeal judge due to age reeks of sewer stench. It attacks judicial independence. And that, in turn, is an attack on our free society ... Bokhary's liberal activism as a top judge has got up the noses of our rulers. They fear his dissenting voice. So when retirement age came they ousted him ... How else can you sensibly explain sticking to the

21 'Retirement of liberal judge'.

22 See K. Bokhary, 'The rule of law in Hong Kong: fifteen years after the handover', *Columbia Journal of Transnational Law* 51, pp. 287–301.

23 *Democratic Republic of Congo* v. *FG Hemisphere Associates LLC* [2011] HKCFA (8 June 2011).

24 *Democratic Republic of Congo* v. *FG Hemisphere Associates LLC*.

25 K. C. Ng, 'Former judge Bokhary: "I was ousted for being too liberal"', *SCMP*, 5 November 2012.

> retirement age for Bokhary but not for his successor? . . . If we remain mute we are allowing sewer stench to infiltrate the independence of our judiciary.[26]

At the end of 2012, Bokhary declared that there was 'a storm of unprecedented ferocity' gathering over the rule of law in Hong Kong.[27] The commitment of the people to the rule of law and freedom in Hong Kong was 'unshakeable',[28] but, as local law professor Eric Cheung pointed out, 'There are tensions between Hong Kong and the mainland . . . and those in authority are not defending our beliefs'.[29] At the time, two pro-China experts declared that all CFA judges should be Chinese nationals, remarks thought to be a criticism of foreign judges on the CFA.[30] This was rejected by the incoming chief justice, Geoffrey Ma, at the opening of the Legal Year in 2013, and Ma later used another speech at Lingnan University to emphasise the 'cardinal importance' of freedom of speech and assembly, and to stress that the Basic Law would continue to be interpreted in a generous manner to protect such rights.[31] In a later speech, Ma spoke again of the need for a 'fearless judiciary' that would deliver judgments regardless of whether they were in line with the government's wishes.[32] In March 2013, Mr Justice Hartman, former judge of the High Court, also wrote an article defending the independence of the judiciary. Seen locally as a judge of integrity, Hartman had ruled against the government on covert surveillance operations and stood up for constitutional rights and the rule of law. The former chief justice, Andrew Li, whilst not commenting directly on the matter, gave a speech in which he insisted that the city must cling to the rule of law with an independent judiciary as a core value that 'must never be shaken'.[33] Given this reaction to Leung's attack on the judiciary, Secretary for Justice Rimsky

[26] M. Chugani, 'Public eye'.
[27] A. Chiu, 'Retiring Court of Final Appeal judge Kemal Bokhary warns of legal turmoil', *SCMP*, 25 October 2012.
[28] Chiu, 'Retiring Court of Final Appeal judge'.
[29] E. Cheung, 'The storm over the rule of law has come', *Ming Pao*, 19 December 2012; 'Safeguard judicial independence', *SCMP*, 28 October 2012.
[30] The CFA has three permanent and fifteen non-permanent judges.
[31] S. Lau, 'Hong Kong's top judge says Basic Law will be interpreted in a generous manner', *SCMP*, 18 March 2014.
[32] P. Moy, 'Trusted judge who fought for legal integrity of city', *SCMP*, 1 April 2013.
[33] Moy, 'Trusted judge'.

Yuen felt it necessary to issue yet another public statement reiterating Hong Kong's commitment to the Common Law world.

However, another opportunity for the government to seek an NPCSC interpretation of Article 158 of the Basic Law arose in 2012, when the Department of Justice asked the CFA to seek an NPCSC interpretation of the Immigration Ordinance.[34] This reflected the increasing judicial review applications in 2011 concerning whether foreign domestic helpers (who typically entered Hong Kong on a series of two-year employment contracts) could be classified as permanent residents entitled to the right of abode.[35] Evangeline Banao Vallejos and Daniel Domingo had succeeded in the Court of First Instance, which ruled that the section of the Basic Law which prevented domestic helpers from being classified as 'ordinary residents' was unconstitutional. This ruling was reversed by the Court of Appeal. A request to the CFA to appeal this decision was sought. In 2013, the government finally attempted to request the CFA to re-visit its controversial 1999 ruling, a decision Lo describes as 'an audacious move for re-calibration'.[36] *Ming Pao* warned that 'one feel[s] the storm is going to break soon. Those who love Hong Kong must stay alert'.[37]Johannes Chan warned that if the government continued to place the CFA in such political dilemmas, one day the public would lose its trust in the court and 'the legitimacy and the authority of the judiciary will be seriously damaged, and such damages are irreversible'. He added that:

> With the rapid development of the mainland after 1997, Hong Kong has started to lose its economic and political power. Its judiciary is the only thing left. Judicial independence and rule of law are the last pillars for Hong Kong ... Hong Kong people should stand up to protect the authority of the judiciary ... people should speak out to protect the judiciary from political pressure.[38]

The CFA averted another crisis by holding that, on a proper construction of article 24 (2) (4) of the Basic Law, foreign domestic helpers were not entitled to be treated as ordinary residents of Hong Kong. It declined to refer a question of interpretation to the NPCSC under

[34] *Ming Pao*, 17 December 2012.
[35] *Vallejos and Others* v. *Director of Immigration* (2013) 4 HKC 239, CFA.
[36] Lo, *Judicial Construction of Hong Kong's Basic Law*, p. 78.
[37] 'A judicial storm would Ruin Hong Kong', *Ming Pao*, 7 November 2012.
[38] P. Moy, 'Johannes Chan, HKU law dean, says Court of Final Appeal's authority at risk', *SCMP*, 24 December 2012.

article 158 (3). Whilst this was victory for the rule of law, it was also a denial of justice to the domestic helpers.

MAINLANDISING THE SYSTEM

Pro-Beijing loyalists' criticisms of the HKSAR courts, as the foregoing suggests, have been sustained. In sum, Lo says, they argue that (i) the CFA was mistaken in its view that it could, on its own and without authorisation by the Central authorities, exercise the power of review; (ii) that by continuing to interpret the Basic Law in the common law tradition, the courts 'distort the relationship between the Basic Law and the common law'; (iii) that the HKSAR does not have 'residual power'; (iv) that the Basic Law does not 'vest the courts with power of review of legislation on consistency with the Basic Law';[39] and (v) that the NPCSC 'should interpret Article 160 of the Basic Law to settle the power and procedure for the NPCSC . . . to review all laws applicable in the HKSAR, be it through the initiative of the NPCSC or by virtue of a "submission" or "request" from the HKSAR'.[40]

However, several commentators have observed that the HKSAR government has been reluctant to pursue the path these criticisms suggest, fearing that it would generate further political controversy. To some, ten years after the handover, it looked as if Beijing had also learnt to live with an independent judiciary.[41] After the first battles, by 2007, public confidence was returning – a survey in August 2006 indicated that 54 per cent of respondents trusted the government; 79 per cent had confidence in Hong Kong's future and 71 per cent were confident in the 'one country, two systems' formula.[42] The government had finally amended the Public Order Ordinance and Societies Ordinance to delete the controversial reference to '*ordre public*'; Chief Justice Andrew Li consistently obtained high levels of public approval. It looked as if early fears were unfounded about the restrictions on the composition and jurisdiction of the CFA – renowned overseas judges had joined the court and several had

[39] Lo, *Judicial Construction of Hong Kong's Basic Law*, pp. 195–6.
[40] Lo, *Judicial Construction of Hong Kong's Basic Law*.
[41] Gittings, 'Changing expectations'.
[42] Hong Kong University Public Opinion Programme (POP) Survey, 22 August 2006. www.khupop.hku.hk.

delivered judgments that expanded the jurisprudence of Hong Kong and linked it to that of the wider common law world.

However, the presence of these independent judges clearly irritated the pro-Beijing lobby, who denounced them as 'parachute judges'.[43] It had also become a tradition of the pro-Beijing loyalists to castigate anyone who opposed Beijing's policies as unpatriotic – China's vice-minister of commerce, An Min, declared that 'loving the country' was tantamount to 'loving the Communist Party. The CCP represents the Chinese people and it should also represent Hong Kong compatriots'.[44] As Zheng and Tok note, this was the first time that patriotism was linked to loving the CCP. Later, in its 2014 White Paper, Beijing would declare that judges were 'administrators' of the HKSAR and, as such, were required to be patriots, prompting for the third time since 1997 a silent march by the legal profession.

Cumulatively, these attacks indicated Beijing's long-term goal of 'mainlandising' the HKSAR legal system and ridding it of its liberal legal supporters. Whilst some of those appointed to leading positions in the legal system have been liberal figures, the general trend has been to appoint known pro-Beijing candidates who – though they reiterate the HKSAR's commitment to the rule of law – could not be relied upon to defend the courts and the judiciary against mainland attacks. They owe their positions to Beijing and must demonstrate their patriotic credentials. Their presence, the NPCSC's interventions and the growing influence of mainland legal scholars all draw Hong Kong's legal system ever more into the mainland's politico-legal system.

Looking back on developments since the handover, one observer commented that the conflicts in the 'one country, two systems' model had become worse much faster than he had seen after the mid-2003 rally:

> As early as the 1990s, I felt increasingly that the conflicts in the 'one country, two systems' would be irreconcilable. This [system] would only be possible if Hong Kong people gave up their most important constitutional values, or if the Communist Party abandoned its one-party dictatorship . . . After 1997, we've seen constant tussles . . . The people of Hong Kong have demonstrated their strong aspirations for democracy and change. It resulted in full-scale control by Beijing . . . It's fair to say Beijing has also changed. They know they have the power . . . The crux

[43] Gittings, 'Changing expectations'.

[44] Gittings, 'Changing expectations'.

> of the problem now is that the NPC Standing Committee has time and again asserted its authority and no longer restrains its power ... Without any power to check the exercise of power by the Standing Committee, Hong Kong people can only influence the process through public opinion and mass movement.[45]

The Basic Law had failed to establish 'a complete constitutional firewall around the HKSAR'.[46] There had been high hopes that the Basic Law Committee[47] would become a 'quasi-constitutional' court linking the two different systems, but the NPCSC had 'effectively reduced it to a rubber stamp', whilst its membership means that 'its advice will be more political than legal'.[48] The Hong Kong deputies to the NPC, meanwhile, acted essentially 'in a symbolic capacity', lacking legal authority both in the mainland and in Hong Kong; elected by a 'small circle', they are invariably drawn from amongst pro-China supporters and are, thus, not genuinely representative of Hong Kong society.[49] As Ghai notes, in the PRC, the law itself is not seen as the will of the people but the will of the ruling class.[50] The NPCSC and the CFA operate, he says,

> under different theories and conceptions of law and functions of interpretation – the CFA places importance on the role of law as limiting power and promoting predictability through it, and the NPC on the task to safeguard the supremacy of political power ... [F]or the NPCSC, the interpretation of the Basic Law is the most powerful and effective tool to exercise the powers of sovereignty.[51]

No amount of public protest is likely to dent the control exercised by the NPCSC over Hong Kong and its courts. Areas of autonomy have been permitted but not where it matters most to Hongkongers.[52] The

45 Gittings, 'Changing expectations'.
46 H. Fu and R. Cullen, 'Two views of Hong Kong's Basic Law: but Hong Kong should seek a better way', *Hong Kong Journal*, Quarterly Online Journal (1 January 2006). www.hkjournal.org/archive/2006_spring/fu.html.
47 Established in 1990, the committee consists of six mainland and six Hong Kong members, each serving a five-year term.
48 Fu and Cullen, 'Two views of Hong Kong's Basic Law'.
49 Fu and Cullen, 'Two views of Hong Kong's Basic Law'.
50 Ghai, 'Themes and arguments', p. 10. 51 Ghai, 'Themes and arguments'.
52 Cummings and Tang note Hong Kong's separation from the PRC in the World Trade Organisation and in the Asia Pacific Economic Conference, where it is known as 'Hong Kong, China'. See L. M. Cummings and J. T. H. Tang, 'The external challenge of Hong Kong's governance', in M. Sing (ed.), *Government and Politics in Hong Kong: Crisis under Chinese Sovereignty* (London: Routledge, 2009), 177.

cracks in Hong Kong's walls of law have widened and may become wider still, given that there was never any mechanism for incorporating the views of the people into the law-making process, no means of enforcing the Joint Declaration, no mechanism for dealing with breaches of the treaty, no rendition agreement between Hong Kong and the mainland, no protections for Hong Kong language or culture, no system of notification of Hong Kong persons lost or detained in China and no provisions for getting them back. Whilst differing legal interpretations between Hong Kong and mainland lawyers offer the possibility of future change and improvements, so far they have also meant that thousands of people have fallen between the 'two systems'. The 1999 film, *From the Queen to the Chief Executive* anticipated just such a problem. Dealing with a story of teenagers sentenced 'at Her Majesty's Pleasure' for a real-life 1985 murder in Hong Kong, what if, it wondered, they fell 'between the legal cracks' and ended up being executed under mainland law after 1997? Yu Man-hon, the right of abode children and civil society activists have an answer to that question that suggests it would not be wise to rely on the government or the walls of law.

HK legal system under continual pressure from Beijing — an aspect of 'mainlandization' — overt via criticisms & interpretations — covert via appointing personnel

13

The culture wars: globalism, nationalism and localism

Attacks on the law walls have encouraged civil society to develop alternative channels of resistance and identity-formation. In this chapter, I explore how global capitalism and mainlandisation have threatened local identity, producing a defiant post-materialist reaction.

HOMO ECONOMICUS

The image of Hongkongers as solely interested in money, not politics, is a profound misrecognition. They have a long tradition of dissent, largely erased by official narratives of Hong Kong history but recovered by revisionist historians. Surveys in the 1990s also showed that 14 per cent of Hongkongers donated money to a political party, three out of every five had signed a petition, 27 per cent had participated in a demonstration, 11 per cent had spoken at such meetings, 15 percent had written to the papers and 18 per cent had called a television or radio talk show.[1] As Vines comments, 'it is hard to imagine such a high level of participation in public affairs in other parts of the world'.[2]

Nonetheless, the conception of Hongkongers as *homo economicus* was instantiated in the Joint Declaration and the Basic Law and reiterated back to the public as the 'authentic' Hong Kong identity. It stressed Hongkongers' durability in the face of hardship, thriftiness and success as 'bootstrap capitalists'. It also preserved in aspic Deng Xiaoping's

[1] Vines, *China's New Colony*, p. 210. [2] Vines, *China's New Colony*.

hedonistic version of their culture as one of dancing, eating, making money and gambling on the horses. The walls of law were framed to safeguard this capitalist lifestyle, preserve the executive-led political system and retain plutocracy. This was supposed to be the politico-legal recipe for economic success. However, it suffered a setback during the Asian Financial Crisis of 1997 and the world-wide recession of 2008. More recently, it was revived in a government campaign to establish Hong Kong as 'Asia's World City'.

The motive behind the 1997 reunion was political but also economic, engineered by politicians and multi-nationals with a view to national hegemony and the furtherance of global capital. Hongkongers are ambivalent about the benefits that economic integration is supposed to bring partly because they feel threatened by what Ohmae calls the 'China mentality',[3] wherein China sees itself as the centre of the universe, putting Hong Kong squarely on the periphery. This fear has turned out to be well-founded.

MEGAPOLIS

Ohmae himself identified the Hong Kong-Pearl River delta as one of the three cross-border regional production systems in the world.[4] Even before the handover, in 1993, Milton Friedman was arguing that Hong Kong was already part of China.[5] Chinese state-owned firms were operating in Hong Kong; China was Hong Kong's largest trading partner; as much as a third of Hong Kong currency was already circulating in China; Hong Kong companies employed three million factory workers in China, about six times as many as they employed in Hong Kong; China was the biggest foreign investor in Hong Kong; and Hong Kong firms were responsible for two-thirds of direct foreign investment in China. Tax breaks, together with a relaxation of rules on the mainland, prompted the mass relocation of manufacturing to cities such as Shenzhen, where entrepreneurs could find a plentiful supply

[3] K. Ohmae, *The End of the Nation State: The Rise of Regional Economies* (London: Harper Collins, 1995).

[4] Ohmae, *The End of the Nation State*. See also J. Shen, 'Cross-border connection between Hong Kong and Mainland China under "Two Systems" before and beyond 1997', *Geografiska Annaler*, series B. Human Geography 85, no. 1 (2003), pp. 1–17.

[5] Milton Friedman, *The Economist*, 18 December 1993, pp. 26–8: 'It's already 1997 in Hong Kong'.

of cheap land and labour and few of the legal restrictions that regulated business in Hong Kong. By 1997, 70 per cent of Hong Kong manufacture had relocated across the border, and 90 per cent of toy-making production had shifted to China.[6] In 1996, more than 150,000 Hong Kong nationals worked in Shenzhen.[7] Senior Guangdong economists predicted that the Shenzhen Special Economic Zone would extend its border to merge with Hong Kong after 1997, sparking rumours that Shenzhen would become part of the future HKSAR.

Before 1997, none of this worried Hongkongers. The economy was booming, Hong Kong was the epitome of laissez-faire capitalism – a free, open economy with no trade barriers and no capital controls, watched over by a small, non-interventionist government. However, observers cautioned that Hong Kong's return to China meant that it was never going to be allowed to go it alone and turn into a world-class, advanced city-state. China planned to integrate it into the Pearl River Delta, joined to the economies of nine southern Chinese provinces and Macau, creating a huge regional economy of 460 million people.[8] Merging Hong Kong and Shenzhen into a 'mega city' appealed to policy advisers with ideas of creating a 'world class metropolis bigger than London, Paris, Chicago or Los Angeles'.[9] Such a mega-city would 'blur the boundary' with China, freeing up the flow of resources and people. The plan included 'fostering cross-border business co-operation, creating multiple-entry electronic smart cards for Shenzhen permanent residents to enter Hong Kong, building a rail line between the two cities' airports, and a joint programme aimed at nurturing talent'.[10]

However, the creation of this megalopolis and the increased economic integration required something more than the movement of money, plant and personnel. It required Hongkongers to identify themselves as members of a common regional culture, with a common language, history, characteristics and destiny – what Lagendijik calls the 'social construction of notion of the region', an illusory, but

[6] P. O'Donovan, 'One night city pays the price of success', *The Guardian*, 9 March 1996.

[7] O'Donovan, 'One night city pays the price of success'.

[8] L. M. Cummings and J. T. H. Tang, 'The external challenge of Hong Kong's governance: global responsibility for a world city', in Sing, *Government and Politics in Hong Kong*, pp. 177–8.

[9] *SCMP*, 13 August 2007. [10] *SCMP*, 13 August 2007.

necessary step to legitimize the logic of global capital.[11] This identification was absent. During the anti-high speed rail campaign in 2009–2010, activists joined villagers whose homes were to be demolished, accusing the government of seeing land only as a commodity for making money and calling for the 'rediscovery of Hong Kong's identity'.[12] This foreshadowed the resistance to subsequent integration measures, including the influx of mainland visitors and mothers.[13]

In January 2010, LEGCO members found themselves under siege by elderly villagers as well as young activists who surrounded the LEGCO building, preventing them from leaving for several hours. The demonstration included a performance by students dressed in white monk's robes slowly processing around the building; every twenty-six steps, they fell prostrate on the ground, marking the twenty-six kilometres of track and the 6.7 billion dollars the rail link would cost. Some sang the 'Internationale' and a version of Woody Guthrie's 'This Land is My Land'. Videos posted online accompanied calls for greater accountability over public spending and accusations that the rail project would only benefit Hong Kong's 'fat cat' developers.

CEPA AND BRAND HONG KONG

In the past, the government and business elites could count on public support for any massive infrastructure project designed to bring economic growth. Post-1997, the promise of growth is no longer sufficient to satisfy Hongkongers concerned with the degradation of their city and the gap between rich and poor, and whose post-materialist values distinguish them from mainlanders. Patriotic measures introduced after the 1 July 2003 march were designed to remedy this deficit. The 2003 Closer Economic Partnership Arrangement (CEPA) was announced during the economic downturn that followed the Asian Financial Crisis. It was billed as the motherland coming to the aid of Hong Kong's economy and included cross-border infrastructure projects, such as a Pearl River Delta bridge and highway linking Hong Kong, Guangzhou and Macau; better access for Hong Kong businessmen to the 'China environment';

[11] A. Lagendijk, 'The accident of the region: a strategic relational perspective on the construction of the region's significance', *Regional Studies* 41, no. 9 (2007), pp. 1193–1208.

[12] Kwong and Yu, 'Identity politics', p. 144.

[13] Kwong and Yu, 'Identity politics'.

and increased competitiveness.[14] It was this agreement that was later blamed for allowing mainlandisation into Hong Kong through the back door.

In Hong Kong itself, the business elite had a different strategy. This was to turn Hong Kong into 'Asia's World City'. Their 'Brand Hong Kong' project began in 1996, amidst concerns that Hong Kong might vanish from the international scene after reunification.[15] It was intended to provide the HKSAR with an identity distinct from other Chinese cities, though publicity materials depicted Hong Kong in terms of its 'usefulness' to China, a 'gateway to China' and a 'hub for business throughout the Asia-Pacific region'.[16] The values extolled in this campaign were those of capitalism 'with Chinese characteristics'. As critics have observed, however, transnational capitalism has a propensity to erase national characteristics. This meant that 'Brand Hong Kong' was somewhat at odds with the discourse of Chinese nationalism, which Beijing was at the same time expounding in Hong Kong.[17]

'Brand Hong Kong' required, amongst other things, a recalibration of legal education to increase the production of high-quality lawyers to service the international market. Corporate law firms, the engines of this process, are international players, driving a shift towards a depoliticized, technocentric law curriculum across the globe.[18] The struggle over reforming legal education in Hong Kong in 2000 embodied the tension between the goals of global commerce and local people's legal needs. There was some attempt to balance the two. One argument was that the legal profession was much more than an adjunct of financial markets, as 'important as those markets are to Hong Kong'. The profession played 'a vital part in the constitutional structure and the maintenance of the rule of law ... the future shape of legal education [should not] be solely determined by reference to the needs of the rich, the powerful, the propertied and the articulate. *All* of Hong Kong's

[14] Hong Kong Democratic Foundation, 'Thinking the unthinkable: what if Shenzhen merged with Hong Kong?' 15 April 1997.

[15] Hong Kong Government press release, 'The Brand Hong Kong'. www.brandhk.gov.hk.

[16] Hong Kong Government, 'The Brand Hong Kong'.

[17] Lu, S. 'Filming diaspora', in P. Fu and D. Desser (eds.), *The Cinema of Hong Kong: History, Arts, Identity* (Cambridge: Cambridge University Press, 2000), p. 285.

[18] M. Thornton, 'The demise of diversity in legal education: globalisation and the new knowledge economy', *International Journal of the Legal Profession* 8, no. 1 (2001), p. 43.

communities and groups ... are entitled to enjoy a set of legal rights and protections that require constant reinforcement and protection'.[19] However, the subsequent reforms emphasized the needs of commerce – greater English language proficiency, the production of more lawyers 'dually qualified' in Hong Kong and mainland law and more clinical legal (transactional) skills. By 2004, the universities had reshaped their law teaching to embrace these priorities, reducing the space available to liberal subjects and considerations of social justice.

There were widespread criticisms of the extent to which the globalising capitalist discourse permeated such policies. Hong Kong writer P. K. Leung attacked those who urged the maintenance of English on the basis that it underpinned Hong Kong's prosperity, or because it was necessary to keep Hong Kong 'useful to China'.[20] Both, he argued, effectively reduced Hong Kong 'to a figure of speech, a useful foil for others ... [granting it] only a marginal existence'.[21] The government's pro-tycoon policies were attacked because they smacked of cronyism and patronage – the award of the 'Cyberport' project to a scion of the Li family was seen as testament to the influence of Hong Kong's most powerful tycoon, Li Ka-shing, popularly reckoned to be more powerful than Jiang Zemin. The government's bias in favour of tycoons and developers was attacked for widening the gap between rich and poor, and its lack of attention to grassroots livelihood issues.

However, civil society activism was still in its infancy in 2002, whereas 'Brand Hong Kong' operated under 'one banner/voice: Business'.[22] Beijing had chosen Tung Che-hwa as the HKSAR's first CE, thought to be appropriate because Hong Kong, as a Chinese capitalist society, needed a patriotic Chinese capitalist at the helm. His appointment put tycoons back at the heart of power and gave them a CE who would resist democracy, something the business elite regarded as inimical to its interests. The 'Brand Hong Kong' campaign identified the city with what Chu calls 'Central District Values' (global capitalism, development and profit) and marginalised all others.[23] These

[19] Response to the Steering Committee on the Review of Legal Education and Training in Hong Kong (Hong Kong: City University of Hong Kong, 2000).

[20] Leung, cited in Armentrout, 'Canto-culture'. [21] Armentrout, 'Canto-culture'.

[22] W. S. Wong, 'Design identity of Hong Kong: colonization, de-colonisation and re-colonisation', Department of Design, York University, Toronto, Canada. www.yorku.ca/wsywong/homepage/articlespdf/proceedings/ead06_id117_final.pdf.

[23] Chu, *Lost in Transition*.

values, however, included the rule of law. Chu notes that, when the then-financial secretary, Donald Tsang, met Jiang Zemin in 1999, he gave him a paperweight inscribed with what he believed to be the four pillars of Hong Kong's success: the observance of the rule of law, the free flow of information, a non-corrupt government and a level playing field.[24] The logo chosen to represent 'Brand Hong Kong' focused attention on the advantages of Hong Kong and listed these as 'the world's freest economy', 'the rule of law' as a defining ideology, a 'free and open society', an 'international business hub', innovation and technology, and law enforcement and anti-corruption efforts, as well as 'an accountable government'.[25]

It was assumed that these values were shared by Hong Kong society but, as critics observed, the government launched its campaign without first trying to develop an 'internal consensus' within the community about 'where Hong Kong was going and [what it was] trying to achieve'.[26] Its business elite supporters simply saw the future as positioning Hong Kong alongside London and New York as host to multinational companies, servicing China. The symbol chosen to spearhead the campaign was a highly stylised dragon, said to represent Hong Kong's links with the mainland's ancient Chinese culture. The dragon was:

> a historical and cultural icon. The flowing lines of the dragon mirror Chinese calligraphy. The dual expression of the dragon image – a combination of modernity and antiquity – also symbolises the meeting of East and West that makes Hong Kong so special . . . the dragon's smooth, fluid shape imparts a sense of movement and speed, recognising that Hong Kong is ever-changing. The dragon image's dynamic and contemporary artwork suggests Hong Kong's passion for the daring and innovative, incorporating a can-do spirit which brings visionary ideas to life.[27]

Launching the brand in Singapore in 2004, Director of the Hong Kong Economic and Trade Office Rex Chang stated that 'the dragon's free-flowing [design] . . . embodies the free spirit of Hong Kong people . . . The Brand Hong Kong Dragon represents our core values – stability, freedom, progressiveness, high quality and opportunity. These

[24] Chu, *Lost in Transition*, p. 44. [25] Chu, *Lost in Transition*.
[26] G. Schloss, 'PR-Puff: the magic dragon', *SCMP*, 12 May 2001.
[27] Schloss, 'PR-Puff'.

underpin the uniqueness of our society and development as a sophisticated economy'.[28]

Critics argued that the design was in fact intended to reflect back to 'westerners' their orientalist image of Hong Kong. It gave the impression that Hong Kong was 'a place without history, without culture, without dissenting views',[29] a place 'where everything can restart all over again without any memory of past history and experience'.[30] The design was a contrived – almost kitsch – stereotype of the Hong Kong 'lifestyle'. The highly stylised version of the traditional Chinese dragon, it was suggested, was an attempt to distance the HKSAR from all-out identification with a very Chinese symbol of power. It managed both to pay homage to the mainland without being identical with it. However, like earlier handover slogans ('Hong Kong People Ruling Hong Kong', 'Stability and Prosperity' and 'One Country, Two Systems') it was abstract, vague, insubstantial and lacking in concrete reference to Hong Kong culture.

In an astonishingly politically-inept move, the brand was launched in Hong Kong in 2001 at the Fortune Global Forum, in front of an audience of over five hundred international business leaders, as well as the former US President, Bill Clinton.[31] This was the site where, under pressure from Beijing, the government had tried to prevent overseas members of the Falun Gong from protesting,[32] provoking doubts about the 'one country, two systems' formula. By choosing such a symbolically potent venue for the launch of a brand supposedly promising freedom and openness, the government managed to identify itself with the suppression of those same values.

The brand proved a HK$9.4 million flop. A survey conducted in 2008 found that 97 per cent of respondents had no idea what the flying dragon represented. Notwithstanding this, Chu observes, 'the government decided to cling to the core values of the Brand Hong Kong programme'.[33] By 2013, the dragon symbol had quietly disappeared from the lapels of top officials, replaced by a new symbol, the 'HK is Our Home' logo.[34]

[28] Hong Kong Government press release, 'Hong Kong Dragon Roars into Lion City', 16 March 2004. www.info.gov.hk/gia/general/brandhk/0316111.htm.

[29] Hong Kong Government press release, 'Hong Kong Dragon Roars into Lion City'.

[30] Wong, 'Design identity of Hong Kong', p. 11. [31] Chu, *Lost in Transition*, p. 71.

[32] Schloss, 'PR-Puff'. [33] Chu, *Lost in Transition*, p. 73.

[34] 'City's dragon symbol flies into the sunset', *SCMP*, 22 August 2013.

COUNTER-CULTURE

In the years after 1997, a counter-discourse emerged in response to these mainlandising and globalising pressures. What Vickers calls the 'belittling or distortion' of Hong Kong's own history and culture formed an integral part of Beijing's strategy for the post-handover re-absorption of the territory.[35] By describing the population as 'residents' and their culture as a 'lifestyle', the Joint Declaration implied there was no such thing as a 'people' of Hong Kong. As Turner says, 'if there is no culture there cannot be said to be a people'.[36] Hong Kong was a 'non-entity'.[37] Gradually, however, conflicts with the mainland in the courts and on the streets have laid clear the error of this view as resistance has emerged in the realms of culture, education and language.

There are no protections for Hong Kong identity in the Joint Declaration. The idea that Hong Kong culture would present any obstacle to re-absorption into the mainland never occurred to its signatories. Beijing saw the Hong Kong variant of Chineseness in wholly negative terms, as 'inauthentic'. It assumed that Hongkongers would show political commitment towards the new government which represented their identity.[38] But instead Siu found 'intensified partisan emotions', 'a visible mixture of scepticism and panic with reference to political leadership' and a 'pervasive feeling that the social fabric is rapidly eroding'.[39] By 1997 Hong Kong was already a fast-moving, brash, unorthodox urban society and a prosperous world metropolis with an irreverence for nationalistic authority.[40]

Hong Kong post-1997 was, Siu argues, experiencing a tension that has long existed in Southern China between the narratives of *minzu*, a cultural definition of being Chinese, *guojia*, the idea of legitimate governance with binding obligations for a population, and *zhengfu*, the apparatus of government. In Imperial China, Siu says, cultural differences were often accommodated by Beijing, but the modern, organised nation state has purged as 'traitors' and 'enemies' those who

[35] Vickers, *In Search of an Identity*, p. 273. [36] Turner, *Hong Kong Sixties*.
[37] See J. Tambling, 'The last governor of Hong Kong', *Public Culture*, Society for Transnational Cultural Studies, 1997, cited in Armentrout, 'Canto-culture'.
[38] H. F. Siu, 'Cultural identity and the politics of difference in South China', in W. M. Tu (ed.), *China in Transformation* (Cambridge, MA: Harvard University Press, 1994) pp. 30–1.
[39] Siu, 'Cultural identity', p. 31. [40] Siu, 'Cultural identity', pp. 30–1.

do not conform.[41] Post-1997, 'all communities [were subsumed] into the imagined Community of nation'.[42] Official campaigns promoted the Basic Law, patriotism, the concept of *kwokga* (nation) and the love of the *jokwok* (motherland).[43] By contrast, colonial rule 'did little to impose the concept of "nation" and loyalty to its sovereign country'.[44] After the handover, however, there was a push for Hongkongers to identify themselves with the culture and history of their motherland[45]: 'For several years now, local television stations have aired a video every evening that showcases the magnificent landscapes and technological achievements of the motherland . . . while playing the national anthem of the People's Republic.'[46] The video was intended, Chow says, to contrast the beauty of the mainland with Hong Kong's postmodern concrete jungle – its lack of grand, stupendous natural landscapes; historic sites; national treasures; and precious monuments.[47] Official propaganda depicted Hong Kong as a place 'whose people showed a careless disregard for the poor and were solely devoted to the pursuit of money and pleasure'.[48] This depiction of Hong Kong as an insubstantial nonentity was accentuated, Leung argues, by a postmodern theory that saw Hong Kong as the epitome of 'hybridity', adopting and discarding identities at the drop of a hat. The 'postmodern' label, Leung argues:

> brushes away all the messy and complicated social phenomena that make up an integral part of Hong Kong culture . . . They say that changes come so fast in Hong Kong that there is no point capturing them in writing, no point in talking about the question of representation. But this in effect is asking us to tie our hands behind our backs and not reflect on the special features of our society and our culture.[49]

[41] Siu, 'Cultural identity', p. 27.
[42] hegelchong, 'Narrating Hong Kong,' February 20 2006, accessed 19 August 2009. http://narratinghk.blogspot.com.
[43] Wong, 'Design identity of Hong Kong'.
[44] Wong, 'Design identity of Hong Kong'.
[45] Wong, 'Design identity of Hong Kong', p. 200.
[46] C. L. Lee, 'Media and metaphor: exploring the rhetoric in China's and Hong Kong's public discourse on Hong Kong and China' in Shi-xu et al., *Read the Cultural Other*, p. 139.
[47] Chow, *Writing Diaspora*, p. 184.
[48] F. C. Peng, and G. Crothall, 'Cities split on return of Hong Kong', *SCMP*, 13 July 1996.
[49] P. K. Leung, cited in Armentrout, 'Cantoculture'.

This propensity for cultural appropriation should not, Leung argues, be taken to mean that Hongkongers are devoid of any sense of identity of their own. Beijing, however, saw Hongkongers as 'watered-down Chinese' interested only in commerce.[50] Their rude slang was 'known for its inventiveness and its use of sexual references', and their cockiness got up the noses of northerners.[51] The mainland, by contrast, was represented as the custodian of permanence, rationality and cultural purity, rooted in China's political centres and its ancient history.[52] Since Hongkongers lacked all this, it was assumed they would welcome reunification with China.[53]

Some in Hong Kong argued, instead, that Hong Kong might 'civilise' the mainland by bringing to it 'the development of the institutions of civil society – a proper legal system, the rule of law[,] . . . secure property rights, professions, a culture of civic responsibility, reduction of corruption and crime'.[54] This touched a sensitive nerve. A long-established CCP view of Hong Kong was that it had been – and could again become – a base for subversion of China by 'peaceful evolution', 'bourgeois liberalism' and 'spiritual pollution'.[55] On the Hong Kong side, however, the task was how to accommodate China whilst avoiding absorbing its mores.[56] This was to prove difficult because economically, CEPA made Hong Kong highly dependent on the mainland.

Hongkongers also feared that by 'looking North' their city would lose its cosmopolitan character and become 'just another Chinese city'. In a farewell speech in 2001, former Chief Secretary Anson Chan observed that 'too many people in Hong Kong . . . have looked towards the mainland at the expense of our traditional links with the rest of the world'.[57] Her comments reignited the debate about whether (and how much) Hong Kong should 'look North' or 'look West', a debate described by one local commentator as 'the most fundamental controversy since the handover'.[58]

50 Cheung, 'Ghost town'. 51 Fenby, *Dealing with the Dragon*, p. 20.
52 Chow, *Writing Diaspora*, p. 184. 53 Chow, *Writing Diaspora*.
54 Chow, *Writing Diaspora*.
55 J. Mirsky, 'The big fact', *The Times Higher Educational Supplement* 26 (November 1993).
56 Mirsky, 'The big fact'.
57 N. K. Lau, 'Hold on to our culture', *SCMP*, 1 May 2001.
58 Lau, 'Hold on to our culture'.

LANGUAGE

Integration has had consequences for Hong Kong culture and language. CEPA gave Hong Kong film-makers easy access to the mainland market, for example, but the use of Cantonese was marginalised because films once made in Cantonese and dubbed in Putonghua are now filmed in Putonghua and dubbed in Cantonese.[59] Such developments, says Kam Louie, have been so dramatic that some commentators have been 'moved to mourn the death of Hong Kong cinema'.[60] Hong Kong was getting lost in China.

The 'language issue', as Geertz calls it, was also always closely related to the essentialist conception of national identity, 'the nationality problem writ small, the "who we are" question'.[61] In Hong Kong's case, what Ng calls the 'nationalist doctrine of unification' was 'based on ethnic and cultural fundamentalism and forceful suppression of differences and heterodoxy'.[62] The wave of anti-colonialism around 1997 was, Chun argues, intended to pave the way for the establishment of a new shared identity with the nation, 'reorienting Hong Kong back to its sino-centric roots'.[63] One means of doing this was through prioritising Putonghua over the native Cantonese language. Although official language policy was 'biliterate trilingualism' *(liang wen san yu)*[64] in Putonghua, Cantonese and English, the aim was to make Putonghua the dominant language. All major constitutional documents and official proceedings were to be conducted in Putonghua.

However, since 1997 Hongkongers have defiantly stuck to Cantonese. When, in February 2014, the Education Bureau website declared that Cantonese was not an official language, the statement provoked such an outcry it had to be removed. A government directive that schools should teach in Cantonese or Putonghua but not English was earlier opposed by schools, pupils and parents.[65] Chan argues that the

[59] Kam Louie, 'Hong Kong on the move: creating global cultures' in Louie, *Hong Kong Culture*, p. 7.

[60] Louie, 'Hong Kong on the move'.

[61] Geertz, *The Interpretation of Culture*, pp. 241–2.

[62] Ng, *Paradigm City*, p. 33.

[63] A. Chun, 'Hong Kong "identity" after the end of history', paper presented to the Institute of Asia-Pacific Studies, University of Nottingham, 19 March 2002.

[64] See Chao Fens Sun, 'Hong Kong's language policy in the postcolonial age' in Chan and So, *Crisis and Transformation*, pp. 283–306.

[65] See E. Y. L. Ho, 'Chinese English, English Chinese: biliteracy and translation', in Louie, *Hong Kong Culture*, pp. 55–73.

'extraordinarily strong and emotional reaction' against the use of mother-tongue education was partly due to the government's failure to understand the social functions of language. In this instance, she holds, use of English served to distinguish Hong Kong people from mainland Chinese and had thus become both cultural and symbolic capital for locals.[66]

This debate intersected with the review of legal education in the HKSAR, which favoured the production of trilingual lawyers sufficiently proficient to serve global capitalism.[67] As Chan, following Bourdieu, notes, linguistic capability 'enables one to apply such cultural capital to other fields in such a way as to advance oneself up the socio-economic ladder'.[68] Locally, English-speakers are sought after by commerce because of their ability to communicate in the global market place. This threatened Cantonese usage.[69] However, Clarke argues, Cantonese speakers have managed to avoid having their language extinguished by employing, in other domains, strategies for evoking it, such as 'the use of spoken Cantonese, where the differences in tones offer possibilities for making verbal puns (conveying meanings unintelligible to those who speak official Putonghua) or the employment of 'already culturally coded items of material culture'.[70] This 'guerrilla' tactic enables Hongkongers to maintain their own modes of engagement. By playing on the differences between spoken Cantonese and Putonghua, local artists are, for example, able to make verbal and visual puns, none of which are readily understood by non-Cantonese speakers.[71] Because certain art materials (such as ink and absorbent paper) are tied to 'pan-Chinese conceptions of high cultural tradition', Clarke says, local artists choose other materials in their work,[72] much of which revolves around the threat of disappearance and erasure of local cultural identity.[73] These projects amount, Clarke says, to 'a serious contestation of official national ideology' both before and after 1997:

66 E. Chan, 'Beyond pedagogy: language and identity in post-colonial Hong Kong', *British Journal of Sociology of Education* 23, no. 2 (June 2002), pp. 271–85.

67 C. A. G. Jones, 'Legal education in Hong Kong: producing the producers' in S. Steele and K. Taylor (eds.), *Legal Education in Asia: Globalisation, Change and Contexts* (London: Routledge, 2009).

68 Chan, 'Beyond pedagogy', p. 272.

69 Chan, 'Beyond pedagogy'.

70 D. Clarke, cited in Armentrout, 'Canto-culture'.

71 Armentrout, 'Canto-culture'.

72 Armentrout, 'Canto-culture'.

73 Armentrout, 'Canto-culture'.

> At a time when patriotic stories, often in the guise of cultural presentations, are being strongly promoted to Hong Kong people in an attempt to interpellate them as citizens of the People's Republic of China, much of the best Hong Kong art is concerned to offer an alternative sense of subjecthood, and one not framed in national terms.[74]

Vickers also argues that the use of non-conventional characters and Cantonese colloquialisms in local comics and newspapers retains the distinctiveness of the everyday spoken and written language of Hong Kong from the standard forms of mainland China and Taiwan.[75] Ironically, he notes, though denigrated by the educated elite, Cantonese is probably the variety of Chinese most closely related to ancient Chinese, 'the source of all of China's present day varieties'.[76] The fact that Hongkongers are able to access these languages and cultures is empowering in the sense that it enables them to 'speak and write by wielding the tools of my enemies'.[77] In the courts – particularly the CFA – it is principally the members of the Bar, proficient in English and often trained in English law schools, who can wield these tools on behalf of individuals against the state.

These 'arts of resistance' are a reaction to the threat of 'disappearance' posed by economism and mainlandisation. At the 26th Hong Kong Film Awards, the band 'Alive' urged Hong Kong to 'keep its own identity, seeing it as the most important thing for Hong Kong culture if it wants to stay *alive*'.[78] Films with uniquely local characteristics reappeared in 2012, along with films containing negative images of mainlanders. They marked the defiant reiteration of Hong Kong identity in the face of mainlandisation.[79]

[74] Armentrout, 'Canto-culture'. [75] Vickers, *In Search of an Identity*, p. 67.
[76] Vickers, *In Search of an Identity*. Vickers cites H. Pierson, 'Cantonese, English or Putonghua', in G. A. Postiglione (ed.), *Education and Society in Hong Kong* (Hong Kong: Hong Kong University Press, 1992), pp. 183–202.
[77] Chow, *Writing Diaspora*, p. 22. [78] Chu, *One Country*, p. 144.
[79] See, for example, films such as *Vulgaria*, '*I Love Hong Kong*', and *Love in a Puff*, which contain Hong Kong themes and 'in-jokes'.

Various mainland threats, resistance — HK distinctiveness variously affirmed

14

The culture wars: creating the nation

China's mission post-1997 is to integrate Hong Kong into the 'Greater China' nation. It does not rely upon law to achieve this goal so much as economics, politics, patriotic education and culture. An essential part of the nation-building process, Featherstone argues, is 'the active encouragement of the *ethnie*, or ethnic core', and the elaboration of a 'common repository of myths, heroes, events, landscapes and memories', which assume a primordial quality. The nation is 'represented through a set of more or less coherent images and memories which deal with the crucial questions of the origins, difference and distinctiveness of a people'.[1] Official narratives of Hong Kong deliberately play up a 'primordialist' conception of China, depicting Hongkongers and their 'mainland compatriots' as being of the 'same blood' with 'a common interest and destiny'.[2] The dominant narrative presents Hong Kong's recovery by China as a 'natural' step in the completion of China's historical mission to create a Greater China. Hong Kong's 'return to the Motherland' was a cause for national pride and joy, a historic wrong now righted.[3] The phrase '*wui gui*' ('return') was posted everywhere on billboards but, as one commentator remarked:

> During *Wui Gui* Hong Kong are told that they have to start learning to be Chinese from now on. Just what is this Chineseness that we

[1] M. Featherstone, *Undoing Culture: Globalisation, Postmodernism and Identity* (London: Sage, 1995), pp. 108–9.

[2] Chief Executive's Policy Address to LEGCO, 2005. [3] *The Times*, 6 April 1993.

> should learn? If we are so much Chinese that the 'return' is a fateful destiny for all of us, then we ARE Chinese already and there is nothing extra to learn. Of course if like me, you don't believe for one second in this 'compatriotic blood is thicker than water' stuff, the whole Chineseness discourse is state manufactured and the promotion campaign for it a form of state control. It is meant to put down local, community experiences and the cultural identity of its people, treating them as worthless indulgence in the colonial past. This is the utmost insult to the 6 million people here, and their forebears, who have worked so hard in the past decades if not centuries for aspirations which go beyond earning a living or wishing a personal fortune. Indeed, while we speak a lively local dialect here we also share the universal voice in calling for justice, peace, and an end to all oppressions in this world.[4]

As this indicates, what Chow calls the 'Realpolitik of coercion of blood, race and soil', but a 'nostalgia for ever-receding origins' did not lead to a rush for reunion by the long-lost native sons of China.[5] For local artists, reunion was marked by 'struggle, instability, transition, anxiety and precariousness'.[6] Only if Hong Kong could maintain its identity, could it sustain itself against China's 'totalising nativist vision'.[7]

1997 saw a wave of metaphor-making. Hong Kong was variously depicted as 'an orphaned child in search of a mother'; a 'helpless maiden' raped by 'Western' colonial powers (China, 'like St George slaying the Dragon', would rescue her); a 'fallen woman', whose cultural purity has been spoiled by 'Western' influences; and a 'bastard child' lacking a core sense of identity which re-adoption by China would supply.[8] One song, 'Homecoming', was 'belted out' during the official handover festivities.[9] It sang of 'a beautiful sun shining on Hong Kong, pride in the homecoming, joy filling every Chinese heart,

[4] 'The Alternative Handover', *Hong Kong Voice of Democracy*, 14 July 1997.

[5] R. Chow, *Writing Diaspora: Tactics of Intervention in Contemporary Cultural Studies* (Bloomington: Indiana University Press, 1993), p. 167.

[6] Wong, 'Design identity of Hong Kong'. [7] Chow, 'Between colonizers'.

[8] See G. W. McDonogh and C. H. Y. Wong, 'Orientalism abroad: Hong Kong readings of the world of Suzie Wong' in D. Bernardi (ed.). *Classic Hollywood Classic Whiteness* (Minneapolis: University of Minneapolis Press, 2001), pp. 210–44.

[9] W. C. Ho, 'The political meaning of Hong Kong popular music: a review of socio-political relations between Hong Kong and the People's Republic of China since the eighties', *Popular Music* 19, no. 3 (2000), p. 347. Ho adds that the lyrics were penned by Betty Tung, the new CE's wife.

the unity of the Chinese people, the wisdom of the motherland, a limitless future, and explicitly, the realisation of "one country, two systems"'.

Lee identifies five metaphors dominant at the time: (i) the Homecoming (which includes returning to the 'embrace of the Fatherland/Motherland', Coming Home to the Big Family and Mother-Child metaphor); (ii) the 'Master' metaphor (which includes metaphors such as 'Own Master', 'True master' and 'Controlling One's own destiny'); (iii) the 'Bridge' metaphor (which includes Hong Kong as a 'bridge', 'window', 'channel', 'door' and 'floodgate'); (iv) the 'Backing' metaphor referring to China's role as a support for Hong Kong; and (v) the 'Lips and Teeth' metaphor (which refers to the relationship between Hong Kong and China as 'lips and 'teeth', 'shoot and root' and 'flesh and blood').[10] Hong Kong people did interesting things with these metaphors. A local drama group scored a hit with a play satirising the essentialism of the 'pure nativist' metaphor. Their play, *The Archaeology Bird*, cleverly employed the metaphor of an archaeological excavation to trace the origins of Hong Kong people back to a clan (the Che clan), which had supposedly been deleted from Chinese recorded history.[11] This kind of cultural work rescued Hong Kong culture from the penumbra cast by the grand narratives of British and Chinese history by ironicising them.[12] In doing so, 'the discourse of race (whether an attachment to *Goumin* 'country-race' or regional ethnicity) was displaced by a more flexible, ambiguous, more generously inclusive, local and popular *cultural* identity.[13]

Another 1997 play, *The Life and Times of Wu Zhong Xian*, documented the disillusionment of a Hong Kong political activist (Wu) who had fought colonialism in the 1960s, supported the Chinese Democracy Wall protesters in the 1970s, protested against the Tiananmen Square massacre, only to die from cancer in 1994.[14] The film – and Wu's life – was seen by some local critics as emblematic both of the fate of Hong Kong's radical activists and – with the handover

[10] Lee, 'Media and metaphor', p. 139.

[11] Tam, 'Missing identity' in Shi-xu et al., *Read the Cultural Other*, pp. 165–76.

[12] R. Lilley, *Staging Hong Kong: Gender and Performance in Transition* (London: Curzon Press, 1998), cited in N. Tapp, 'Post-colonial anthropology: local identities and virtual nationality in the Hong Kong-China Region'. http://suzi1.lib.hku.hk/hkjo/view/44/4400844.pdf.

[13] Turner, 'Hong Kong sixties'.

[14] See www.aptfs.org/pastact/info/WuZhongXian.htm.

looming – the end of youthful idealism.[15] John Woo's *A Better Tomorrow* (1986) and *Bullet in the Head* (1990) were also seen as allegories of post-1997 Hong Kong, with themes such as the loss of traditional values (honour and loyalty) and individuals' attempts to maintain their individual agency against the pressure to conform to the demands of (sometimes corrupt) organisations.[16] The popular movie 'Election'[17] (in which an election for the leadership of a triad results in a 'one triad, two leaders' deal, with fatal consequences for the upstart) parodied both Hong Kong's lack of democracy and 'one country, two systems'. According to Ryan, what drove such films as *A Better Tomorrow*, *Sworn Brothers*, and *The Tragic Hero* was the problem of, 'tortured fraternity, in a world where old rules do not apply . . . [they] dismiss certain kinds of Chinese rhetoric, particularly the idea that there is one China . . . Are Hong Kong's gangster films a call to political arms – to embrace the Communist elder brother? Or fight him off?'[18]

Lee argues that the post-handover government in fact tried to tweak the inflexion of metaphors to achieve a sense that Hong Kong was close but not identical with China.[19] Tung Chee hwa, for example, used the phrase 'family reunion' to describe Hong Kong's return to China, rather than the phrase 'returning to the big family of the land of the forefathers', employed by Jiang Zemin at the handover ceremony. Whilst Jiang's phrase cast Hong Kong in the role of a child returning to the long-lost family, Tung's indicated no status difference, only a reunion between two equal 'family members'. Thus, Lee argues, whilst they drew on shared metaphorical forms to connect them, there were also subtle differences in the words and idioms being employed.[20] Metaphors such as that of 'long-lost child returning to the mother' were greeted cynically or with indifference by local people, who complained of having to repeatedly perform celebrations of the handover on 'decorated floats, with singers singing handover songs, celebrating the coming handover, which weave through streets and alleys'.[21] Primary

[15] www.aptfs.org/pastact/info/WuZhongXian.htm.

[16] See J. A. Sandell, 'A better tomorrow?' *Bright Lights Film Journal* 31 (January 2000).

[17] The film contrasted two competing visions of Hong Kong, a city run by gangster triad leaders and the 'rule of law'.

[18] B. Ryan, 'Blood, brothers, and Hong Kong gangster movies: pop culture commentary on "One China"' in J. A. Lent (ed.), *Asian Popular Culture* (Boulder, Colorado: Westview Press, 1995), pp. 61–76.

[19] Lee, 'Media and metaphor', p. 161.

[20] Lee, 'Media and metaphor'.

[21] Lee, 'Media and metaphor'.

students in Yuen Long district, Lee notes, had to act out a play with the theme of '*baby swallows returning to their nests*' in every hall of their district, while festooned vehicles paraded noisily through 'indifferent crowds and murmuring tramps.'[22]

Vickers also notes that, in 1997, mainland studios released three films all carrying messages about the importance of 'national unity, morally upright political leadership, and resistance against foreign schemes to divide, dominate and exploit China'.[23] By contrast, three local 1998 productions (*Who Am I?*, *Lucky Guy*, and *Young and Dangerous Part V*) focussed on Hong Kong identity.[24] Hongkongers may have embraced economic integration, but they were 'holding more tightly to a local Hong Kong identity', manifested in films with distinct Hong Kong stories and identities.[25] Young people in particular lacked identification with China, prompting changes to the school curricula to strengthen their identification with the Chinese nation-state.[26] The government reiterated that there would be no 'hard sell' on patriotism but launched a 'soft' campaign ('Ideal Citizen') emphasising national songs, flags, emblems and patriotism.[27] There were already 'patriotic holidays' on 1 July and 1 October, accompanied by festivals of fireworks, traditional Chinese music and dance, but these largely failed to create allegiance to the new sovereign. Hongkongers either enjoyed the day off or turned these state-sponsored public ceremonies into occasions of mass protest.[28]

As the conflicts in the courts and on the streets, and the widening gap between rich and poor testified, the 'one blood' discourse did not resonate with ordinary Hongkongers. Instead, they poked fun at the image and at their leaders. Comic strips, such as 'Silly Old Tung', 'Broomhead Ip' and 'Bowtie Monk' were runaway successes in

22 Lee, 'Media and metaphor'. Quotes in original text.

23 Vickers, *In Search of an Identity*, p. 69. The three films were *The Opium War*, *Red River Valley* and *The Soong Sisters*.

24 Chu, *Lost in Transition*.

25 L. K. Pang, 'Postcolonial Hong Kong cinema: utilitarianism and (trans)local', *Postcolonial Studies* 10, no. 4 (2007), p. 425, cited in Chu, *Lost in Transition*.

26 T. K. C. Tse, 'Civic education and the making of a deformed citizenry: from British colony to Chinese SAR', in Ku and Pun (eds.), *Remaking citizenship*, p. 58.

27 Q. Chan, 'Patriotism campaign treads softly', *SCMP*, 28 July 1997. One survey found that patriotism took a back seat to the rule of law.

28 H. T. Dickinson, *Liberty and Property* (London: Weidenfeld and Nicolson, 1977). Dickinson argues that such occasions afford the crowd opportunities to challenge the state's legitimacy by attacking symbolic targets of power.

a territory previously unremarked for its political satire. Their publisher, Jimmy Pang, saw his publishing house as having a responsibility to 'point out society's injustices and protect the truth in a world populated by spin doctors'.[29] In 2005, he published a comic book about patriotism, which he argued was popular because the public were becoming hostile to being force-fed the national anthem every day before the evening news.[30] His 2012 comic book poking fun at the new CE (*Secretary Leung)* was another hit, as was another volume taking a swipe at patriotism (*Heng's Heartfelt Ties to His Homeland*) by documenting the experiences of ten secondary school students on a national education tour of the mainland, 'an experience they described as "brainwashing"'.[31]

The Hong Kong Book Fair, at which such works debuted, became a platform for mainland writers whose critical works face censorship in the mainland itself, whilst mainland visitors attended to gain access to books outlawed on the mainland. In 2012, the book fair was billed as the 'most political that the public has ever seen,[32] 'an expo of knowledge and ideas, where the Chinese-speaking world's leading authors and publishers can present, exchange, and contest their ideas regardless of political background or personal agenda . . . This peaceful co-existence and civility deserves serious attention . . . Genuine cultural and political diversity . . . epitomises the success of the book fair. Indeed, it epitomises the success of Hong Kong'.[33]

Hong Kong's leaders tried to conceal this swelling resistance from visiting mainland dignitaries. Protestors have, for example, been kept well away from official venues – in 2011, when Vice-Premier Li Keqiang visited Hong Kong, so concerned were the authorities about public protests that the media were barred from many of the events:

> Mainland-style core security zones, unmarked protest-free areas, were implemented; one man sporting a Tiananmen T-shirt was carted away; . . . and police allegedly locked three students from the University of Hong Kong in a stairwell . . . Although it is banned on the mainland, many people

[29] J. Cheng, 'King of satire, defender of the truth', *SCMP*, 16 July 2012. Pang's publishing company is Sub-Culture.
[30] Cheng, 'King of satire'.
[31] Cheng, 'King of satire'. The author of *Heng's Heartfelt Ties to his Homeland* is Lau Sze-hong.
[32] Cheng, 'King of satire'.
[33] O. Chou, 'Great reconciliation at the book fair', *SCMP*, 30 July 2012.

> have read the dystopian sci-fi novel *The Fat Years* by Shanghai-born, Hong Kong educated author Chan Koonchung. In it he imagines a Chinese population which happily trades freedom for material wealth. This is a tale that Beijingers know well – and one that Hongkongers, it seems, will do anything to avoid.[34]

What Vickers calls the 'kinship myth' of Chinese nationalism failed to translate into popular support for the Chinese state. The experience of living in Hong Kong, he says, has created amongst local people 'what amounts to a strong "ideological consciousness" of their own distinctiveness'.[35] As Clarke writes of the generation of artists who emerged in the 1980s and 1990s:

> They felt no requirement to engage with national cultural traditions on the one hand or to adopt the look of recent western art on the other . . . Art participated in [a] desire to affirm Hong Kong identity or subject-hood and even to some extent helped give birth to it . . . Oriented towards the post-handover future, it often used the strategy of disaffirming notions of Chinese national identity in order to open up an alternative space of Hong Kongness.[36]

As this suggests, by 1997, Hong Kong people already possessed a well-established local identity which marked them as 'different from other Chinese communities'.[37] However, Chinese leaders' long-term plans for Hong Kong's economic and political development require the sublimation of difference. Their policies have provoked wide-ranging forms of resistance.[38]Along the fault lines of reunification, hegemonic and counter-hegemonic struggles are occurring in the courts of law, in popular culture and in the myths and beliefs they create and sustain through culture.[39]

Beijing efforts at top-down patriotism fail – HK identity is clear → locals affirm it

[34] C. Sebag-Montefiore, 'City scope: HK "addicted to causing trouble"', *SCMP*, 25 September 2011.
[35] Vickers, *In Search of an Identity*, p. 57.
[36] D. Clarke, 'The culture of a border within: Hong Kong art and China', *Art Journal* (Summer 2000).
[37] M. K. Lee, cited in C. K. Lau, 'Futures on the line', *SCMP*, 24 June 1995.
[38] Lau, 'Futures on the line'.
[39] T. Cresswell, *In Place/Out of Place: Geography, Ideology and Transgression* (Minneapolis: University of Minnesota Press, 1996), pp. 12–13.

15

The culture wars: education and the cultivation of identity

When Mao Zedong proclaimed the founding of the PRC in 1949, Ho tells us, education and music were 'claimed as instruments for the transmission of new beliefs and values to build a socialist revolutionary society'.[1] Cultural identity was to be 'constructed and imposed by a centrally controlled ideology'. At the core of the sixtieth anniversary celebrations of the founding of the PRC, in 2009, Beijing began a round of 'unprecedented patriotic education' across the nation.

Hong Kong's own national education campaign followed the 1 July 2003 demonstration. The government tried to gloss over the differences which that protest expressed by creating a sense of 'harmony with the nation'. It depicted the territory as a model of equity for all China, a place where:

> people live and work in harmony and with mutual respect, whether they come from different provinces in the mainland or are overseas Chinese or ethnic Chinese, or nationals from all corners of the globe. We encourage the promotion of cultural diversity ... Hong Kong is a city steeped in Chinese culture but with many institutions and practices common to other major cities worldwide. People from all over the world feel at home here.[2]

[1] Ho, 'The political meaning of Hong Kong popular music', pp. 341–53.
[2] Chief Executive's Policy Address to LEGCO, 2005–2006, 'Strong governance for the people'. www.policyaddress.gov.hk/05-06/eng/pdf/speech.pdf.

The government also revived old stereotypes of Hong Kong people as hardworking. 'Bootstrap' entrepreneurs were revived to create a sense of community: 'We have grown up with Hong Kong and, collectively with "Our Hong Kong Spirit", endured many trials. With their bare hands, Hong Kong people have built a vibrant world city that is caring and just, without compromising efficiency. Over the past eight years, these same people have, through their perseverance and wisdom, overcome the most serious economic difficulties in half a century. We have finally emerged from rainy weather to embrace sunny days'.[3] At the same time, however, Hongkongers were exhorted to identify with the nation:

> The successful launch this morning of Shenzhou VI spacecraft, designed and built by our own country, marked yet another important development in our country's modernisation, but also manifested the Chinese people's grand ambition. We face excellent prospects. Being in the right place at the right time, we now have the right climate for social harmony and good governance. This is an epochal opportunity for Hong Kong and we must seize it for future generations.[4]

The message was clear: unity brought fortune, disunity harm: 'We should have fewer arguments to avoid missing good opportunities through idleness and indecision. With all sincerity I hope and urge everyone to unite and focus on seizing every chance to build a better tomorrow for Hong Kong'.[5] Hongkongers – especially the younger generation – were unconvinced. The government's response to their indifference to patriotism was a programme of patriotic education. Education is a classic technology of imperial rule, enabling the subordination of indigenous culture and values, and the transmission of the cultural values of the ruler. Where a society is changing, or there are alternative cultures, 'education can become a contested area and one group's "education" can become another group's "indoctrination"'.[6] The difference between 'education for oppression' and 'education for freedom' was well understood by Freire and his followers, who advocated an education for freedom that was 'a critical

[3] Chief Executive's Policy Address to LEGCO, 2005–2006, 'Strong governance for the people'.
[4] Chief Executive's Policy Address to LEGCO, 2005–2006.
[5] Chief Executive's Policy Address to LEGCO, 2005–2006.
[6] R. Billington, S. Strawbridge, L. Greensides and A. Fitzsimmons, *Culture and Society* (Basingstoke: Macmillan Press, 1991), p. 67.

challenging process, committed to, and engaged with the oppressed in finding a voice for their silenced culture'.[7]

This is especially true of history (the control of the past), language, and literature. Immediately after 1997, the Tung administration embarked on reshaping Hong Kong education to accommodate the culture and values of the new ruler. It introduced 'Chinese culture' into the curriculum of schools and universities. Putonghua became the official language of Hong Kong, though the native language is Cantonese.

Overall reaction to this drive was lukewarm – there was no rush to follow the CE's exhortation to become 'more Chinese',[8] nor did Hong Kong designate a 'Reunification Square' or 'Motherland Avenue'.[9] The valorisation of mainland culture placed Cantonese culture on the margin of Chinese civilisation, raising uncomfortable questions about exactly what constituted 'Chinese culture', and where Cantonese culture stood in relation to its canon.[10] The HKSAR government also urged its people to 'put the past behind' them, but, as Cohen argues, during periods of intensive social change communities often 'drop their heaviest cultural anchors' in order to resist transformation.[11] Since 1997, the past has become more important to Hongkongers, much to the chagrin of the HKSAR administration and its attempts to inculcate a different version of their identity through education.

Governments have long used the school curriculum as a vehicle for disseminating political ideologies 'with a view to transforming societies and subjecting them to more effective state control'.[12] In post-1997 Hong Kong, the classroom has proved a key site for the promotion of the national identity. The curriculum content has been redesigned with the construction and reproduction of hegemony in mind. As Tse says, through education the HKSAR administration has tried to construct citizens proud of their national identity and cultural heritage.[13] In his public speeches, Tse notes, Tung repeatedly 'reaffirmed fine traditional

[7] Billington et al., *Culture and Society*, p. 154.
[8] Fenby, *Dealing with the Dragon*, p. 51. [9] Fenby, *Dealing with the Dragon*.
[10] Shields, *Places on the Margin*, p. 29.
[11] Cohen, *Construction of Community*, p. 102.
[12] M. Lall, 'Introduction' to M. Lall and E. Vickers (eds.), *Education as a Political Tool in Asia* (London: Routledge, 2008), p. 1.
[13] T. K. C. Tse, 'Civic education and the making of a deformed citizenry: from British colony to Chinese SAR' in Ku and Pun, *Remaking Citizenship*, pp. 60–1.

Chinese values and emphasised individuals' fulfilment of obligations and acceptance of responsibilities rather than pursuit of their rights'.[14] Along with national reunification and nation-building, Tse argues, it became a 'cultural hegemonic' state project to create 'unquestioning political commitment and strengthen social order through the promotion of a unifying Chinese identity . . . to the exclusion of a distinctive Hong Kong cultural identity'.[15]

NATIONAL AND MORAL EDUCATION

Some efforts were made after the 1984 Joint Declaration to prepare Hong Kong students for the retrocession, but these were principally concerned with encouraging pupils 'to understand and appreciate their Chinese cultural heritage and the workings of the political and economic system in the PRC'.[16] This programme ran alongside an emphasis on the acquisition of skills and proficiencies required for participation in the global economy, what Chan calls neo-liberal restructuring of education.[17] After the handover, in 2001, efforts to inculcate national identity became more explicit. The government specified that the school curriculum should 'nurture a Chinese identity' in students. Schools organised cultural trips to China, as well as flag-raising ceremonies. They incorporated China-related topics into the curriculum. In 2002, guidelines were issued identifying 'National Identity' as a key theme.[18] According to Morris, the revised curriculum provided pupils with a 'soft portrayal' of Chineseness, which promoted sentimental affinity and common cultural and ethnic heritage. Kindergartens were provided with a package of materials ('I Love China'), including songs and activities designed to promote patriotism.[19] In 2003, a visit to Hong Kong by China's first astronaut was earmarked to boost patriotic feelings in the HKSAR.

These measures provoked a reaction. In November 2004, the secretary for education was asked whether the 'I Love China' programme

[14] Tse, 'Civic education'. [15] Tsc, 'Civic education'.

[16] P. Morris, 'Education, politics and the state in Hong Kong', in Lall and Vickers, *Education as a Political Tool in Asia*, 83–101.

[17] A. Chan, 'The making of the "ideal citizen" in schooling processes: gender, differences and inequalities', in Kun and Pun, *Remaking Citizenship*, pp. 74–94.

[18] Morris, 'Education, politics and the state', p. 97.

[19] Morris, 'Education, politics and the state', p. 98.

would teach kindergarten students to distinguish between 'I Love China' and 'I Love the Communist Party of China'. His negative response was critically reported in the newspapers.[20] A popular discourse emerged which held, 'We love the classic culture, long history, ordinary people and beautiful landscape of China but not the regime'.[21] In 2004, a TV clip called 'Our Home Our Country', introduced alongside the national anthem before the evening news, was popularly denounced as 'brainwashing'.[22] A 2005 video series designed to promote social harmony in the wake of recent political dissent (the 2003 march) also provoked controversy.[23] In 2006, the third in the series focussed on the national anthem. Designed to promote national identity as well as 'Chinese virtues and arts', it covered customs and practices such as filial piety, perseverance and harmony.[24] Ironically, as a Chinese-language broadcast, it had to carry subtitles in Cantonese. Featuring local celebrities, the series was accompanied by calls from pro-Beijing supporters for schools to fly the national flag. Local commentators drew a comparison between the series and the June 4 commemorations, contrasting the very different way in which Hongkongers expressed their 'love and hope for the nation'.[25]

On the tenth anniversary of the handover in 2007, President Hu Jintao encouraged Hong Kong to foster a strong sense of national identity amongst its young people.[26] Schools were exhorted to undertake more flag-waving and mainland study trips, and to focus more on teaching the Basic Law rather than human rights, rule of law and democracy.[27] Between 2006 and 2010, government spending on National Education rose from HK$5 million to HK$96 million.[28] In

[20] Kwong and Yu, p. 133. [21] Kwong and Yu, 'Identity politics'.
[22] 'Hong Kong Promotes Motherland', *SCMP* 12 March 2007.
[23] A. Leung, 'Brainwash denied over longer TV anthem', *SCMP* 19 May 2005.
[24] W. Yeung, 'Subtitles to feature in new series of national anthem broadcasts on TV', *SCMP* 30 September 2006.
[25] C. Yeung, 'What identity crisis?' *SCMP* 23 May 2005.
[26] T. Cheung, 'A history of how national education was introduced in Hong Kong', *SCMP* 9 September 2012.
[27] Tse, 'Civic Education', p. 62.
[28] *Ming Pao*, 2012, cited in P. Morris and E. Vickers, 'Schooling, Politics and the Construction of Identity in Hong Kong: The 2012 "Moral and National Education" Crisis in Historical Context', unpublished paper, delivered to the Taiwan Research Group 2013–14 Seminar Series, London School of Economics.

his policy address to LEGCO in October 2010, the CE declared that moral and national education was to become a compulsory school subject.[29] Activities were to include understanding the Basic Law, supporting the national sports teams, singing the national anthem and appreciating Chinese culture and ideas, such as filial piety, broad-mindedness and solidarity.[30]

Opinion polls between 2002 and 2008 show that, for a time, a majority of respondents had begun to identify themselves as 'Chinese'. This reached a peak in 2008, the year of the Beijing Olympics. However, polls thereafter revealed an increase in those identifying themselves as 'Hongkongers' (twice as many as saw themselves as 'Chinese').[31] This was a direct consequence of the mainland's interventions in Hong Kong affairs and the push to instil a greater sense of patriotism. A 2007 survey indicated that, amongst the population as a whole, 55 per cent still saw themselves primarily as 'Hong Kong people'; their sense of Chinese identity began to drop, 'reaching a 13-year low'.[32]

Any national patriotism flowing from China's successes in space and the Beijing Olympics dwindled. The school curriculum was criticised as one-sided. It praised the 'Motherland' whilst omitting any mention of controversial events such as 4 June 1989. The teaching materials (the textbook, *The China Model*) had a clear political bias in favour of the Communist Party, having been developed by a pro-Beijing organisation, the Hong Kong National Education Services Centre.[33] Government ministers insisted that national education was simply a means of instilling a sense of national pride and civic responsibility. Opponents called it indoctrination:

> I am over 40 . . . I don't pretend I represent the views of HK people, but I represent myself, my freedom of thoughts. I don't normally support drastic measures, in fact I hate them. I love my country, its history, culture, language and inventions. I don't belong to any political party, but I am a patriot because my conscience and my instincts tell me that

[29] Cheung, 'History of national education'.
[30] Kwong and Yu, 'Identity politics', p. 133n19.
[31] Kwong and Yu, 'Identity politics', p. 126. [32] Kwong and Yu, 'Identity politics'.
[33] Morris and Vickers, 'Schooling, politics and the construction of identity'.

> I should support my motherland, pray for it, and fight against Japanese imperialism. National education is not patriotism, because it will only do harm to our country, unless it teaches everything that is both good and bad about the government, otherwise it is no more than brainwashing. You don't have to agree with me because I don't force my opinion on anyone. You are free to disagree with it, and that is the distinction I draw with forced education.[34]

Another commentator reported that her three-year-old daughter had come home from school waving a Chinese national flag she had made at kindergarten:

> This indoctrination of patriotism is coming a bit too early, I thought ... Chinese officials ... do not understand why numerous trade deals aimed at boosting Hong Kong's economy have failed to win over the hearts of its citizens ... I took one look at the new teaching materials and knew the plan was a step [too] far ... I was one of tens of thousands of people who braved scorching heat ... saying no to the government's plan ... [The] government-funded handbook ... touts the superiority of the Communist regime, depicting its one-party rule system as 'progressive, selfless and united'. It decries multiparty democracy as unfavourable to the livelihoods of ordinary people because, it says, 'malicious fights between political parties leads to people's suffering'. [It] makes no mention of the 1989 Tiananmen Square crackdown, the Cultural Revolution, or other political movements that led to the deaths of millions of people. It simply praises the government without mentioning its faults – the lack of democracy and free speech, the ubiquitous human rights abuses and the widespread corruption. I could accept the handbook's guidelines if the praise of the Communist Party was balanced by a discussion of its failures. But this one-sided version of history is alarming ... I want my children to love our country, but I don't want them to be in love with a false image.[35]

In August 2012, the Executive Council and Editorial Board of the Hong Kong Institute of Education Students' Union published a paper in which they argued that 'moral education' was out of tune with the Hong Kong educational system.[36] Large-scale opposition to the proposals followed, involving parents, students, teachers and social

[34] jimmybabe, *SCMP*, 9 September 2012, www.scmp.com/news/hong-kong/article/1032368/hong-kongs-leung-backs-down-chinese-patriotism-lessons?page=all.
[35] V. Yu, 'Chinese indoctrination in Hong Kong', *New York Times*, 2 August 2012.
[36] 'PRC-style national education not wanted', *Ming Pao*, 8 August 2012.

activists but led by Scholarcism. A mass march on 29 July 2012 saw over 90,000 protesters call for the subject to be scrapped. To the accusation that their position made them 'unpatriotic', they responded that loving one's country did not entail loving its government. Writing textbooks 'to glorify communist rule' was, they argued, a 'clear departure from the declared objective of giving students multi-faceted knowledge about the nation'.[37]

These protests continued throughout the summer of 2012. In the run-up to the handover anniversary in July 2012, the Home Affairs Bureau tried to win over its youthful opponents using 'populist' tactics, such as 'anti-establishment'-style graffiti in large red and yellow letters promoting pro-Beijing messages (such as 'Glorify' and 'Return to China') accompanied by images of the Chinese flag flying over the harbour. Rock music played by young, long-haired musicians was introduced into the official celebrations for the first time to offset the usual fare of classical Chinese music. But anti-national education graffiti sprang up every time the government tried to erase it. At City University, students organised a 24-hour guard to prevent the authorities from removing graffiti painted in big characters on the university concourse ('Freedom of Thought. Academic autonomy. Never give in. Resist to the end').[38] In September 2012, 120,000 protestors marched to government headquarters. For nine consecutive nights, 'an ocean of black T-shirts swamped the Tamar site';[39] overseas Chinese also joined in the protests.

In the 2012 elections to LEGCO, national education made the pro-government candidates more unpopular. In a television interview, the chief secretary conceded that the situation partly arose from a lack of trust in the government and a fear of the Communist Party.[40] In October 2012, during one clash with the police, protestors chanted, 'Withdraw brainwashing national education now'.[41] The British colonial flag was raised by a handful of activists calling for Hong Kong to become an independent city-state with a separate identity as

[37] 'National education must be impartial', *SCMP*, 16 July 2012.

[38] J. Chiu, 'City University students guard anti-national education graffiti', *SCMP*, 25 September 2012.

[39] D. Chong, 'Black day for national education as Tamar site is swamped', *SCMP*, 8 September 2012.

[40] Chong, 'Black day for national education'.

[41] Chong, 'Black day for national education'.

'Hongkongers' not 'Chinese'.[42] On 9 October 2012, in an attempt to rebuild mutual trust, the national education guidelines were dropped. Like Article 23, they were placed on hold until a future date.

[42] Chong, 'Black day for national education'.

16

The culture wars: history, identity and nostalgia

Of all subjects in the school curriculum, history offers the state one of the best means of inculcating nationalism. Carroll notes that when school began in September 1997, the Chinese history textbooks 'were noticeably thinner than in previous years'.[1] This was because, in 1995, the Chinese Vice Premier Qian Qichen declared that history textbooks should be rewritten, whereupon local Hong Kong publishers started deleting topics that might prove offensive or controversial (e.g., Taiwan, Tibet, the Great Leap Forward, and mainland pro-democracy protests). Other changes followed. A new museum, the Hong Kong History Museum, opened with an exhibition 'The Hong Kong Story' which, Ng argues, 'inscribed a specific political ideology for the new Hong Kong'.[2] Chinese history (which had been optional) became compulsory. Secondary school civics classes were redesigned to place more emphasis on China, its geography, political system and culture. Hong Kong's history was subsumed within the history of the nation. Chinese history became the main thread of history lessons, Confucianism central to the teaching of Chinese philosophy.[3] References to 'Hong Kong society' and 'Hong Kong people' disappeared from the new secondary school history curriculum.[4]

[1] Carroll, *Concise History of Hong Kong*, p. 236. [2] Ng, *Paradigm City*, p. 45.
[3] C. Wan and M. Wong, 'Chinese history to be compulsory in schools', *SCMP*, 14 July 2001.
[4] Vickers, *In Search of an Identity*, p. 260.

As Vickers argues, whilst the British were more interested in what was *not* taught in Hong Kong's schools, the PRC leadership is more interested in what *is* taught, resulting in what he calls a 're-politicisation' of national history for the purposes of promoting uncritical patriotism.[5] For Beijing, patriotism involves a version of 'Chineseness' which stresses unity, primordial blood ties, an immutable set of beliefs and practices and loyalty to the government. As Siu notes, however, Southern China – of which Hong Kong forms a part – has long adhered to a different variation of Chineseness.[6] She charts the history of the various inhabitants of pre-colonial Hong Kong, not all of whom were of Han origin. Indeed, she cites a 1950 survey carried out by a mainland body that identified several ethnic groups in south China, including the Yao, the Dan and the Zhang as well as the Han.[7] A Heritage Commission Consultation Paper issued in 2002 nevertheless insisted that Hong Kong culture had its roots in traditional Chinese culture 'without which Hong Kong's cultural position would be obscure, cultural exchange meaningless, and Hong Kong . . . unable to contribute to the further development of Chinese culture'.[8] Hong Kong should 'not attach importance to culture only for the sake of its own development; it should also assume an active role in the modernisation of China and the development of the Chinese culture in this century'.[9] For the Hong Kong Chinese, Chu argues, this sort of top-down national consciousness was alien. They identified, rather, with the image of themselves in the iconic documentary and song, *Under the Lion Rock*, and in local films, Cantopop, television programmes and everyday experience.[10] As Ng argues, these form an experiential grid through which a social ethos, sentiments, history and national identity can be written.[11]

THE NOSTALGIA MOVEMENT

Whilst the state was busy re-engineering education and history, local people were fashioning their own versions of the past. A 'nostalgia

[5] Vickers, *In Search of an Identity*, pp. 243–51.
[6] H. Siu, 'Cultural identity and the politics of difference' pp. 19–44.
[7] Siu, 'Cultural identity'.
[8] Hong Kong Culture and Heritage Commission, *Policy Recommendation Report*, 2003, cited in Chu, *Lost in Transition*, p. 132.
[9] Chu, *Lost in Transition*.
[10] Chu, *Lost in Transition*, p. 133.
[11] Ng, *Paradigm City*, pp. 4–5.

craze' movement developed around the preservation of sites associated with Hong Kong's colonial past, often in the face of international business and property developers.[12] Protesters rallied around the preservation of the Star Ferry Pier in Central as well as the Central Police Station/Central Magistracy/Victoria Prison complex on Caine Road.[13] A coalition formed of artists, students and cultural and heritage activists as well as workers from NGOs.[14] They mounted information boards and displayed banners and placards, and were joined, Cartier notes, by 'countless numbers' of local people who left tributes and mementos of their association over the years with the place, especially the clock tower. Performances were also staged 'to demonstrate concern about the loss of local heritage and sense of place'.

The overall aim was to 'raise public interest about the issue and promote wider understanding about the meaning of public participation and local democracy'.[15] Films such as *Echoes of a Rainbow*, *Once Upon a Time in China*, *Rouge*, *Centre Stage*, *He Ain't Heavy*, *He's My Father*, *Days of Being Wild*, *Lee Rock* and *To be Number One* expressed this wave of nostalgia.[16] Postcolonial nostalgia in filmmaking, fashion, pop music and literary and historical writings expressed a 'mourning for the past' and the need to maintain and rediscover identities.[17] The search for 'who we are, what we are about, and whither we go', was, Chan says, 'a way of rewriting the history of the past, a revision of the present, and a speculation of the future';[18] it represented a cultural response in which identity, political anxiety, loss and collective memory were dominant themes. Brett Erens sees the film, *Summer Snow*, for example, as cinematic reflection on the loss of identity, focussing as it does on an old man losing his memory. Perhaps, Erens writes, 'the film represented a latent fear among Hongkongers that as the colony merged with the mainland, it would lose its distinctiveness. All that would remain of Hong Kong identity would be the long-ago past'.[19] Others also saw the defence of heritage sites not so much as a

12 N. S. H. Chan, 'Rewriting history: Hong Kong nostalgia cinema and its social practice' in P. Fu and D. Desser (eds.), *The Cinema of Hong Kong: History, Arts, Identity* (Cambridge: Cambridge University Press, 2000).

13 A. Leung and H. Wu, 'Conservationists' last battle cry', *SCMP*, 2 August 2007.

14 Cartier, 'Power plays', pp. 38–9.

15 Cartier, 'Power plays'.

16 Chu, *Lost in Transition*, p. 117.

17 Chan, 'Rewriting history', p. 264.

18 Chan, 'Rewriting history'.

19 P. Brett Erens, 'The film work of Ann Hui' in Fu and Desser, *The Cinema of Hong Kong*, p. 189.

longing for the colonial past as a fight against the loss of individual memories and experiences, 'a nostalgia and fondness for public places of personal and community experience'.[20] The yearning for yesterday, Chan argues, 'serves not only as a possible way for the people of Hong Kong to escape the uncertainty brought about by the 1997 issue but also as an alternative form of the colony's history'.[21]

For Williams, the popularity of films depicting the old 'lawless days' also owed much to the idea that people could survive and succeed even in bad situations, countering the notion that 1997 represented a historical and cultural apocalypse.[22] In the midst of the pessimism that surrounded the Tung administration, remembrance of times past bolstered the 'survival myth' central to Hong Kong's identity. The nostalgia boom expressed what Tapp describes elsewhere as dissatisfaction, unease or disenchantment with the present, as well as a yearning for an imagined 'what-went-before'.[23] It recreated a 'vanished community . . . a sense of community which has been destroyed'.[24] Another cultural critic observed that the strong public emotions over heritage protection stemmed from a need to feel rooted.[25] The heated protests against the demolition of the Star Ferry, Chu observes, flowed from its being widely seen by Hongkongers to be a vehicle as well as a symbol of Hong Kong.[26] The Star Ferry was remembered, for example, as the scene of anti-government riots in 1966. It was listed by National Geographic as one of the fifty 'must see' sites in the world and was thus an international icon. The government's own report on development of the area acknowledged its historical value.[27] Such sites, Kam Louie says, encapsulated fond personal and collective memories, rather than

[20] Kam Louie, 'Hong Kong on the move: creating global cultures' in Louie, *Hong Kong Culture*, p. 3.

[21] Chan, *Rewriting History*, p. 256.

[22] T. Williams, 'Space, place, and spectacle: the crisis cinema of John Woo', in Fu and Desser, *The Cinema of Hong Kong*, pp. 137–57.

[23] N. Tapp, 'Postcolonial anthropology: local identities and virtual nationality in the Hong Kong-China region', *Journal of the Royal Asiatic Society Hong Kong Branch* 39 (1999).

[24] Tapp, 'Postcolonial anthropology'. See also G. Matthews, (ed.) 'Heunggong Yahn', *Bulletin of Concerned Asian Scholars* (1997), pp. 3–13.

[25] Lau, 'New debate', citing Bono Lee and Kam Nai-wei.

[26] Chu, *Lost in Transition*, p. 53.

[27] M. K. Ng, 'Outmoded planning in the face of new politics', in Cheng, *The Hong Kong Special Administrative Region*, p. 625.

colonial history.[28] However, as Chu notes, neo-liberal logic won, and the Central Pier was demolished in 2008.[29]

Protests (and legal action) occurred wherever moves were afoot to re-develop old colonial sites, 'neutralize or hide the colonial past' or empty history of its critical potential.[30] As Lee notes, 'Each government project of urban renewal in Hong Kong has been challenged with a spontaneous outpouring of popular protest ... This new up-rising in popular consciousness betrays a certain mental desperation – to hold on to whatever remains from the past, for otherwise there will be nothing left'.[31]

SPACE, PLACE AND MAINLANDISATION

The threat of Hong Kong 'disappearing' into China reemerged in 2012 with government plans to build three new towns in the North East New Territories. The government claimed that the houses were needed to house ordinary Hong Kong people, but on social media, objectors argued that it was a 'political project' designed to blur the physical and psychological border between Hong Kong and southern China. It would 'benefit the developers a hundred times more than the homeless' and set up 'a foothold, a headland, for mainlanders to invade the rest of Hong Kong. This whole plan is to dissolve the Hong Kong-China border, integrating Hong Kong with Shenzhen, nullifying Hong Kong as its own city-state!' The government was accused of following Beijing's wishes, 'to connect Hong Kong to greater Shenzhen ... once they kick down the wall in the near future'. With no borders separating the area from the rest of Hong Kong, 'there is nothing that can stop mainlanders flooding into the rest of Hong Kong'. In 2011, an Action Plan for the Pearl River Delta Bay Area was attacked for annexing Hong Kong to Guangdong, 'thus bringing a de facto end to the SAR's high degree of autonomy'.[32]

28 Louie, 'Hong Kong on the move', p. 3. 29 Louie, 'Hong Kong on the move'.

30 A. S. Ku, 'Postcolonial cultural trends in Hong Kong: imagining the local, the national and the global', in M. K. Chan and A. Y. So (eds.), *Crisis and Transformations in China's Hong Kong* (Hong Kong: Hong Kong University, 2002), pp. 343–62.

31 L. O. F. Lee, *City Between Worlds* (Cambridge, MA: Harvard Belknap, 2010), pp. 272–3.

32 Kwong and Yew, 'Is Hong Kong dying?' in in Kwong and Yew, *Hong Kong under Chinese Rule*,, pp. 176–7.

Ng argues that these unpopular decisions about the use of space are a result of a system that excludes the public's voice from planning decisions – when developments choices are made, 'the legal framework . . . confines decision-making rights to a privileged few at the apex of the power pyramid'.[33] Citizens are not, Ng notes, invited to participate in the vision for their city. The interests of the powerful – 'progress' and 'development' – are prioritised over other social, cultural and environmental considerations, such as heritage and a sense of belonging. As a result, since 1997 there have been a series of protests against developments such as the Cyberport, a Disney theme park, the Lok Ma Chau Spur line, the Star Ferry demolition, re-zoning initiatives in the urban area, and further reclamation work in Central District. All were related to 'the long neglected social and natural or cultural heritage issues in the development process'.[34] Judicial review did not, in many cases, prevent the erasure of these sites.

A 2012 survey indicated that respondents identifying themselves as Hong Kong citizens stood at a ten-year high, whilst the figure for those identifying as 'Chinese citizens' hit a twelve-year low.[35] In seeking to rewrite history and erase the past, then, the government had succeeded only in underscoring its importance to Hong Kong identity and exacerbating resentment towards mainlandisation.

[33] M. K. Ng, 'Outmoded planning in the face of new politics', in Cheng, *The Hong Kong Special Administrative Region*, pp. 601–13.

[34] Ng, 'Outmoded planning'.

[35] Ng, 'Outmoded planning'. For the survey, see www.hkupop.hku/English/index.html.

Arguments about identity – nostalgia –
debates about urban form

17

The culture wars: freedom of the press

Before 1997, there were fears that Beijing would impose restrictions on the freedom of the press and that there would be an increase in censorship or self-censorship. In 1998, less than a year after the handover, a prominent local pro-Beijing supporter, Xu Simin, attacked the radio talk shows that criticised government policies and called upon RTHK to air government propaganda. Xu accused RTHK of being a 'remnant of colonial rule' and, despite the fact it was publicly funded, that it used the 'pretext of editorial independence' to criticise the Tung administration.[1] The Hong Kong *Voice of Democracy* responded that 'a free, open and responsible press is a cornerstone of a just and fair society. Curbing media freedom is to rule out a forum for views, dissenting opinions'.[2] It went on to liken Xu's arguments to Orwell's 'Big Brother' society in which words were erased from textbooks and independent thought stifled. It asked whether Xu's comments were a 'mere quirk' or the signs of things to come.

The next few years witnessed a struggle to preserve freedom of the press, prevent the rewriting of school textbooks, and keep propaganda at bay. Journalists and some academics began to report pressure to 'self-censor' articles. In 2002, Hong Kong was ranked 18th in the world in a press freedom index.[3] By 2011, it had fallen to 54th, with arrests,

[1] 'Broadcaster's autonomy at stake', *Hong Kong Voice of Democracy*, 6 March 1998.
[2] 'The doomed fate of a noiseless society', *Hong Kong Voice of Democracy*, 5 March 1998.
[3] A. Binitez, 'HK tops Asia press freedom ratings', *SCMP*, 24 October 2002.

assaults and harassment being cited as 'worrying' by *Reporters Without Borders*.[4] In 2002, as debates were taking place about Article 23, the chair of the Hong Kong Journalists Association, Mak Yin-ting, observed that the mainland's position was one reason why many in Hong Kong were worried about the proposed anti-subversion legislation. This could affect the SAR's definition of 'press freedom'.[5] In the same month, an opinion poll showed that the public's confidence in civil liberties, freedom of the press, freedom of speech and freedom to publish had dropped to a two-year low, following police crackdowns on activists and the Article 23 legislation.[6] Finally, Beijing's reaction to the mass anti-Article 23 demonstration of 1 July 2003 was to increase controls not only on pro-democracy politicians but also the press.

Radio phone-in programmes, the subject of much controversy in the 1990s, now function as an important 'surrogate democracy' able to create 'instantaneous communities over the territory among those with coexistent interests and passions . . . leading the public to challenge the government'.[7] However, there was a cost. Attacks on talk show hosts after the 2003 march (and on magazines such as *Next* and *Apple Daily* and their proprietor) are widely believed to have been orchestrated by Beijing or pro-Beijing elements. Albert Cheng's office was vandalized in 2004; his subsequent resignation was held to be due to political intimidation. Survey data for 2004 indicated that 59.8 per cent of respondents 'believed that the talk show hosts quit their jobs due to political pressure'.[8] Yuk-man Wong was attacked by gangsters and subsequently left Hong Kong. In 2004, Allen Lee also left his radio show.[9] Jimmy Lai has also frequently been the target of attacks, as have his publication outlets in Hong Kong and on the mainland.

In 2011, Hong Kong's main broadcaster, Radio Television Hong Kong, became a target when the government appointed a new director, a former administrative officer with no experience of broadcasting, sparking fears that he would curtail RTHK's editorial independence

[4] Cited in K. M. Kwong and C. P. Yew, 'Is Hong Kong dying?' in Kwong and Yew, *Hong Kong under Chinese Rule*, p. 176.

[5] Binitez, 'HK Tops Asia press freedom ratings'.

[6] M. C. Ng, 'Public concerned about freedoms', *SCMP*, 23 October 2002.

[7] So and Lee, 'The radio phone-in talk show', p. 832.

[8] So and Lee, 'The radio phone-in talk show', p. 832.

[9] So and Lee, 'The radio phone-in talk show', pp. 846–7.

and turn it into a government mouthpiece.[10] A previous RTHK chief had already been unexpectedly posted to Japan following a broadcast that featured a Taiwanese spokesman. The mass media are not permitted to air any programme in which independence for Taiwan is advocated, even by a visiting speaker. In 2009, an RTHK host, Lee Siu-mei, was criticised as 'anti-communist' when she mentioned the June 4 movement in a discussion about the collapse of former communist regimes in Eastern Europe.[11] Lee's supporters argued that the attack was an attempt to 'mainlandise' the broadcaster and turn RTHK into another mainland station.

In 2013, another controversy arose over the refusal by EXCO to grant a free-to-air licence to HKTV chairman, Ricky Wong. Tens of thousands of people wore black t-shirts to protest against what they saw as a breach of the rule of law. In this instance, it was EXCO's failure to follow the rules regarding the regulation of such matters, coupled with the secrecy of its decision-making and its refusal to give reasons for its decision. This was, in effect, a demand for the observance of fair procedures as well as greater transparency in decision-making. Protestors saw the episode as a threat to Hong Kong's core values:

> It was a sea of black outside government headquarters – formed by protesters in matching T-shirts – and everyone from families and students to keen television viewers and those who barely watch television wanted to make their voices heard. They called for justice and the preservation of Hong Kong's core values. Protesters clutched placards which read 'Don't kill the media' and chanted slogans such as 'Demand justice! Don't kill our dream'.[12]

On appointment to Asia Television in 2008, Wong had wanted to 'de-mainlandise' the station, for which he was criticised by the pro-Beijing lobby; he resigned shortly afterwards.[13] Mainlandisation of ATV and the media more generally is, Lo argues, inevitable – the family which dominated ATV's ownership was pro-Beijing. Ownership of the *SCMP* shifted to a pro-Beijing tycoon, and in 2006 TVB was bought out by pro-Beijing tycoon Yeung Kwok-hung. However,

[10] P. So, 'Black carpet welcomes RTHK's new boss to his first day in broadcasting', *SCMP*, 16 September 2011.
[11] Lo, *Competing Chinese Political Visions*, p. 221.
[12] 'This is not just about television', *SCMP*, 21 October 2013.
[13] Lo, *Competing Chinese Political Visions*, pp. 212–13.

18

Conclusion: lost and found

In his book, *Lost in Transition: Hong Kong Culture in the Age of China*, Chu Yiu-wai argues that, although Hong Kong culture has not disappeared since 1997, the rise of China 'has led to the fall of Hong Kong culture'.[1] When Lo argued that Hong Kong is being recolonized, he was referring to a process whereby 'a powerful metropole is exerting influence on its colonial enclave politically, economically, socially and culturally'.[2] Far from enjoying a high degree of autonomy under the 'one country, two systems' arrangement, the HKSAR is, he argues, 'already another PRC colony . . . To put it bluntly, the HKSAR has become a colonial appendage of the PRC, both in terms of the power to control the polity and influence the economy'.[3]

It seems clear that, since 1 July 2003, Beijing has stepped up its political, legal and cultural efforts to control Hong Kong, often via united front organisations and offices. Similarly, after the 2012 protests regarding national education, it appointed a new Liaison Office head, Zhang Xiaoming, and replaced several other officials. In one of his first public statements, Zhang called on the HKSAR to implement Article 23. In mid-July 2014, another Beijing official

[1] Chu, Lost *in Transition*, p. 157.
[2] Lo, 'Mainlandization and recolonization', in Cheng, *The Hong Kong Special Administrative Region*, pp. 222 and 227.
[3] Lo, 'Mainlandization and recolonization', pp. 222 and 227.

reiterated that candidates for the CE elections must not challenge the Communist Party's one-party rule.

This authoritarianism was predicted before 1997 – in 1990, Nihal Jayawickrama pointed to the irony that, just as the peoples of Eastern Europe were freeing themselves of authoritarian rule, Hong Kong prepared 'to capitulate to a similar, and equally arbitrary, accord thrust upon it'.[4] But Hongkongers have not accepted their subordination. By 1997, they had already come to regard themselves as distinct from the mainland Chinese, and post-1997, their identity has become a 'dual process of dissociation from colonial cultural domination as well as from the social and political life of the mainland'.[5] Beijing, however, requires Hongkongers to become part of a unified people with a single identity, common history and language.[6] It has disdained Hong Kong culture as inauthentic, suggesting a deeply evolutionary hierarchization of cultures.[7] For Hongkongers, on the other hand, it seemed ridiculous that a society riven by crime, corruption and instability should represent itself as superior to one with an established reputation in the world for prosperity, stability, fairness and social harmony.

In responding to Hongkongers' reluctance to surrender their identity, China has the advantage shared by developing countries everywhere, which is to learn from the mistakes of those who have gone before. One lesson to be learnt from British colonialism in Hong Kong is that repression as a strategy for dealing with the natives is usually counterproductive. Hongkongers taught Britain this lesson in the 1960s. Then, the continuance of an unrepresentative government remained possible only because the state created channels to absorb conflict, including multiple channels of grassroots consultation and regional political bodies, an apolitical civil service, a strong anti-corruption agency, clean government and the rule of law. In this 1970s hegemonic project, the rule of law was a handy tool for the manufacture of consent and delaying democracy.

[4] N. Jayawickrama, 'The Right of Self-Determination' in *Hong Kong's Basic Law: Problems and Perspectives*, p. 85.

[5] B. Leung, *Perspectives on Hong Kong Society* (Hong Kong: Oxford University Press,1996), p. 68.

[6] P. Cuttitta, 'Points and lines: a topography of borders in the global space', *ephemera* 6, no. 1 (2006), pp. 27–39.

[7] N. Thomas, *Colonialism's Culture: Anthropology, Travel and Government* (Princeton: Princeton University Press, 1994), p. 6.

GLOBALISM, NATIONALISM AND DEMOCRACY

Post-1997 Hong Kong is experiencing a double-colonialism. Global capital erases the local, including practices, sites and memories. As observers of global city developments note, this process is insensitive to the associations these have for local people, manipulating space according to efficiency and economics. In doing so, they 'hollow out' the sense of space, sever its associations and curtail its symbolic value to the community.[8] In this regard, the strategies of global capital dovetail with Beijing's desire to erase local culture in Hong Kong. Problematically, however, precisely because it erases the 'local and diverse', global capitalism also undercuts the narrative of a distinctive, national 'Chinese civilisation'.[9] Perhaps therefore, as Stoler and others have suggested, differences of interests and sensibilities make the 'colonisers' less homogenous than we imagine (though she was referring to colonisation by countries not commanded by democratic centralism).[10]

Globalisation is a double-edged sword for Beijing in another respect. As Sing points out, global commerce regards law and democracy as an aid, not a hindrance. Research shows that democracy promotes political stability, whilst cross-national research suggests that it promotes economic growth, especially in the long-run.[11] The World Bank's barometer for gauging good governance includes voice, accountability, political stability, government effectiveness, regulatory burden, rule of law and clean government.[12] However, Sing says, since 1997 Hong Kong has been beset with questions on virtually every aspect. Anti-Occupy Central groups argue that democracy will harm stability and therefore jeopardise Hong Kong's prosperity. A video released in June 2014 predicted that Occupy Central's proposed sit-in would lead to deaths, fires and the total shutdown of all transport routes in and out of Hong Kong Island. Barclays issued alarmist statements predicting a fall in property prices; the 'Big Four' accountancy firms declared their opposition to the proposed sit-in. A cartoon in a local paper summed

[8] E. Relph, *Place and Placelessness* (Toronto: Pion Ltd., 2008), p. 41.

[9] Relph, *Place and Placelessness*, p. 118.

[10] A. L. Stoler, 'Re-thinking colonial categories: European communities and the boundaries of rule', *Comparative Studies in Society and History* 31 (1989).

[11] M. Sing, 'Hong Kong at the crossroads: public pressure for democratic reform', in Sing, *Politics and Government in Hong Kong*, pp. 120–1.

[12] Sing, *Politics and Government*, p. 2.

up this 'doom and gloom' prognosis with a picture of two fat cats above the caption: 'What's next? The plague of boils and rivers of blood rating?'[13] Against this discourse of disaster, another observer, a financial commentator, remarked that:

> International investors welcome political dissent and positive change towards a more civil society rather than outright insurrection. Similar protests regularly come and go in London and New York without invoking the apocalyptic scenarios ... Any attempt to achieve a more democratic society through free elections is good for any financial centre. Ultimately, financial markets and international investors want to see strong, publicly accountable institutions in Hong Kong and on the mainland ... Hong Kong's economic oligarchs and an unrepresentative and unresponsive government are seen to be the very source of instability in the lives of average people, making Hong Kong an almost impossibly expensive place to live and raise a family.[14]

This description captures the damage that the post-1997 regime has inflicted on the 'Hong Kong Dream'. Under colonial rule, this dream held out the promise of a society in which everyone could prosper on the basis of merit, a promise secured by the rule of law. Since 1997, that dream has vanished. The dominance of business tycoons and pro-Beijing parties has led to 'the very worst kind of politics of exclusion and divisiveness', as well polarisation along class lines.[15] Under this regime, the elites have been the winners, the poor the losers. Hong Kong has become a highly unequal society. The top 20 per cent of the population own about 50 per cent of all wealth, while the bottom 20 per cent holds about 6 per cent. The top 10 per cent have about 44 per cent of the HKSAR income, while the bottom 10 per cent has 1.8 per cent.[16] In June, 2012, the Gini Co-efficient stood at its highest point ever. Figures from the Organisation for Economic Co-operation and Development for 2013 placed Hong Kong's elderly as among the poorest in the developed world; about 20 per cent of the city's total

13 'Harry's View', *SCMP*, 8 July 2014.

14 P. Guy, 'Occupy Central is Hong Kong's "mad as hell" moment', *SCMP*, 30 June 2014.

15 M. K. Chan, 'The HKSAR in flux' in Chan and So, *Crisis and Transformation*, pp. 10–11.

16 B. Sautman, 'Hong Kong as a semi-ethnocracy: "race", migration and citizenship in a globalised region' in Ku and Pun, *Remaking citizenship*, p. 127.

population was living in poverty.[17] In such circumstances, the rule of law is not enough. The disadvantaged want a change in the way their society is organised, which is to say a part in electing the rule-makers. Law – and lawyers – alone cannot overcome structural and political inequality.

Belatedly, Lu Ping recognised that, in the run-up to 1997, Beijing paid too much attention to Hong Kong's tycoons and not enough to other sectors of society.[18] In failing to address the concerns of the grassroots, mainland leaders encouraged the development of the very thing they most wished to avoid – a more politically assertive civil society.[19] The rows with China over the rule of law, the attempts to curtail local culture and rising mainlandisation have accelerated this politicisation. Without significant change, Hong Kong may become, as some predict, ungovernable.

LAW AND LAWYERS

My argument has been two-fold. First, I have tried to demonstrate that rule of law has become firmly embedded in Hong Kong as a core cultural value, central to people's civic identity. This is chiefly because it offers post-1997 Hongkongers hope that China's authoritarian rule in the territory can be restrained. Second, I have suggested that, as the walls of law have been breached, culture in its many forms has become a locus of resistance to domination. Often subversive and ephemeral, cultural identity may seem too insubstantial to provide a coherent and organised realm of resistance to domination. However, the same qualities make it difficult for the state to reach and contain. Evidence from other places and other times suggests that it is quite capable of outlasting even the most determined efforts to erase it. Lo thinks it probable that Hong Kong's civil society is robust enough to deter any 'further attempt at diluting Hong Kong's values of freedom, the rule of law, and . . . civil liberties'.[20] If so, the rule of law will remain an important restraint on authoritarianism.

[17] J. Ngo, 'One in three old people in Hong Kong are living below the poverty line', *SCMP*, 27 January 2013.
[18] S. Vines, 'The flaws in Beijing's notions of Hong Kong', *SCMP*, 25 May 2007.
[19] Vines, 'The flaws in Beijing's notions of Hong Kong'.
[20] Vines, 'The flaws in Beijing's notions of Hong Kong'.

Since 1997, Ghai argues, the CFA's role in interpreting the Basic Law *has* been gradually weakened, and its role in protecting the HKSAR's autonomy against onslaughts from the national government has been marginalised.[21] Nevertheless, the CFA has also 'strenuously and often eloquently protected human rights against considerable resistance from China'.[22] More generally, the ideology of the rule of law is a source of political culture and a resource for civil society. Writing of the role of the Basic Law, for example, Tai argues that it provides the necessary conditions for Hong Kong's civil society to blossom: 'It expressly protects Hong Kong citizens' freedoms of association, of assembly, of procession, and of demonstration'.[23] Ghai also sees the Basic Law as a positive resource. It instantiates promises made in the Joint Declaration about the safeguarding of human rights and the democratisation of Hong Kong. It may, he says, 'be more far-reaching in its protection of the autonomy, economy, and way of life than is generally realised'.[24] More importantly, given Beijing's assertion of control in its 2014 White Paper, the Basic Law cannot be amended unilaterally by the NPCSC. The Joint Declaration, Ghai points out, was:

> a solemn international treaty and undertaking, the fundamental principles on which Britain transferred responsibility and sovereignty over Hong Kong to China, the assurances given by both to the people of Hong Kong, and their participation in its preparation premised upon the principles of the Joint Declaration – all point to an instrument which, though enacted by one party, represents the will of several parties. As such, its unilateral amendment would be contrary to good faith and justice.[25]

The 'walls of law', then, may still provide some space within which liberal society can survive. What then of the lawyers? Can they become *porte parole* (spokespeople) on behalf of – and in association with – civil society's fight for rights and freedoms?[26] A structural obstacle makes this problematic. Hong Kong has a split legal profession, divided amongst barristers and solicitors. The barristers have been in the

[21] Ghai, *Themes and Arguments*, p. 7. [22] Ghai, *Themes and Arguments*, p. 19.

[23] Tai, 'An unexpected chapter two of Hong Kong's constitution: new players and strategies', in Sing, *Politics and Government in Hong Kong*, pp. 227–8.

[24] Ghai, 'The Basic Law: a comparative analysis', p. 21.

[25] Ghai, 'The Basic Law: a comparative analysis'.

[26] Halliday, Karpik and Feeley, *Fighting for Political Freedom*, p. 4.

vanguard of the fight for rule of law and human rights; the solicitors have typically supported the government. The legal profession is not, therefore, unified. The Bar is a relatively small group with very limited political reach within the Chinese state. The Bar's advocacy role is limited to the Hong Kong courts and courts in other common law jurisdictions, whilst barristers who have entered politics as pro-democracy legislators are barred from election to the HKSAR's top post. As far as Beijing is concerned, the Bar is fairly marginal.

By far the largest swathe of the legal profession comprises solicitors, mainly working in local and expatriate law firms specialising in corporate work. They have no substantial history of activism. Under British colonialism, few spoke out against the injustices of colonial rule, seeing their primary role as handmaidens to capitalism, a view which many still take. With some exceptions, they traditionally demonstrated little investment in what Dezalay and Garth term 'legal virtue'.[27]

Like the large transnational accountancy firms, these law firms have expanded into China. This lends them a structural vulnerability – they have the biggest stake in not offending Beijing. Therefore, though the Bar and the judiciary enjoy a high level of social capital in their defence of liberalism, they cannot rely on the support of the profession as a whole. Moreover, ranged against them are mainland legal experts who *are* close to state power.

Moreover, until the 1990s, even the barristers were not what Halliday, Karpik and Feeley term 'active agents' in the construction of a liberal political regime.[28] Though since then a significant number have become more engaged with civil society, their roots in civil society are relatively new and weak. Few barristers or solicitors engage in public interest work, which means that the profession as a whole lacks connections to grassroots networks and civil society organisations, though a small number of high-profile barristers have support as politicians.

In between these groups stand other lawyers – sometimes expatriates, sometimes mainlanders – often trained overseas in common law jurisdictions. In the past, many of these have brought to Hong Kong liberal legal values and a culture of engagement in public interest law. Whilst not connected to state power, many of these transnational lawyers are keen to cultivate China's market, and so cannot be relied upon to

[27] Y. Dezalay and B. Garth, *Asian Legal Revivals: Lawyers in the Shadow of Empire* (Chicago: University of Chicago Press, 2010).

[28] Halliday, Feeley and Karpik, *Fighting for Political Freedom*.

support liberal values against Beijing's opposition. However, like the international accountancy firms, the transnational law firms may find themselves called to account in their home countries by domestic publics concerned with human rights. This position may mitigate any tendency on their part to become what Dezalay and Garth call 'servants of power'.

Alone, however, courts and lawyers cannot win the fight against authoritarianism. This requires links to civil society and to international networks beyond Hong Kong. Without these, it is questionable whether Hong Kong's lawyers can effectively resist the mainlandisation of the legal system itself, let alone translate their socio-legal capital into political success. Their politicisation also makes them a potential target of repression – on the mainland itself, the CCP has already taken authoritarian measures to rein in its rights lawyers. It may bring these measures to Hong Kong. It already seems to be the case that Beijing has the overseas judges on the CFA in its sights. It may be hoped that support would be forthcoming from the wider Common Law world, but this is by no means certain.

As Dezalay and Garth argue, without strong connections outside the law, it is generally the case that even 'well-functioning and well-established legal institutions ... cannot by themselves hold back authoritarianism'.[29] The question then becomes, do Hong Kong's lawyers-cum-statespersons have these connections? Their answer is that the Hong Kong Bar generally lacks the domestic or foreign resources to challenge the controlling Hong Kong merchant alliance with the Chinese state.[30] To this bleak diagnosis one must add a further consideration: that Hong Kong's commercial elites, who currently support the rule of law, will cease to have any utility for Beijing. Tai argues that, whilst business people are important to the governance of Hong Kong, after the failure of the Tung regime, 'the Beijing government considered them a group which must be respected but cannot be trusted with the direct authority to govern Hong Kong'.[31] Once pro-Beijing loyalists are in place, China's leaders will no longer need the support of the Hong Kong business elite to govern. If the commercial elites, traditional supporters of the rule of law, lose their political traction, who then is left in the corridors of power to argue for the rule of law?

[29] Dezalay and Garth, *Asian Legal Revivals*, p. 216.
[30] Dezalay and Garth, *Asian Legal Revivals*, p. 258.
[31] Tai, 'An unexpected chapter', p. 238.

Beijing is, in any case, ambivalent about the rule of law, regarding Hongkongers' attachment to it as evidence of Britain's clandestine mission to use its 'soft power' to influence Hong Kong and subvert China.

With global capitalism, however, rule of law ideology has obtained global hegemony. This means that, to retain any semblance of legitimacy, the PRC's rule in Hong Kong has to be conducted through a discourse of legality. As Halliday and others argue, 'even where illiberal states resist the construction of political liberalism or seek to undermine and dismantle it, they must engage in the pretence of legality'.[32] If China wishes to participate in the global economy, it must at least be seen to pay lip service to global legal norms:

> political elites are impelled to legitimise domestically or internationally their regimes on legal grounds. They increasingly need some kind of legal system to support expansion of the market economy. Here repressive rulers play a complicated and potentially dangerous game. While they may roll out all the soft strategies of repression, through law and alongside law, [the legal profession] ... may mobilise subversively through law. Moreover, law ... never is entirely domestic. It retains juridical concepts that span frontiers and its draws upon claims to universality that are embodied in jurisprudential traditions and global institutions. To legitimate their repression on legal grounds, therefore, political elites risk exposing themselves to the erosion of their repression also on legal grounds.[33]

This partly explains why Beijing's resistance to universal suffrage must be framed in terms of Basic Law interpretations. But it also suggests that, whilst at times defeated, lawyers can live to fight another day, on a terrain they know, and with weapons with which they are familiar.

LAW VS. DEMOCRACY

There is, however, a proviso to be added to this narrative of how rule of law has become embedded in Hong Kong culture. As critics of the rule of law argue, whilst it promises many things, in practice it simply makes the unjust appear just. The whole point of the law, they argue, is to 'legitimize the assertion of power in the eyes of those who are

[32] Halliday, Feeley and Karpik, *Fighting for Political Freedom*, pp. 35–6.
[33] Halliday, Feeley and Karpik, *Fighting for Political Freedom*.

disenfranchised and dispossessed. By throwing them morsels of legal victories every now and again, they may be mollified by the law's formal equality'.[34]

Outright repression, as Gramsci reminds us, signals a failure of hegemony, as the British discovered in 1960s Hong Kong. The rule of law can provide another form of hegemony to an iniquitous regime by lending it a liberal face. Thus, whilst the rule of law may have made Hong Kong more liberal and marginally more democratic, it is worth recalling that it can also be used to shore up an inequitable economic and political system. This was why it appealed to the ruling class of eighteenth-century England, Thompson reminds us. Faced with challenges to its rule, the need to impose ever-more repressive measures, and the instabilities this in turn brought, this ruling class had a choice: 'either dispense with the rule of law, dismantle their elaborate constitutional structures, countermand their own rhetoric and exercise power by force; or submit to their own rules and surrender their hegemony'.[35] Nevertheless, Thompson concludes, ultimately the rule of law is an unqualified human good. It is especially appealing where the alternative is the arbitrariness of authoritarianism. Moreover, to be effective as an ideology, rule of law must deliver justice at least some of the time for:

> If the law is evidently partial and unjust, then it will mask nothing, legitimize nothing, contribute nothing to any class's hegemony. The essential precondition for the effectiveness of law, in its function as ideology, is that it shall display an independence from gross manipulation and shall seem to be just. It cannot seem to be so without upholding its own logic and criteria of equity; indeed, on occasion, by actually being just.[36]

Rule of law may be an ideology that benefits the elite, but it must also make good on its promise of justice for subordinate groups. The rulers themselves must also not be seen to constantly flout the law, or else the general public will not accept and respect law as a legitimate social institution.[37] The problem for Hong Kong is that, because rule of law is so widely valorised and so deeply entrenched in local culture,

[34] A. Merritt, 'The nature of law: a criticism of E.P. Thompson's Whigs and hunters', *British Journal of Law and Society*, 7 (1980).

[35] E. P. Thompson, *Whigs and Hunters: The Origins of the Black Act* (Harmondsworth: Penguin Books, 1975), p. 269.

[36] Thompson, *Whigs and Hunters*, p. 263.

[37] Thompson, *Whigs and Hunters*, p. 269.

Hongkongers themselves may be pacified by measures from Beijing that offer them legal instead of political answers to their demands. Lawyers and civil society must therefore remain aware of the implications of this possibility. As Leung Ping-kwan warns, Hong Kong is 'a fragile, vulnerable space … easily appropriated by other forces, political or economical. This space that is open to us could easily be lost to us'.[38]

[38] P. K. Leung, 'Homeless', in 'Homeless Poems and Photographs', *NuNaHeDuo (Dislocation)* 2.2 (Public Vs Image Issue), pp. 1–2, cited in R. Chow, 'Things, common/places, passages of the port city: on Hong Kong and Hong Kong's author Leung Ping-kwan', *Differences* 5, no. 3 (Fall 1993), pp. 179–204.

INDEX

BOOKS IN THE SERIES

Diseases of the Will
Mariana Valverde
The Politics of Truth and Reconciliation in South Africa: Legitimizing the Post-Apartheid State
Richard A. Wilson
Modernism and the Grounds of Law
Peter Fitzpatrick
Unemployment and Government: Genealogies of the Social
William Walters
Autonomy and Ethnicity: Negotiating Competing Claims in Multi-Ethnic States
Yash Ghai
Constituting Democracy: Law, Globalism and South Africa's Political Reconstruction
Heinz Klug
The Ritual of Rights in Japan: Law, Society, and Health Policy
Eric A. Feldman
The Invention of the Passport: Surveillance, Citizenship and the State
John Torpey
Governing Morals: A Social History of Moral Regulation
Alan Hunt
The Colonies of Law: Colonialism, Zionism and Law in Early Mandate Palestine
Ronen Shamir
Law and Nature
David Delaney
Social Citizenship and Workfare in the United States and Western Europe: The Paradox of Inclusion
Joel F. Handler
Law, Anthropology and the Constitution of the Social: Making Persons and Things
Edited by Alain Pottage and Martha Mundy
Judicial Review and Bureaucratic Impact: International and Interdisciplinary Perspectives
Edited by Marc Hertogh and Simon Halliday
Immigrants at the Margins: Law, Race, and Exclusion in Southern Europe
Kitty Calavita
Lawyers and Regulation: The Politics of the Administrative Process
Patrick Schmidt
Law and Globalization from Below: Toward a Cosmopolitan Legality
Edited by Boaventura de Sousa Santos and Cesar A. Rodriguez-Garavito

Public Accountability: Designs, Dilemmas and Experiences
Edited by Michael W. Dowdle
Law, Violence and Sovereignty among West Bank Palestinians
Tobias Kelly
Legal Reform and Administrative Detention Powers in China
Sarah Biddulph
The Practice of Human Rights: Tracking Law Between the Global and the Local
Edited by Mark Goodale and Sally Engle Merry
Judges Beyond Politics in Democracy and Dictatorship: Lessons from Chile
Lisa Hilbink
Paths to International Justice: Social and Legal Perspectives
Edited by Marie-Bénédicte Dembour and Tobias Kelly
Law and Society in Vietnam: The Transition from Socialism in Comparative Perspective
Mark Sidel
Constitutionalizing Economic Globalization: Investment Rules and Democracy's Promise
David Schneiderman
The New World Trade Organization Knowledge Agreements: 2nd Edition
Christopher Arup
Justice and Reconciliation in Post-Apartheid South Africa
Edited by François du Bois and Antje du Bois-Pedain
Militarization and Violence against Women in Conflict Zones in the Middle East: A Palestinian Case-Study
Nadera Shalhoub-Kevorkian
Child Pornography and Sexual Grooming: Legal and Societal Responses
Suzanne Ost
Darfur and the Crime of Genocide
John Hagan and Wenona Rymond-Richmond
Fictions of Justice: The International Criminal Court and the Challenge of Legal Pluralism in Sub-Saharan Africa
Kamari Maxine Clarke
Conducting Law and Society Research: Reflections on Methods and Practices
Simon Halliday and Patrick Schmidt
Planted Flags: Trees, Land, and Law in Israel/Palestine
Irus Braverman
Culture under Cross-Examination: International Justice and the Special Court for Sierra Leone
Tim Kelsall
Cultures of Legality: Judicialization and Political Activism in Latin America
Javier Couso, Alexandra Huneeus, Rachel Sieder

Courting Democracy in Bosnia and Herzegovina: The Hague Tribunal's Impact in a Postwar State
Lara J. Nettelfield
The Gacaca Courts and Post-Genocide Justice and Reconciliation in Rwanda: Justice without Lawyers
Phil Clark
Law, Society, and History: Themes in the Legal Sociology and Legal History of Lawrence M. Friedman
Robert W. Gordon and Morton J. Horwitz
After Abu Ghraib: Exploring Human Rights in America and the Middle East
Shadi Mokhtari
Adjudication in Religious Family Laws: Cultural Accommodation: Legal Pluralism, and Gender Equality in India
Gopika Solanki
Water On Tap: Rights and Regulation in the Transnational Governance of Urban Water Services
Bronwen Morgan
Elements of Moral Cognition: Rawls' Linguistic Analogy and the Cognitive Science of Moral and Legal Judgment
John Mikhail
A Sociology of Constitutions: Constitutions and State Legitimacy in Historical-Sociological Perspective
Chris Thornhill
Mitigation and Aggravation at Sentencing
Edited by Julian Roberts
Institutional Inequality and the Mobilization of the Family and Medical Leave Act: Rights on Leave
Catherine R. Albiston
Authoritarian Rule of Law: Legislation, Discourse and Legitimacy in Singapore
Jothie Rajah
Law and Development and the Global Discourses of Legal Transfers
Edited by John Gillespie and Pip Nicholson
Law against the State: Ethnographic Forays into Law's Transformations
Edited by Julia Eckert, Brian Donahoe, Christian Strümpell and Zerrin Özlem Biner
Transnational Legal Process and State Change
Edited by Gregory C. Shaffer
Legal Mobilization under Authoritarianism: The Case of Post-Colonial Hong Kong
Edited by Waikeung Tam
Complementarity in the Line of Fire: The Catalysing Effect of the International Criminal Court in Uganda and Sudan
Sarah M. H. Nouwen

Political and Legal Transformations of an Indonesian Polity: The Nagari from Colonisation to Decentralisation
Franz von Benda-Beckmann and Keebet von Benda-Beckmann
Pakistan's Experience with Formal Law: An Alien Justice
Osama Siddique
Human Rights under State-Enforced Religious Family Laws in Israel, Egypt, and India
Yüksel Sezgin
Why Prison?
Edited by David Scott
Law's Fragile State: Colonial, Authoritarian, and Humanitarian Legacies in Sudan
Mark Fathi Massoud
Rights for Others: The Slow Home-Coming of Human Rights in the Netherlands
Barbara Oomen
European States and their Muslim Citizens: The Impact of Institutions on Perceptions and Boundaries
Edited by John R. Bowen, Christophe Bertossi, Jan Willem Duyvendak and Mona Lena Krook
Religion, Law and Society
Russell Sandberg
The Experiences of Face Veil Wearers in Europe and the Law
Edited by Eva Brems
The Contentious History of the International Bill of Human Rights
Christopher N. J. Roberts
Transnational Legal Orders
Edited by Terence C. Halliday and Gregory Shaffer
Lost in China?: Law, Culture and Society in Post-1997 Hong Kong
Carol A. G. Jones

Lightning Source UK Ltd.
Milton Keynes UK
UKOW06n2234260415

250366UK00002B/26/P

9 781107 093379